MAHESH DUTT SHARMA

No part of this publication can be reproduced, stored in a retrieval system or transmitted in any form or by any means, electronic, mechanical, photocopying, recording or otherwise, without prior permission of the author. Rights of this book are reserved with the author.

Published by
PRABHAT PRAKASHAN PVT. LTD.
4/19 Asaf Ali Road,
New Delhi-110 002 (INDIA)
e-mail: prabhatbooks@gmail.com

ISBN 978-93-5562-061-3
GAUTAM ADANI: A COMPLETE BIOGRAPHY
by Mahesh Dutt Sharma

© Reserved

Edition
2025

Price
₹ 500.00 (Rupees Five Hundred Only)

Printed at
Siddhi Press, Delhi

Author's Note

Gautam Adani was born in a lower middle class family. Today, he is counted among the select ten billionaires of the world. The journey to become a successful businessman has not been an easy one for Gautam Adani.

During their initial days of struggle, the Adani family lived in the Sheth Chawl in the Pol area of Ahmedabad. 'No business is small or big and there is no religion greater than the business'. Implementing this maxim in his life, Gautam Adani left the narrow streets behind and became the most famous businessman in India. Today, he is recognised all over the world.

As his struggles in life continued and when the question of livelihood arose before he could complete his studies, he left his BCom degree course from Gujarat University halfway. One day, Adani came to Mumbai with some money. Very soon, he tasted success. Adani made his fortune through sheer hard work.

He founded the Adani Group in the year 1998. At present, Gautam Adani's business is diversified in many areas. While on one hand, he has become the largest contract miner in the field of coal mining, on the other hand, he has the country's most efficient coal-based power plant. He also has a strong presence in the port sector through Mundra port.

With 33 years of experience in business, Gautam Adani is a first-generation entrepreneur in his family. At present, Adani is worth about ten billion dollars. He has the largest export company in the country. He bought his own Beechcraft jet in 2005 and Hawker jet in 2008. He has achieved all this in just three and a half decades.

Gautam Adani's business instinct is very sharp and his rags-to-riches story is another example of the finely developed business acumen of the people of his coastal state.

An interesting and inspiring life story of India's famous industrialist.

❑

Contents

The Story of Brand Adani

Everyone salutes the rising sun but it dazzles everyone's eyes when it shines bright at midday. One such successful personality is Gautam Adani. Gautam Adani was born in a lower middle class family. There was a time when he had to give up his studies midway due to the poor financial condition of his family, whereas today he is counted among the chosen hundred billionaires of the world. The journey to be a successful businessman has not been an easy one for Gautam Adani. He did not achieve this success easily. He also faced various criticisms and allegations.

Gautam Shantilal Adani is an Indian billionaire businessman, who is the chairman and founder of the Adani Group. He founded the Adani Group in the year 1998, which now deals in coal trading, coal mining, oil and gas exploration, ports, commodities, power generation, agriculture, edible oil, transmission, and gas distribution.

Birth and family

Gautam Adani was born on 24th June 1962 in a Gujarati Jain family in Ahmedabad. Adani's father had migrated from Tharad town to this northern part of Gujarat for a livelihood. Adani has six siblings. During their initial days of struggle, the Adani family lived in Sheth Chawl in Pol area of Ahmedabad.

'No business is small or big and there is no religion greater than the business'. Implementing this maxim in his life, Gautam left the narrow streets behind and became the most famous businessman in India, and today he is recognised all over the world.

In Mumbai after raising a hundred rupees

The struggles in life continued and even before he could complete his studies, the question of livelihood arose. As a result, although he took admission to BCom in Gujarat University after intermediate, he could not continue his studies. Leaving his studies halfway before completing his BCom, one day, Gautam came to Mumbai with some money. At that time, he was only 17-18 years old. Adani made his fortune through his hard work. When his family was struggling with financial constraints, he decided to quit college and forge his own path. His father Shantilal Adani was not too happy with his decision. But a determined Gautam Adani did what he wanted to do.

After coming to Mumbai, he started working at Hindra Brothers for a salary of only three hundred rupees. But Gautam Adani had come to Mumbai with the determination to achieve something in life. So, he was not going to be satisfied with just this. Two years later, at the age of twenty, he became a diamond sorter and within a few years, he started his own diamond brokerage firm in Zaveri Bazar, Mumbai. Fortune smiled on him and in the very first year, the company had a turnover of a few lakhs. After spending a few years in

Mumbai, Adani returned to Ahmedabad at the behest of his brother Mansukhlal to work in his brother's plastic factory. Here Gautam decided to start importing PVC, i.e., polyvinyl chloride and entered into global trading. PVC is used extensively in making plastic.

The launching of Adani Group

From the capital raised from the plastic business, Gautam laid the foundation of Adani Exports Limited in 1988. The company started operating in the sectors of power and agricultural commodities. The export business kept gaining momentum gradually. When he tried his hand in many businesses including ports, he found success everywhere.

PVC imports continued to grow and in 1988, the Adani Group was officially incorporated into Power and Agro Commodity. Due to economic reforms in the year 1991, Adani's business quickly diversified and he became a multinational businessman. The year 1995 proved to be extremely successful for Gautam Adani when his company received the contract to operate Mundra port. Gautam Adani continued the diversification of his business and in 1996 Adani Power Limited came into existence. After 10 years, the company also entered into the power generation business.

At present, Gautam Adani's business is diversified in many areas. On one hand, he became the largest contract miner in the field of coal mining, and on the other hand, he built the country's most efficient coal-based power plant. Through the Mundra port, he had already registered his strong presence in the port sector. Then he set his sight on setting up a cement factory, on road construction, defence production and railways in the infrastructure sector. He had already formed a railway track management company by consolidating his 6-7 small railway lines.

Swift life events

With 33 years of business experience, Gautam Adani is a first-generation entrepreneur in his family. Till the 1980s, people used to see him riding pillion on the scooter of his childhood friend Malay Mahadeviya in the city of Ahmedabad. There was also a particular reason behind this friendship and that was Adani's weak but Mahadeviya's good English. His old friend Mahadeviya still reminisces about the bygone days of this unlikely billionaire from Ahmedabad. He narrates how Gautam Adani used to travel with his childhood friend (Malay Mahadeviya) on the backseat of his grey-coloured Bajaj Super scooter in the 1980s. Originally a dentist by profession, Malay is now associated with the Adani Group in the capacity of a Director at Adani Port and SEZ Limited. Malay Mahadeviya used to play an important role along with his friend Adani. The reason was that Adani was not very comfortable when speaking English and found it difficult to communicate with government officials.

At present, Gautam Adani is worth about $10 billion. He has the largest export company in the country. He bought his own Beechcraft jet in 2005 and Hawker jet in 2008. He has achieved all this in just three and a half decades. Recently, Adani announced an investment of ₹ 35,000 crores in Uttar Pradesh.

Coping with difficulties

Gautam Adani has overcome many adversities. Once in the 90s, he was kidnapped for ransom. So, now his personal security system is very strong. The incident of his kidnapping in the year 1997 shocked everyone. He was present in the Taj Hotel in Mumbai during the terrorist attack of 26th November 2008 , but managed to escape, unharmed.

The political parties in opposition in the country have levelled many accusations against him. Aam Aadmi Party leader

Arvind Kejriwal had attacked BJP's prime ministerial candidate Narendra Modi while releasing a picture of him disembarking from a plane that belonged to Adani. Kejriwal has repeatedly made accusations that only the industrialists like Gautam Adani and Mukesh Ambani have benefitted from Modi's so-called 'gross capitalist' policies. Congress leader Rahul Gandhi also joined in and attacked Modi over the alleged Modi-Adani ties in his election rallies. Adani, however, clarified that he rents out his aircraft to the BJP or whoever asks for it at the market rate. Adani says, "We have four choppers." His chopper is also used by the chief minister of Gujarat and he pays for it. As far as the prime minister of India, Narendra Modi is concerned, he also does not use the chopper for free, rather he uses it by paying a fee.

Tax evasion: On 27th February 2010, the Central Bureau of Investigation arrested Rajesh Adani, Managing Director of Adani Enterprises Limited, on charges of custom duty evasion of ₹ 80 lakh.

In August 2017, Indian Customs alleged that the Adani Group was remitting millions of rupees from the company's books to the Adani family's tax havens abroad. Adani was accused of diverting funds using a Dubai-based shell company. The details about diversion of $235 million were obtained and published by *The Guardian*.

In 2014, the Directorate of Revenue Intelligence traced a complex money trail connecting India to Mauritius via South Korea and Dubai. The company is owned by Gautam Adani's elder brother Vinod Shantilal Adani.

Even today, on many fronts outside the country, he is faced with difficult situations. He got an opportunity to mine from the largest coal mine in Queensland, Australia, at a cost of about $16.6 billion, for which he was also given a loan of about $1 billion by the Australian Government, but the project ran into controversy. Australian environmentalists protested saying that this project was harmful to the environment. The controversy around this project has not stopped even today.

Adani's diamond mine project in Madhya Pradesh has also been in the limelight. It is being said that the Adani Group and the billionaire Anil Agarwal-controlled Vedanta Resources Group are working together to get this diamond project. The mine is estimated to have 32 million carats of diamonds. In fact, even though Adani is accused of being close to Narendra Modi, he has had many friends in Congress-led governments during the expansion of his business in Odisha, Haryana, Maharashtra, Madhya Pradesh and Rajasthan. He is also said to be close to Sharad Pawar and senior Congress leader Kamal Nath.

His ability to make friends is not limited to the borders of India. He is also believed to have built a good rapport with people in Australia's top political circles, with plans to invest a total of $6 billion in the Adani Group's coal mine and a port near Brisbane.

Joining the 100 billion club

Gautam Adani has reached this envied position on his own. When he enrolled in Gujarat University for his BCom, his family was faced with a crisis of livelihood. He abandoned his study under such difficult circumstances. He turned his back on college and embarked on a challenging journey to earn money. He was hard-working and talented. It is said that Adani, who started his commercial journey with a Maruti-800, today has a fleet of BMW vehicles, a Ferrari, a total of three helicopters, three Bombardiers and a Beechcraft aircraft.

Gautam Adani has not achieved this success easily in his journey. Especially from the time that Narendra Modi became the prime minister of the country, Adani has been facing various types of taunts and allegations. It is said that when Narendra Modi took over as the prime minister in May 2014, Adani's personal wealth was about $5 billion, which according to the Bloomberg Billionaires Index has grown to 63,000 crores today and he is 14th on the list of the world's richest people. In Asia, only Reliance Industries chairman, Mukesh Ambani ($76.3 billion) is ahead of him.

Of the six listed companies of the Adani Group, five have a market cap of more than ₹ 1 lakh crore. The group's six listed companies have a combined market cap of over $100 billion. After Tata Group and Reliance, the Adani Group is the third business house in the country to achieve a market cap of over $100 billion. Adani's business spans mines, ports, power plants, airports, data centres, and defence sectors. His net worth has grown tremendously.

Today, Adani Group's business spans the globe in coal trading, mining, oil & gas distribution, ports, multi-modal logistics, and power generation and transmission. The condition of Gautam Adani's home was such that he could never even dream of becoming a billionaire. But he did it on the strength of his passion and vision. This is the real success story of a college dropout student! He proved that to become big, it is not necessary to have a college degree but the quality to think big.

Adani started Adani Power Limited on his own. His success can be gauged from the fact that he was included in Forbes magazine's top 10 Indians. According to the statistics of 2019, his wealth stands at ₹ 7,65,48,89,00,000 i.e., $1100 million. The Adani Group's business has been growing at a rate of around 35 per cent per annum in the last 10-15 years. The Adani Group is currently the country's largest seaport operator and also the largest private airport developer. Apart from this, the group's business is also spread across sectors such as energy, mining, gas, renewables, aerospace, defence, logistics, gas distribution, and agro-commodities.

Gautam Adani's father's name is Shantilal Adani and his mother's name is Shantaben Adani. His wife's name is Preeti, who is a dentist by profession and heads the Adani Foundation. Adani has two sons—Karan and Jeet. Gautam Adani loves Gujarati cuisine. He is shy by nature and avoids going to parties. He lives in Ahmedabad with his family. In the initial years, the group's focus was on agro-commodities and power. By 1991, the company was doing well in both sectors, but Adani believed that it was the right time to enter another business.

World's largest solar power producer

Indian renewable energy company 'Adani Green' is ranked as the world's number one solar power company in terms of capacity. Adani Group has become the top developer in solar power with a capacity of 2.3 GW. The Adani Group is ranked as the number one global solar power generation asset owner in the latest ranking of global solar companies.

Adani Group has been ranked as the top global solar power generation company by Mercom Capital in its ranking of global solar companies. According to a Mercom study, Adani Green's solar portfolio has now reached 12.32 GW, which is more than the total installed capacity in the US in 2019.

The company has under-construction projects of 10.1 GW. The company is also on top in this regard. Commenting on this ranking, Gautam Adani, Chairman, Adani Group says, "Achieving this ranking is a direct result of our commitment to creating the necessary infrastructure for an eco-friendly energy future. We expect our renewable energy platform to create new possibilities for our core business. We are confident that this business will scale new dimensions." Gautam Adani estimates that many business models are going to be impacted in the coming decade as the grasp of renewable energy trends and technology will be better.

Target of 25 GW by 2025: The company said that on the basis of under construction and active capacity, Mercom Capital has named Adani Green as the world's largest solar power company in a time span of just five years. The company aims to reach an installed capacity of 25 GW by 2025.

The company established its first solar project in the year 2015 and in the year 2017 itself, the company completed two solar projects. The company was listed in the year 2018. After the announcement by Mercom, the company's shares rose by 10 per cent to reach a price of ₹ 546.

Game changer contract

The year 1995 proved to be extremely successful for Gautam Adani when his company won the contract to operate Mundra port. The Gujarat government's decision to hand over the operation of Mundra port and SEZ in Kutch to a private company proved to be a turning point in Gautam Adani's life. He got control of this port and today it has become the largest private sector port. Adani Power Limited came into existence in 1996.

Business expansion abroad

He ventured into businesses like mines, ports and railways in Australia and Indonesia. In 2010, he started a mining business in Indonesia. In 2011, the Adani Group bought the Abbot Point coal terminal in Australia for $2.72 billion. During the last one year, despite Covid, his acquisitions and infrastructure projects have added to his fortune. Based on the market cap, six of the Adani Group companies have entered India's 100 most valued companies.

During the years 2020 and 2021, Gautam Adani added several ports, airports, data centres, solar PV manufacturing plants, power and coal generation capacity, etc., to his company's assets. These are either directly owned by the Adani Group or are managed by group companies.

Fortune brand products

In 1999, the Adani Group formed a joint venture with Wilmar International, through which the FMCG (fast-moving consumer goods) business is carried out. It is one of the fastest growing food FMCG companies in the country. It deals in many products under the Fortune brand.

Biggest deal in the renewable sector

Recently, Adani Green Energy Limited (AGEL), a part of the Adani Group, entered into a major deal with SoftBank of Japan and Bharti Group of India. Under this deal, the company will acquire SB Energy India. This will add a capacity of 4,954 MW to Adani's renewable energy portfolio. The deal is worth $3.5 billion (approximately ₹ 25,500 crore).

Control over seven airports

Gautam Adani joined the big league by bidding heavily for the operation of Ahmedabad, Jaipur, Thiruvananthapuram, Mangalore, Guwahati and Lucknow airports. Adani Group holds 74 per cent stake in Mumbai International Airport. The group bought the Mumbai airport stake from GVK Airport Developers.

The shares of Adani Enterprises were listed on the BSE on 25th November 1994. On that day, the shares of the company opened at ₹ 360 on BSE and closed at ₹ 375. On the same day, the company's stock saw a high of ₹ 400 and a low of ₹ 360. And despite the tough global business environment today, the Adani Group successfully introduced seven bonds totalling $4.26 billion (₹ 31,098 crore) in the world markets in 2019-20.

Secret of success

This incident is from the late 1990s. An employee of Adani Exports Company took a wrong decision in relation to sugar trading which caused a loss of ₹ 20 crore to the company. Afraid of being fired from his job, the employee immediately apologised for his grave mistake and also submitted his resignation letter. At that time, Gautam Adani tore his resignation letter and said with a smile, "I know that due to the lessons you learnt from this incident, you will never make such a mistake again in the future. So, why should I let the next appointee take advantage of your learning when I have incurred a loss due to it?"

❑

Adani Group: Gradual Growth

Adani Group is an Indian multinational conglomerate headquartered in Ahmedabad, Gujarat, India. It was founded by Gautam Adani in 1988 as a commodity trading business with the flagship company Adani Enterprises Limited (earlier Adani Exports Limited). The group's diversified businesses include energy, resources, commodities (logistics), agribusiness, real estate, financial services, defence and aerospace. With operations in 70 locations in 50 countries, the group has an annual revenue of over US$13 billion. It is India's largest port developer and operator with ten ports and terminals, including Mundra port which is its largest port. The group is a co-owner of India's largest edible oil brand, Fortune Oil, through a joint venture with Wilmar International in Singapore.

In April 2014, it added a fourth unit of 660 MW at its Tiroda thermal power station, making Adani Power India's largest private power producer. In 2015, Adani was ranked as India's most trusted infrastructure brand by 'The Brand Trust

Report-2015'. The group operates mines in India, Indonesia and Australia and supplies coal to Bangladesh, China and countries in South-East Asia. In 2018-19, the group carried a total cargo of 200 mega tonnes.

The group made its biggest investment in the controversial Carmichael coal mine in Queensland, Australia. In January 2018, the group's commodity and SEZ arm, Adani Ports & SEZ, added equipment and machinery becoming the largest dredger fleet in India. It is also the first group to manufacture high-voltage DC in India. The system was launched in May 2012.

Adani Group started as a commodity trading firm in the year 1988. In the year 1990, the Adani Group developed its port at Mundra to provide a base for its business operations. Its construction started in the year 1995 in Mundra. It became the top net foreign exchange earner in the year 1998. The company started coal trading in the year 1999. It then started a joint venture in edible oil refining with the formation of Adani Wilmar in 2000.

The group's second phase began with the creation of large infrastructure assets. The company established a portfolio of ports, power plants, mines, ships and railway lines in and outside India.

Adani handled 4 million tonnes of cargo at Mundra in the year 2002, which became India's largest private port. Later, in the year 2006, the company became the largest coal importer in India by handling 11 MT of coal. The company expanded its business in the year 2008 by purchasing the Bunyu mine in Indonesia, which has 180 metric tonnes of coal reserves. In the year 2009, the firm started producing 330 MW of thermal power. It created an edible oil refining capacity of 2.2 million tonnes per annum in India.

Adani Enterprises became India's largest coal importer with a 60 per cent market share. It also supplies coal to

NTPC. The Adani Group became India's largest private coal mining company after Adani Enterprises acquired the rights to the Odisha mine in 2010. Dahej port started operations in the year 2011 and later its capacity increased to 20 metric tonnes. The company also purchased the Galilee Basin mine in Australia with 10.4 gigatonnes of coal reserves. It also commissioned a 60 MT handling capacity for the coal import terminal at Mundra, making it the largest port in the world. In addition, in the same year, Adani Group also bought Abbott Point Port in Australia which had a 50 MT handling capacity. It commissioned India's largest solar power plant with a 40 MW capacity. As the firm achieved 3,960 MW of capacity, it became the largest private sector thermal power producer in India. In 2012, the company shifted its focus to three business groups—resources, commodities, and energy.

Adani Power emerged as India's largest private power producer in 2014-20. Adani Power had a total installed capacity of 9,280 MW. During the financial year 2013-14, Mundra port, Adani Ports, and SEZ Limited (APSEZ) handled 100 million tonnes. On 16th May of the same year, Adani Ports acquired Dhamra port on the east coast of India for ₹ 5,500 crore. Dhamra port was a 50-50 partnership venture between Tata Steel and L&T Infrastructure Development Projects, which was now acquired by Adani Ports. The port started operations in May 2011 and handled a total cargo of 14.3 MT in the year 2013-14. With the acquisition of Dhamra port, the group was successful in its plan to increase its capacity to over 200 MT by the year 2020.

In 2015, Adani Renewable Energy Park of the Adani Group signed an agreement with the government of Rajasthan for a 50:50 joint venture to set up India's largest solar park with a capacity of 10,000 MW. In November 2015, the Adani Group started construction at the Vizhinjam port in Kerala.

Adani Aero Defence Systems & Technologies Ltd signed an agreement with Elbit-ISTR and Alpha Design Technologies to work in the field of Unmanned Aircraft Systems (UAS) in India in 2016. In April, Adani Enterprises secured approval from the Gujarat government to start work on solar manufacturing. In September 2016, Adani Green Energy (Tamil Nadu), the renewable energy arm of the Adani Group, commenced operations at Kamuthi in Ramanathapuram, Tamil Nadu with a capacity of 648 MW at an estimated cost of ₹ 4,550 crore. In the same month, the Adani Group inaugurated a 648 MW single-location solar power plant. At the time of its installation, it was the largest solar power plant in the world. In December, the Adani Group inaugurated Punjab's largest 100 MW solar power plant in Bathinda.

On 22nd December 2017, the Adani Group acquired the power arm of Reliance Infrastructure for ₹ 18,800 crore.

Subsidiaries: Adani Enterprises

Adani Enterprises is one of the major subsidiaries and primary holding companies of the Adani Group. The company focuses on setting up other new businesses in the energy and infrastructure sectors. It acts as an incubator, which converts opportunities into thriving or successful businesses. Till now, Adani Enterprises has expanded its presence in various industries and has emerged as a market leader. The company has three subsidiaries—Adani Wilmar, Adani Airport Holdings, and Adani Road Transport.

The company is so successful that it was listed on the 'Bombay Stock Exchange' and the 'National Stock Exchange of India'. Since its inception and listing in 1994, the company has come a long way to reach a market cap of ₹ 22,909 crore. So far, companies such as APSEZ, Adani Power, Adani Transmission, Adani Green Energy, and Adani Gas have separated from Adani Enterprises to list independently on the Indian stock exchange market.

The objective of the company is to provide sustained value, maximise returns for the stakeholders and help in nation-building activities. The vision of Adani Enterprises is to build infrastructure for airports, water, roads, data centres, and solar manufacturing and create sustainable value.

Adani Ports and SEZ

Adani Ports and SEZ (APSEZ) is known as the largest commercial port operator in India as it accounts for more than one-fourth of the cargo transportation in the country. Adani Ports and SEZ (APSEZ) was originally known as Mundra Port and Special Economic Zone Limited until it was renamed in 2012. The company started its operations at Mundra port, which grew to ten ports. Today, Adani Ports and SEZ (APSEZ) is India's largest private port company and Special Economic Zone. The company is headed by APSEZ CEO Karan Adani. The company's operations include port management, commodity and special economic zones. The company operates at the following ports—Mundra, Dahej and Hazira in Gujarat; Dhamra in Odisha; Kattupalli in Tamil Nadu and Vizhinjam in Kerala.

In addition, the Adani Group manages terminals at Mormugao, Ennore, Visakhapatnam and Kandla ports. The commodities arm was initially scaled up by the Mundra Port Infrastructure Development Company, a venture of the government of Gujarat and Adani Port. The company started operations at Mundra port in October 1998. With a concession agreement with the government of Gujarat and the Gujarat Maritime Board in February 2001, the group was given the rights to operate and develop the Mundra port located at the Navinal Island in the Kutch region for 30 years. In August 2020, Mundra port became the largest container port in India, surpassing the Jawaharlal Nehru Port Trust.

Mundra port: This port is also well equipped to handle a wide variety of cargo ranging from dry goods, liquid goods, and raw materials to containers. Mundra SEZ is spread over 8,000 hectares, making it the largest port operation and notified multi-product SEZ in India. It offers investment options such as Free Trade and Warehousing Zones (FTWZs) and Domestic Industrial Zones in India.

It also helps large scale industries with manufacturing set-up based on cluster-based development for various industries. APSEZ has also undertaken mangrove afforestation activities to help the environment, and in 2016, it also announced that all ports and townships were being prepared to run on 100 per cent renewable energy.

Adani Power

One of the biggest portfolio companies of the Adani Group is Adani Power Limited. Even though our per capita energy consumption is well below half of the global average, our energy needs are burgeoning.

The three primary energy sources, meeting over 80% demand are coal, oil and solid biomass. Coal remains a staple in electricity generation and industrialisation. Rapid urbanisation, vehicle ownership and trade expansion have driven oil imports and consumption. Biomass is used mainly as a cooking fuel.

India has traditionally been a coal-dominated energy market. Amongst their peers, both India and China are expected to have large forecasted shares of global coal consumption (2024), at 13% and 52%, respectively, as per a report by Capital Monitor.

Despite the fact that India is the third-largest producer and consumer of electricity worldwide, with an installed power capacity of 408.71 GW as of October 31, 2022, we have our fair share of challenges in this sector, ranging from low access to modern energy sources, heavy dependence on fossil fuels, weak sector institutions and utility governance.

Adani Power was established in August 1996. Adani Power is another major business subsidiary of the Adani Group. The company is headquartered in Ahmedabad, Gujarat, and is recognised as the largest private thermal power producer in India.

The company has thermal plants in Gujarat, Maharashtra, Karnataka, Rajasthan and Chhattisgarh and has a power generation capacity of 12,450 MW. It also operates a massive 40 MW solar power plant in Kutch, Gujarat.

The company develops and maintains power projects in India. The firm has a combined installed capacity of 10,440 MW with four thermal power projects across India. The company runs the following subsidiaries:

✓ Adani Power Maharashtra Limited

✓ Adani Power Rajasthan Limited

✓ Adani Power Dahej Limited

✓ Mundra Power SEZ Limited

✓ Adani Power (Overseas) Limited

In 2014, Adani Power overtook Tata Power to become India's largest power producer. The third phase of Adani Power Limited's (APL) thermal power plant at Mundra, Gujarat is the world's first coal-based plant to receive carbon credits from the United Nations Framework Convention on Climate Change (UNFCCC). Adani Power's Udupi power plant has been awarded the 'Power Award' by the government of Karnataka.

This Indian company is also the first company in the world to set up a coal-based thermal power project registered under the Clean Development Mechanism (CDM) of the Kyoto Protocol. The company is also working on a plan to set up a 1,600 MW plant at Godda, Jharkhand.

According to the latest report released on the National Power Portal, the private sector accounted for 48.1% of India's total power generation installed capacity as of October 31, 2021, which stood at 391,091 MW. State government utilities had a share of 26.7% followed by Central government agencies that took up the remaining 25.2%.

Adani's expansion in the power sector began in the early 2000s, when the Adani Group launched the first power plant in Mundra in 2006. Around that time, they were the largest importers of coal, supplying more than half of the country's by the Mundra terminal, which housed the world's largest coal import terminal, the group scaled rapidly in the power generation business. It operates in the segment along with other players, such as Tata Power, Jindal and public sector enterprises like NTPC.

It is now the largest private thermal power producer in India, with a power generation capacity of 12,450 MW comprising thermal power plants in many states across India, including Gujarat, Rajasthan, Maharashtra, Karnataka, and Chhattisgarh and a 40 MW solar power project in Gujarat.

Power projects execution in India require Power Purchase Agreements (PPA); most of the PPAs are with the state government, and this outlines the rate at which the state government purchases power. The variables which define a company's profitability are immense - raw material costs, transport, logistics. It is here that Adani's astuteness again is at play - by backward and forward integration, he has ensured that he has access to as many supply chain components as possible. This renders an overall price advantage of 10-20%, which is commendable in the infrastructure business.

Mundra was built to run largely on coal imports from Bunyu Island, Indonesia, unlike its peers around the same time. The sourcing is governed under a 15-year supply agreement with

Adani Enterprises. The Mundra project was built across four phases of 2 × 330 MW, 2 × 330 MW, 2 × 660 MW supercritical and 3 × 660 MW supercritical units. In efforts to reduce sulphur oxide emissions, the 1980 MW Phase IV also constitutes flue gas desulpherisers.

The plant has set global benchmarks for efficiency and sustainability. Water system of the plant, seawater from the Gulf of Kutch is used, which is transported using large-diameter glass- reinforced pipes, making the Mundra plant the first project in India to use such technology.

Adani Power supplies approximately 1,000 MW from Phase I to Gujarat Vitran Nigam. Under a 15-year supply agreement, additional 221MW power from Phase II is sold to AEL. Other purchase agreements include the supply of 1,424 MW from Phase IV to Uttar Haryana Bijli Vitran Nigam and Dakshin Haryana Bijli Vitran Nigam under 25- year PPAs. Around 1,000 MW from the Mundra power station is transmitted to Power Grid Corporation of India at Degham, Gujarat, via a 433 km long 400kV transmission line. In addition, a dedicated 989 km long and 500kV bi- pole, high-voltage, direct current transmission line was laid to transmit power from Mundra to Mohindergarh in Haryana. The line has the capacity to transmit 2,500MW from Phase IV.

The energy infrastructure business is extremely challenging, demanding huge investments, with projects having long gestational periods. It is also hugely dependent on efficient energy infrastructure. Despite getting orders, sometimes projects are held up because of executional challenges. However, Adani ensured that his team is fully prepared to circumvent any challenges. One such example is when the team undertook the mammoth task of commissioning India's biggest transmission line, nearly 1000 km long, through Haryana, Gujarat, and Rajasthan.

Adani Power Limited had acquired an order to provide 1424 MW power to Haryana for 25 years. Though the order was huge, it came with considerable challenges. The Mundra Dehgam transmission system was catering to the maximum at that time, 1200 MW.

The company evaluated all possible options and after extensive brainstorming, empirical calculations macro- economic analysis and weighing long-term business opportunities, a High Voltage Direct Current (HVDC) Transmission system was identified as a possible solution. At that time, incidentally, Haryana was constructing a 400 KV substation at Mohindergarh which was expected to become the hub for other load centres in the state.

It was decided that HVDC transmission system would act as a bulk power highway with capacity to transmit 2500 MW of power from Mundra (Gujarat) to the load Centres in the National Capital Region (NCR) through an inverter station at Mohindergarh (Haryana) in a single hop of about 1000 kilometres. This was the first time that any private player was getting into constructing a transmission network to build such a system.

HVDC was a challenging technology – finding talented professionals to execute the project was difficult. Training and knowledge sharing forums were organised for staff in erection and commissioning, expert site visits were organised for assessment and addressing doubts, lectures and on-site training by industry partners and visits and trainings at similar HVDC station under operation such as Talcher - Kolar and Balia – Bhiwani were organised.

The project was completed in a record 24 months and was the first of its kind project registered in Clean Development Mechanism (CDM), again attesting to the never-say-die attitude of the founder.

Adani did not rest after getting the first power plant commissioned in Mundra. Mundra (Phase III) is the first coal based thermal power project in the world to be granted carbon credits by United Nations Framework Convention on Climate Change (UNFCCC). The company was also the first to develop a methodology for High Voltage Direct Current power transmission lines and got it approved from UNFCCC.

The plant has continually invested in technology and efficiency generation. It effortlessly worked upon improved quality of raw material sourcing, increase in plant efficiencies leading to reduction in carbon emissions. The plant also managed a significant, around 106%, reduction in pollution by fly ash utilisation in FY21.

Many of Adani Power plants have achieved the highest level of operational excellence through business process transformation initiative setting highest benchmark in operational efficiency parameters. The highest standards of safety and housekeeping have enabled the group to secure many industrial awards and recognitions.

For transmission and generation assets, asset availability is critical. To avoid system overloads, seamless availability ensures smooth transfer of power in a grid. To enable active monitoring of Adani assets, a centralised dashboard application capturing the availability of various sites was developed in-house by the team Adani in 2020. The centralised application helped enable active real time monitoring of system availability and also helped in diagnosing operational issues well in advance, thus aiding fast and accurate decision making.

Adani Transmission

Adani's journey in the transmission industry started long before the inception of Adani Transmission Limited in the year 2006. The company, integrated in the year 2013, handles the commissioning, operation and maintenance of the electric power transmission system. Adani Transmission Limited Company has a total transmission capacity of 16,200 MW and is currently one of the largest private sector power transmission companies in India. Adani Transmission Limited (ATL) is one of the largest private sector transmission companies – it owns and operates various High Voltage AC (Alternate Current) transmission lines and substations of 132kV, 220kV, 400kV, 765kV voltage level and also High Voltage DC (Direct Current) transmission lines and substations of +/- 500kV voltage level. With a portfolio of more than 18,500 km of circuit transmission lines and around 38,600 MVA of power transformation capacity, Adani is set to upset the transmission business as well.

By 2020, the company operates a total network of 12,200 circuit kilometres and an additional 3,200 circuit kilometres are under various stages of construction. Adani Transmission was founded by Gautam Adani and is headquartered in Ahmedabad. The company entered the distribution space in 2018 with the acquisition of Reliance Infrastructure's power generation, transmission and distribution business in Mumbai.

Now Adani Electricity Mumbai Limited, which operates under Adani Transmission, caters to over 3 million customers and their electricity needs in Mumbai. The company aims to establish 20,000 circuit kilometres of transmission lines by 2022 with the help of organic and inorganic growth opportunities. It is the first private power sector player in the country to achieve an international investment grade rating.

In 2020 and 2021, it purchased assets of Kalapataru Power Transmission, Maharashtra State Electricity Transmission Company, and Essel Infraprojects respectively.

Outpacing its peers, ATL has grown 18% CAGR from 2016 to 2022, against the industry growth of 6% annually. Revenue growth for the past five years was at 23.34% CAGR.

At the ET Awards 2022, Adani Transmission won in the Emerging Company of the Year category. The jury members voted in its favour recognising the company's growth and profitability over the past decade.

Adani Green Energy

The distribution arm of the Adani Transmission Limited (ATL), Adani Electricity Mumbai Limited (AEML) is India's largest private sector power distribution utility, distributing electricity for over nine decades in Mumbai. A 100% subsidiary of Adani Transmission Ltd, AEML is into power generation, transmission and retail electricity distribution.

Adani Electricity meets close to 2,000 MW of power demand in Mumbai, serving 31.5 lakh households and establishments in Mumbai. In the Ministry of Power's 11th edition of the 'Annual Integrated Rating & Ranking' of country's power distribution utilities, Adani Electricity was honoured with the 1st rank with Grade A+ and the highest integrated score of 99.6 out of 100.

Adani Green Energy is the renewable energy arm of the group, whose portfolio includes 5,290 MW of wind and solar power plants. This Adani subsidiary is one of the largest renewable energy companies in India with a current project portfolio of 13,990 MW. Adani Green Energy is known to develop, operate, build and maintain solar and wind power projects. The power generated is supplied to central and state government institutions or even government-backed corporations. The company has now expanded to more than 11 Indian states.

The company uses the latest technologies in its projects and has an impressive portfolio of 54 operational projects and 12 under-construction projects. It is leading India in its renewable energy journey and aims to provide a cleaner, better and greener future for the country. The company operates one of the largest solar photovoltaic plants (Kamuthi Solar Power Project) in the world.

Adani Green Energy also has over 39 subsidiaries and has won the world's largest solar bid of 46 billion rupees by the Solar

Energy Corporation of India. The company is known to manage over 5,290 MW of wind power and solar power plants.

Biggest deal in the renewable sector: The Adani Group took over the management of seven airports in the country in less than two years. With this, the company controls almost one-fourth of India's air traffic. Adani Green Energy has set a target to increase its renewable energy capacity by about eight times by the year 2025. The company also signed the biggest deal in the history of the renewable energy sector. It signed a deal to buy SB Energy for about 26,000 crores. With this acquisition, the total capacity of Adani Green has gone up to 24,300 MW.

Adani Green is the only Indian renewable energy company which launched an Investment Grade-rated Green Bond. The Group also conceptualised the world's first single- use plastic-free solar plant and the first water positive plant at its solar plant in Kamuthi. Adani Green also became the first company to receive renewable generation asset issuance from India with Investment Grade rating from all three rating agencies (Fitch, Moody's, and S&P), further attesting to the relentless innovation and continuous improvement credo of its founder.

Adani Green Energy Limited (AGEL) has a number of firsts to its credit – it invested in India's largest bi-facial and tracker-based solar project; the first to use string invertors, enhancing energy stability; commissioning of India's first hybrid energy park, which reconciles solar and wind renewable energy infrastructure within the same location, improving return on land and empowering the company to generate power through all 24 hours.

COVID – induced supply chain disruptions put the spotlight on integration of resources. Adani has acknowledged how COVID was an eye opener for the Indian solar industry and the government. China, Vietnam and Malaysia are the major exporters of more than 80% of solar equipment needed in India.

Since 2021, imports of solar equipment have touched over 800 MW per month. According to the All India Solar Industries Association (AISIA), domestic manufacturers make only 4 GW of solar cell and 16 GW of modules, a pithy fraction of the total demand. Domestic manufacturers are further rendered uncompetitive due to lack of basic raw materials like ingots and wafers and poly silicon. Our import dependence makes us further vulnerable to price hikes as was witnessed during COVID, when China raised prices by 50–60% thus adversely impacting the Indian solar industry.

As a visionary entrepreneur who understands the value of integrated supply chains, Adani has been working upon a big green solar manufacturing ecosystem in Mundra, investing $4 billion. The facility will also support the entire Group's green hydrogen ambitions. This venture is projected to be backed by green funds. Adani Green, the group's renewable energy arm, was the first energy utility from India to raise $2 billion Global Medium-Term Notes (GMTN) or Sustainability Linked Bonds (SLB).

Adani has always propounded business adjacencies, leading the Group's expansion from ports to power, energy, oils to defence. The business adjacencies of the port-to-airports majorly leave it with considerable heft in the markets it operates in. The Group's infrastructure journey started with the Mundra Port, acknowledged to be a jewel in the Group's crown, and it led to other businesses such as APSEZ, power generation, and subsequently into transmission and distribution. The Mundra Thermal Power Project, that began operations in 2009, is the backbone of the $4.7 billion Adani Power.

The Adani Group owns more than 200 ports, airports, power stations, cement plants, mines, defence factories, renewable energy farms, electrical facilities and gas distribution networks across 23 states and Union Territories.

The backward-forward integration strategy ensures that the Group exploits available synergies and gets unrestricted access to transport and logistics for any new business.

Adani Wilmar

Adani Wilmar was created out of a joint venture between the Adani Group and the Singapore-based company Wilmar International Limited. Wilmar is one of the fastest growing food FMCG companies in India and Asia's leading agribusiness conglomerates. The company has the largest range of edible oils like soya, flax, mustard, rice bran, groundnut and cottonseed oil.

Apart from oil, it also manufactures other products like basmati rice, pulses, soya chunks, *besan*, Fortune wheat flour, *rava*, *sooji*, all of which are well-known products in India. Brands such as Fortune, Kings, Bullet, Raag, Opportunity, Pilaf, Jubilee, Frayola, Alpha, Alife and Aadhar operate under Adani Wilmar.

The company has the largest distribution network among all the branded edible oil players in India as it has more than 95 stock points, 5,000 distributors, and 1.5 million outlets across the country. Adani Wilmar has become internationally successful after selling its edible oil to the Middle East and is now exporting its products to over 19 countries such as Middle Eastern countries, South-East Asian nations, countries in East Africa, Singapore, Australia and New Zealand.

Adani Gas Limited

It is an urban gas distribution company and a subsidiary of Adani, that primarily serves industrial companies and residential customers in Indian states. Adani Gas currently uses the city gas distribution network to supply piped natural gas to commercial, domestic and industrial companies in the country. The company also supplies compressed natural gas to the transportation sector.

Adani Gas has so far established a city gas distribution network in cities like Ahmedabad and Vadodara in Gujarat, Faridabad in Haryana, and Khurja in Uttar Pradesh. Natural gas is not only environmentally friendly but it is also convenient and reliable, allowing consumers to enjoy a high level of safety, convenience and economic efficiency.

Initiative in sports

Adani Group has taken great initiative in promoting sports. The 'Garv Hai' programme launched in 2016 to prepare athletes for the Rio Olympics is a nationwide programme to promote sports and support athletes in India.

In 2021, it was launched for the second time to prepare athletes for the Tokyo Olympics-2022, Asian Games and Commonwealth Games. The programme focuses on archery, shooting, athletics, boxing and wrestling. The 'Garv Hai' pilot project beneficiaries of 2016 include Ankita Raina (tennis), Pinki Jangra (boxing), Shiva Thapa (boxing), Khushbir Kaur (athletics), Inderjit Singh (athletics), Mandeep Jangra (boxing), Malaika Goel (shooting), Deepak Punia (wrestling), K T Irfan (race walking) and Sanjeevani Jadhav (athletics). Another initiative is the Surguja Football Academy in Chhattisgarh. So far, 11 players from Surguja have been selected to play for the national Indian football team.

Awards and recognition

- ✓ Adani Ports and Special Economic Zone (APSEZ) Limited won the 'Emerging Company of the Year 2014' award at the 'Economic Time Awards'.
- ✓ In January 2018, Adani Green Energy Limited, a division of the Adani Group, entered the 'Global Top 15 List' of solar power developers by GTM Research, the market analysis and consulting arm of Greentech Media.

- ✓ Adani Ports and SEZ (APSEZ) received the 'India's Container Port of the Year, 2016' award in Mumbai. The port developer and commodity arm of the group was honoured at the seventh edition of the 'All India Maritime and Commodity Awards' (MALA).
- ✓ Adani Ports and Special Economic Zone (APSEZ) Limited won the 'Non-Major Port of the Year 2015' award by the 'All Time Maritime and Logistics Award'.

Philanthropy

The 750-bed GK General Hospital in Bhuj, established by Gujarat Adani Institute of Medical Sciences, provides treatment to many people. The foundation has started village development projects in the villages of Bada Gram Panchayat.

Adani Foundation implemented the 'Rice Intensification System' on 4,000 acres of farmland spread over 42 villages and empowered over 2,000 farmers.

Adani Foundation established 'Adani Vidya Mandir', schools for underprivileged children at three different locations in Ahmedabad, Bhadreshwar and Surguja, offering them free education. Other schools funded by the foundation include Adani DAV Public School, Adani Vidyalaya and Navchetan Vidyalaya. The foundation provides education to 1,00,000 children through 600 schools and kindergartens.

In 2020, the Adani Foundation donated ₹ 100 crore to the 'PM Cares' fund to fight the outbreak of coronavirus. The foundation contributed ₹ 5 crore to the Gujarat CM Relief Fund and ₹ 1 crore to the Maharashtra CM Relief Fund. Adani Group employees contributed ₹ 4 crore to Adani Foundation for Covid-19 relief measures.

In March 2021, the Adani Group announced that it would reimburse the charges for Covid-19 vaccination paid by employees and their families.

Summary

The CEO of Adani Group is Gautam Adani and under his guidance, Adani Group has emerged as a global integrated infrastructure player with interests in resources, commodity and energy verticals. The Adani Group is headquartered in Ahmedabad, Gujarat. Adani Group is a leader when we talk about business operations in sectors such as energy, resources, logistics and agriculture. Adani Group's subsidiaries are Adani Gas Limited, Adani Wilmar, Adani Green Energy Limited, Adani Transmission Limited, Adani Power Limited, Adani Ports and Special Economic Zone Limited, and Adani Enterprise Limited.

Over the past three decades, the Adani Group has continued to develop to establish itself as a global leader in various sectors such as energy, resources, commodities, coal trading and mining, real estate, aerospace, public transport infrastructure, consumer, finance, solar manufacturing, defence, gas distribution and agriculture. The company has also benchmarked global standards across all sectors. The company has been successful so far due to its many successful subsidiaries and will continue to reach greater heights in the future.

Family

Gautam Adani is married to Preeti Adani and they have two sons. The name of the elder son is Karan Adani and the name of the younger son is Jeet Adani. Preeti is a dentist and contributes to Gautam's work as managing trustee of the Adani Foundation, particularly in matters of education. She runs many campaigns for the education of children. Karan Adani has completed his graduation in Economics from Purdue University, USA. After completing his studies, he joined his father's business.

Karan was appointed as the CEO of Adani Ports and SEZ (APSEZ) with effect from 1st January 2016. He has been overseeing the development of Adani ports across India since 2009. He married Paridhi Shroff, the daughter of Cyril Shroff in the year 2013. Shroff is arguably the biggest name in the corporate law sector of India.

Karan fully handles the responsibility of Adani Group. In the Adani Group, he oversees the day-to-day operations.

Valuable thoughts from Adani

- ✓ It was my dream to become something from the beginning and this is the test of your perseverance.
- ✓ The main objective of the infrastructure sector is to create wealth for the nation, it is a part of nation-building.
- ✓ I dislike politics. I am not associated with any political party, but I have friends in all political parties.
- ✓ I decide my investment policy keeping in mind the interest of the nation, which never changes.
- ✓ I am a school dropout. I moved to Mumbai at the age of 16 to try my luck in business.
- ✓ You are either an introvert or an extrovert; I am an introvert. I am not a social person; I dislike going to parties.
- ✓ Either you sit by accumulating your capital or keep growing continuously.
- ✓ I have my own method of analysis; it's very simple. There is no web of words. If someone complicates his point, I don't like it at all.
- ✓ Business itself means taking risks, uncertainty, and restlessness.

❑

Goodness is Essential for Development: Adani

The existence and emergence of the Adani Group have been an integral part of India's resurgence. Over the past three decades, it has reached millions of people who believed in it, inspired them to be ambitious, inspired them to achieve those ambitions, and disciplined them in order to set new standards in everything.

According to Gautam Adani: "Today, as the world takes India into its most defined stage of development, the Adani Group's responsibility towards the nation assumes greater importance. I believe that our responsibility to give back to society makes us who we are. Wherever we work, our ability to contribute there will define our future and hold us together as a global organisation.

"As we continue to work towards bridging the urban-rural divide and creating equitable growth opportunities across geographies, we will also explore new horizons that meet the changing aspirations of a new India.

"It is increasingly being recognised that development is incomplete if it is devoid of any good for the nation and the society as a whole. I believe that development should infuse prosperity and harmony and above all, it should spread happiness!

"In the last 30 years, we have created fundamental and lasting assets for nation-building. The vision for the future should be to increase the factor of goodness. It should be to tap new opportunities—within India as well as across the world.

"When I say goodness, it is broadly divided into three dimensions:

"First, our presence in businesses that matter to a nation must have a definite impact on the lives of the millions of people affected by our projects. Whether it is delivering LPG to fuel-starved rural kitchens or safeguarding the nation's staple food produce, our actions should contribute to the nation's happiness index.

"Second, we must ensure that our immediate communities around our business sites are empowered by our presence and become self-sustaining in the shelter of our expansion.

"Third, we must continue to enter the areas where the country needs a foothold. We will see these opportunities as part of our national duty.

"At Adani Group, we believe in enriching lives through state-of-the-art infrastructure and our contribution to nation-building. We believe in growth with goodness.

"India remains the fastest growing economy in the world. Recently, the World Economic Forum predicted that India would lift 25 million more households out of poverty over the next decade, reducing the share of families below the poverty line to

5 per cent. These are staggering statistics considering the sheer size of our country and are a harbinger of hope and optimism for the country as a whole. No doubt, there will be challenges and unpredictable circumstances. But there is no denying the fact that the aspirations of our nation are taking shape in a transformative and exciting way and India is at a turning point.

"Despite being one of the fastest growing economies in the world, the per capita electricity consumption in India is about one-third of the global average. Given our demographics and projected economic outlook, there is significant room for growth. The availability of electricity will play an important role in meeting the country's ambitious development goals in the next decade.

"During the fiscal year 2019, India's annual electricity demand grew by 5.15 per cent, while generation capacity grew by only 3.5 per cent, slowing investment in baseload capacity. Thermal power continues to be the mainstay of baseload power accounting for more than 50 per cent of the installed GW capacity in the country. Efficiently operating thermal power plants meeting the country's baseload requirements are likely to remain important as the demand for electricity continues to grow.

"Various regulatory and judicial orders, which provide for compensation for higher fuel costs and bearing costs for regulatory claims, will help in improving financial strength and achieving a greater degree of certainty for future earnings. However, there is a need for continuous reforms and equitable measures to encourage private sector investment to achieve the objective of 24×7 reliable electricity for all. Critical issues are improving the availability of domestic fuel and actively addressing the challenges posed by a greater share of intermittent power generation in the grid.

"APL is committed to providing electricity to those who need it most.

"As India's largest private thermal power producer, we are committed to meeting the growing electricity demand in India as well as in our neighbouring countries. We will also continue to explore select high-quality stressed assets with attractive valuations for inorganic capacity development opportunities.

"Our 1,600 MW power project in Godda, Jharkhand will supply electricity to Bangladesh through a dedicated transmission line. This project marks our foray into 'ultra-supercritical technology', which provides greater plant efficiency with lower emissions.

"These investments are a reflection of our belief that a baseload, partially met by thermal power, is vital to helping provide opportunities to our nation's 300 million people who need the power to help transform their lives.

"We are equally committed to continuing to strengthen our corporate governance practices while increasing our focus on financial and operational performance.

"Accordingly, we have implemented a strict policy for related party transactions. We will include evaluation by internal business teams, review through an external agency and due diligence by an executive committee consisting of the board of directors, to ensure transparency and that all transactions are at arm's length. These steps are in addition to the existing regulatory requirements.

"The Adani Foundation continues its mission of making a difference to the lives of the various communities of the group.

"Our initiative is now touching more than 5,00,000 households in 18 states and 2,250 villages and towns. This goodness along with the growth of the business makes our efforts meaningful.

"I would like to thank all our stakeholders for their continued support and conviction in our philosophy of 'Growth with Good'.

We are committed to continuing our exciting journey of growth with the support and guidance of our customers, employees, shareholders, bankers, governments, and the board. We will continue to be an active contributor to nation-building, adding value to our product portfolio and exploring new opportunities that contribute to the growth of our business and nation."

❑

Key Features of Adani Group

Gautam Adani says, "We are an inter-generational holder of equity. We remain focused on creating long-term sustainable value for our partners, our minority investors and ourselves."

- ✓ The Adani Group through Adani Enterprises Limited (AEL) made its foray into the airports in diversified groups and today one out of every four passengers in India flies from Adani airport.
- ✓ Adani Green Energy met its renewable energy target of 25 GW four years ahead of schedule.

On Covid-19 crisis

Adani says, "History has shown that many lessons are learnt from every pandemic crisis and I believe that India and the world have become wiser while going through this pandemic. India will be a 5 trillion dollar economy and then become a 15 trillion plus economy in the next two decades. India will emerge as one of the largest global markets, both in terms of consumption size and market capitalisation."

$100 billion market cap

The performance of the listed entities of the Adani Group has propelled its portfolio to cross $100 billion in market capitalisation. This valuation is a milestone and a first for a first-generation Indian company. Although there is reason to be proud, evaluation is the only outcome that really matters to the Adani Group. It is the path that led it to this point, and more importantly, the path it has taken. The Adani Group attributes its performance and resilience to the core values it believes in. These values further its objective of nation-building.

Consolidated EBITDA (earnings before interest, tax, depreciation and amortisation) for the listed portfolio for FY 2021 stood at over ₹ 32,000 crore, registering a year-on-year growth of 22 per cent. All the shares of Adani gave more than 100 per cent returns and the businesses ensured that they return about ₹ 9,500 crore to the equity shareholders. This is an increase of 166 per cent in profit after tax on a yearly basis.

The Adani Group is an inter-generational holder of equity. They focus on creating long-lasting sustainable value for their partners, their minority investors and themselves. Recently, some media houses made reckless and irresponsible reporting related to the administrative actions of the regulators. This led to unexpected volatility in the market price of Adani's shares. Unfortunately, some small investors in the Adani Group were influenced by this distorted narrative, with some commentators and journalists implying that companies have regulatory powers over their shareholders and companies can force disclosure.

Such diversions will not affect the Adani Group in the long term. It has always been a trusted organisation, which has faced challenges that few would have dared or imagined. Adani Group

Chairman Gautam Adani says, "Every challenge before us makes us stronger and better prepared."

Ukraine crisis

Asia's richest man, Gautam Adani, who built his empire on coal-based businesses, says that the world's attention has been drawn to green energy solutions after the Ukraine war forced countries to scramble for supplies of fossil fuels.

Adani wrote in a May 26 note after attending the 'World Economic Forum' in Davos, "Few are willing to accept that there has been a shift in favour of green solutions and technologies. This fragility has been fully exposed by the crisis in Ukraine."

He said, "Russia's invasion of Ukraine has disrupted global supply chains, pushing crude and coal prices to a record high in many years."

Adani, a first-generation entrepreneur whose net worth has soared to $99 billion this year, will also face the challenges of green energy as he seeks to replace fossil fuel-based electricity used at his ports with green energy. According to Adani, "We want to build green data centres—a huge energy consumption business—and aim to become the world's largest renewable electricity producer by the end of this decade. If India is to be made one, she has to be made one of the key players in aiming to be carbon net-zero by 2070."

Apart from energy security, Adani said the talks in Davos this year were heavily targeted towards border security and self-reliance in defence capabilities. He underlined how much the world has been shaken by the war in Ukraine.

He said, "Almost every leader I spoke to and some explicitly stated that a new and more sophisticated arms race could now take place, and alliances would now be built around defence agreements. Many countries may prioritise defence manufacturing and procurement as a non-negotiable aspect of self-reliance."

Adani is one of the top gainers with his assets increasing by 96 per cent. His net worth increased to ₹ 1,01,307 crore from ₹ 51,612 crore last year.

Over the past 25 years, the group has established itself as a leading infrastructure conglomerate in India. His company reported 3.11 per cent growth in consolidated net profit at ₹ 350.55 crore for the third quarter ending December 2017-18.

Adani claims that his company is focused on incubating diverse nation-critical businesses to address the country's growing need for energy, food and infrastructure.

❑

Learning Different Things

Malay Mahadevia, who has known Adani since 1974 and is the director of Adani Group, says, "He talks very less. He hates boasting about his success."

Adani is a first-generation entrepreneur who rose from a modest background and built a huge business empire worth ₹ 30,000 crore in a short span of time. But the shy Adani, who runs a conglomerate spanning ports, power and coal trading, doesn't like comparisons. He says, "I request you not to make comparisons. I like Dhirubhai's vision. Even during the licence raj, he saw the bigger picture and set up world-class facilities." He quickly adds, "But he's not a role model. I like to imbibe different things from different people."

Adani, whose family comes from a community of entrepreneurs in Tharad, northern Gujarat, speaks slowly, with long pauses. English is not his first language and he takes his time searching for the right words. When he answers a question, he is not to be fooled.

Unlike Dhirubhai, Adani is a product of liberalised India. After spending a few years as a diamond merchant in Mumbai in the early 1980s, he established Adani Enterprises as an export-import company in 1988, just three years before the end of the licence-permit raj by Manmohan Singh. Adani rejected any suggestion of secret deals. "Dealing with the government doesn't mean you have to give bribes. From my experience of working with bureaucrats and politicians, they will definitely help you if you are a credible business group. At the end of the day, they also want development—in their constituency, state or country."

He says that he prefers to keep a safe distance from politics. Adani says, "I don't like politics. I am not associated with any political party. I have friends in all political parties. But I never discuss politics with them, I only talk to them on development issues."

He is clear about the kind of politicians he likes. "I am not attracted to politicians who do not have a vision and just want to make money. I like those who have farsightedness."

Vision is an important word in Adani's vocabulary. He says, "Each era has its own compulsions and opportunities." Dhirubhai saw opportunities in the obstacles. In the early 1990s, Adani competed with Reliance by importing PVC which was being indegeneously manufactured by Reliance and selling it at cheap rates.

Adani insists that his personal wealth is just a number. "Money doesn't drive me. I love challenges where you feel like you are a part of nation-building. I could have built many different businesses. But I feel more satisfied when I create something that can be a part of India's growth journey."

In the year 1995, he got the right opportunity. The government of Gujarat decided to invite a private player to run the Mundra port in Kutch for the first time in India. Adani acquired control of the port in 1993 from the then Chimanbhai Patel government, though the formal announcement came two years later. Today it is the largest of the 12 private sector ports in the country.

"I can assure customers of the power at the lowest cost if I have coal, ports and transportation," says Adani. "We go public only when the risks are taken care of. Mundra went public in 2007 and Adani Power in 2009. I bought a big mine in Australia for $10 billion. I have realised that there is uncertainty here. It is not wise to have such a large part of electricity generation which is Indian fuel-dependent."

❑

Realisation of Adani's Vision: Mundra Port

Gautam Adani's business instincts are very sharp and his rags-to-riches story is another example of the finely developed business acumen of the people of his coastal state.

His business spans a wide range of industries such as power, oil and gas exploration, export-import of pulses and fruits, and port development. The group is divided into various divisions—energy verticals include coal trading, mining, shipping, power generation and distribution, oil and gas exploration, oil bunkering and logistics.

Agribusiness includes edible oil business and export-import of pulses and fruits among others. In other business, the real estate includes all commercial and residential properties in Mumbai, Ahmedabad, Mundra, Cochin and New Delhi.

Adani real estate sector is getting ready for the big game. Mumbai's biggest deal for the uninitiated was done by Mr Adani, when he bought 8-10 acres of land in Bandra-Kurla for over ₹ 2,000 crore, which was the largest real estate transaction in the city.

The Adani Group is today the largest coal importer of India. The company is also engaged in the development of coal mines in Indonesia through its wholly owned subsidiary, which will prove to be a major asset to its power plants as well as the coal trading business.

The 2,640 MW plant at Mundra and the 2,000 MW plant in Gondia district of Maharashtra will require a total investment of ₹ 20,000 crore and large imports of coal. Adani says, "We plan to install 10,000 MW by 2016 and be a part of India's growth story." The group is currently looking for additional coal assets in Indonesia and Africa.

The group is now setting up the world's largest coal receiving terminal at Mundra for Tata Power, which is building a 4,000 MW power plant. The 40 million tonne terminal, which will support a coal-fired power plant with a discharge rate of 6,000 metric tonnes per hour, is being set up just outside the SEZ.

What makes it interesting is the carefully designed forward/ backward integration along with the full range of logistics. Adani Shipping, currently a division of Adani Enterprises, may be spun off and is likely to be relocated to Singapore. The division has ordered two bulk carriers and is looking to buy two more. The company has successfully commenced a bunkering business—supply of fuel to ships through a unit at Mundra SEZ.

A few years back, the company was embroiled in major controversies over its market operations, forcing market regulator SEBI to temporarily suspend its promoters. Later, the company came out of the bad phase and became the darling of the market. Its share price has gone up and so has its market capitalisation.

Thanks to the commodity cycle, its various divisions are performing well. Agribusiness has written a success story. Adani

Agri Fresh, its wholly owned subsidiary, is the first company in India to successfully implement controlled atmosphere storage facilities (CASF) for storage and trading of fruits and vegetables under controlled climatic conditions.

Adani Agro Logistics, its wholly owned subsidiary, is setting up fully mechanised silos for food grain storage and has entered into a long-term contract with the Food Corporation of India. Adani Wilmar, a 50:50 JV with Singapore-based Wilmar Group, is a leader in the branded edible oil segment with its brand 'Fortune'.

The company is one of the leading exporters of iron ore. Through its wholly owned subsidiary, Adani Global FZE, it continues to be the largest importer of iron scrap in India. A consortium, where the company is the majority stakeholder, has been given two onshore blocks for oil and gas exploration--one in Gujarat and one in Assam—under the government's NELP-IV. The group has also been awarded an onshore block in Thailand for oil and gas exploration.

If you travel through Bhuj airport, you pass through a long desolate stretch of land. As soon as you reach Mundra, you see India's deepest and fastest growing private port; it is a thriving industrial township. The first investment in Mundra port was made in 1998 when the government liberalised the port policy.

At that time many people did not support this move of Adani. There were no roads and no rail connectivity. But the group's chairman Gautam Adani had the vision to enrich the barren land.

The port today handles about 200 million tonnes of miscellaneous cargo such as coal, wheat, fertilisers, steel, edible oils, chemicals, and various oil and petroleum products.

The vast 'Special Economic Zone' (SEZ) is attracting traders from across the country and abroad. Several cargo berths and two container terminals, rail connectivity, and a vast tank farm and container stack-up yard are part of the rapidly growing port company.

The port provides the shortest land route from any port in the vast hinterland of western and northern India, accounting for two-thirds of India's GDP. It is an ideal gateway for Asian, European, American and African markets and is well connected to the national railway network.

A 57-km stretch has been developed privately to connect the port with Adipur, the nearest railhead. Various broad-gauge conversions on the Mundra-North Bharat route have resulted in mileage of up to 200 km from Mumbai. The rail track is capable of hauling double-stack container trains, resulting in substantial freight savings.

On the road front, the port is connected to the NH grid by several national and state highways. There are two commercial airports—Bhuj and Kandla—which are about 60 km from the port. Adani has developed an airstrip in Mundra for personal use.

MPSEZ—Logistics Management, is the result of the merger of two group companies to leverage the vast expertise acquired in Gujarat Adani Port Limited (GAPL) and Mundra Special Economic Zone.

MPSEZ is the operating and holding company for the three port projects—Mundra, Dahej and Dholera, and the giant SEZ at Mundra. The cost of all the projects taken up by the MPSEZ was estimated to be around ₹ 4,000 crore. While Mundra and the proposed Dholera port are wholly owned by Adani, Dahej port is being developed in a joint venture with Petronet LNG.

Adani Group holds a 50 per cent stake. The multi-purpose port at Dahej is a mandatory condition as part of the agreement between Petronet, India's largest LNG importer, and the Gujarat government. The facilities at the port are unmatched.

Importers of coal and wheat prefer to import through Mundra, irrespective of the cargo sourcing.

The port has eight operational multi-purpose berths with a draft of up to 17.5 metres, which can handle dry-bulk, breakbulk and liquid cargo. These berths are also capable of handling post-Panamax and Capsize ships.

DP World-operated Mundra International Container Terminal (MICT) has two berths with a draft of 17.5 metres and a capacity to handle 1 million TEU. The second container terminal built by Adani is currently being operated by the group itself.

The port hosts over a dozen container freight stations (CFS) operated by various players. It carries adequate infrastructure to handle all types of dry cargo, meet the storage and warehousing needs, round-the-clock internal transport, and cargo loading and unloading.

It is well equipped to handle a range of liquid cargo such as chemicals, vegetable oils and petroleum products. The port provides the largest tank farm storage area inside any port in the country. It also has an 8 km offshore Single Buoy Mooring (SBM) terminal with a depth of 32 m for crude oil handling.

Institutional investors and merchant bankers in Mumbai say that Mr Adani's business acumen and knowledge base are unparalleled. "Gautam is totally a performance-focused entrepreneur. Mundra port is a classic story of a world-class infrastructure facility, which has emerged as one of India's major ports," says Tapseej Mishra, Head of 'I-Banking' at Mumbai-based SSKI, which has carried out the highest number of financial deals for the Adani Group.

There is also a philanthropic element in the personality of Gautam Adani. Adani and his family of four are devoted Jains and they travelled to 'Sammed Shikhar', a Jain community pilgrimage site with about 2,000 poor people from their native village, in Gujarat's Banaskantha district. He hired an entire train and travelled with his family in second class comfortably and hosted the villagers at the temple for 15 days.

Adani is running a school in Ahmedabad for the benefit of children from low/middle-income groups. The school provides free transportation, education and food for gifted children.

During the 2001 Gujarat earthquake, Adani and his wife set up a kitchen for the poor. His wife Preeti and several cooks from Ahmedabad cooked food for the displaced people and provided them shelter.

Jayesh Buch, an old-time confidant, says, "Due to the efforts of Gautam Bhai, we were the first to provide electricity to a secondary school in Bhuj city, where many people who were devastated by the earthquake were given shelter. A key feature of his success story is that what is more surprising than his business acumen is his quick response to changes in the economy and dealing with problems within the legal framework."

❑

World's Fifth Richest Person

Gautam Adani became India's second largest cement maker after acquiring a controlling stake in two of India's leading cement companies—Ambuja Ltd and ACC Ltd—from Swiss major Holcim Ltd in a $10 billion mega-deal. Earlier, his group had bought a 49 per cent stake in the digital news platform 'Quintillion Media'. From old economy businesses to new age platforms, Adani wants to carve a niche for himself in every field.

Those who know Adani say that to him, scale matters the most. Thus, he creates wealth for himself and his investors. A decade ago, in 2011—with a net worth of nearly $10 billion—Adani was hardly known outside his home state, Gujarat. Now, he is in the limelight, sharing space with the world's richest people, surpassing famed billionaire Warren Buffett to become the fifth richest on *Forbes'* real-billionaires list in April 2022 with a net worth of $123.7 billion.

Gautam Adani is continuously climbing the ladder of success. Raising the flag of Indians among billionaires around the world, he has now become the fifth richest person. According to the Forbes Real Time Billionaires Index, Adani has moved up to the fifth spot with a net worth of $123 billion, while Warren Buffett who occupied this position slipped to sixth place with a net worth of $121.7 billion. Tesla's Elon Musk, Amazon's Jeff Bezos, Bernard Arnault and Bill Gates are now ahead of Adani. Gautam Adani is behind Microsoft's Bill Gates by only $7 billion.

Industrial mogul and chairman of port and energy conglomerate Adani Group, Gautam Adani became the fifth richest person in the world, surpassing investor Warren Buffett, with an estimated net worth of $123.7 billion, while Buffett has a net worth of $121.7 billion.

Industrialist Adani added $43 billion to his wealth in the year 2022, which increased his portfolio by 56.2 per cent.

Gautam Adani is the founder and chairman of the Adani Group, whose businesses span multiple sectors, including energy, edible oil, airports, power generation and distribution. There are seven companies listed under the Adani Group—Adani Power, Adani Total Gas, Adani Green Energy, Adani Transmission, Adani Enterprises, Adani Ports and Special Economic Zone, and the recently listed edible oil major Adani Wilmar.

These subsidiary companies have zoomed by 19-195 per cent so far in the year 2022, while Adani Wilmar's shares gained 235 per cent and Adani Power gained 170 per cent compared to their issue price.

Recently, Abu Dhabi-based investment firm 'International Holding Company' (IHC) announced an investment of $2 billion in three companies of the Adani Group, including Adani Green Energy. Thus, the Adani Group is backed by some of the most respected financial names and capital-raising companies and has one of the largest renewable portfolios in the world.

In April 2022, the group announced the purchase of Ocean Sparkle, India's largest marine services company, for $220 million.

Reliance Industries Chairman Mukesh Ambani is at the eighth position on the Forbes list of the world's richest people. That is, two Indians are included among the 10 richest people in the world. Ambani's total net worth has been estimated at $103.7 billion.

Tesla and SpaceX chief Elon Musk occupies the first place on this list. His total net worth is estimated at $269.7 billion. Amazon's Jeff Bezos is second with a net worth of $170.2 billion. The net worth of France's Bernard Arnault and his family is estimated at $166.8 billion. He occupies the third position on the list. Bill Gates is ranked fourth. His net worth is estimated at $130.2 billion. Larry Ellison is seventh on the list. His total net worth is $107.6 billion. Larry Page is ranked ninth on the list with $102.4 billion. Sergey Brin is ranked 10th with a net worth of $98.5 billion.

The jump in Gautam Adani's net worth in the past few weeks is a result of a sharp rally in the shares of several Adani Group firms. The shares of Adani Group firms rose this year, helping him not only become a centibillionaire but also climb up the list of billionaires.

Three companies of the Adani Group have given multi-bagger returns in the year 2022 so far. Adani Wilmar is up 235 per cent over its issue price, while Adani Power has jumped 170 per cent. Adani Green Energy also gained 110 per cent. Other companies in the group have grown by 17-55 per cent in the current year. Now Adani Power has become the sixth firm in the group to cross the market valuation of ₹ 1 lakh crore, with its stock hitting an all-time high of ₹ 272. Adani

Green Energy, Adani Transmission, Adani Total Gas, Adani Enterprises, and Adani Ports and Special Economic Zone have already achieved this milestone.

Recently, at the 'India Economic Conclave-2022', Adani said that India can become a $30 trillion economy by 2050. He said, "We are about 10,000 days away from the year 2050. During this period, I hope we would add about $25 trillion to our economy. This adds up to an additional $2.5 billion in GDP every day. I also hope that during this period, we will eradicate all kinds of poverty."

Significantly, amid the huge fall in the stock market, shares of five out of seven companies of Gautam Adani, India's and Asia's richest person, have been steadily rising. Shares of Adani Power and Adani Wilmar rose over four per cent. In fact, the shares of Adani Power touched the upper circuit.

❑

The Hunger for Risk

People from the olden days still remember Adani, the billionaire from Ahmedabad, who rode his grey Bajaj Super scooter during the 1980s, while his childhood friend Malay Mahadevia who is a dentist, now works with the group as a Director of Adani Ports and SEZs Ltd.

Several years ago, a photo of BJP's PM candidate Narendra Modi landing from one of his aircraft was released by AAP leader Arvind Kejriwal. However, Adani says that he rents out his plane to the BJP or whoever asks for these services at market rates.

Even after the NDA government was voted out in 2004, Adani never tried to hide his close ties with Modi. But he hasn't really depended much on him. He cultivated friends in the UPA and other parties to expand his power business in Haryana, Maharashtra, Madhya Pradesh and Rajasthan, besides bidding for ports in Odisha, Andhra Pradesh and Tamil Nadu.

Several senior Congress ministers are believed to have helped him in the early days. His ability to make friends extends beyond the shores of India. He is also known to have developed excellent relationships with top political officials in Australia, where the group invested $6 billion in a coal mine and port near Brisbane.

With an estimated net worth of ₹ 25,000 crore, Adani presides over an empire spanning coal, power, logistics, real estate, agro-products, oil and gas. Employing 10,000 people, the conglomerate built the country's largest private port and also emerged as the top private electricity producer in the country.

Mahadeviya says, "He has diverse interests, but I will always call him the seaman of India. He has almost single-handedly changed this field in India." Like Mahadeviya, those who work closely with Adani think that he is a visionary, who always thinks bigger than anyone around him.

Bakul Dholakia, former director of IIMA, who is now associated with the Adani Group's educational and CSR initiatives, says, "There are very few people who can match Gautam Adani in terms of risk appetite and risk absorption capacity. There are many who take great risks, but very few have the ability to face adversity with courage and conviction." Close aides say that Adani has great potential to win over people, be it political or otherwise.

When the Mundra port was being constructed, a consultant came up with a new idea of constructing floating water to stop the sea waves at a cost of ₹ 7 crore. But this experiment sank within 20 minutes of its execution. Adani, watching the disaster calmly, went to the adviser and placed his hand on his shoulder. Before leaving Adani said, "It was a good try." The adviser burst into tears and worked for the group for the next 15 years.

While much has been said about his close ties with Modi, Adani was also very close to the previous governments in Gujarat led by Shankersinh Vaghela, Chimanbhai Patel and Keshubhai

Patel. All these regimes allotted land to Adani in Mundra and its surrounding areas at cheaper rates than the Modi government.

In 2003, when most of the veteran industrialists stayed away from an investment meeting organised by the then Gujarat Chief Minister Modi, a group of Gujarati businessmen led by Gautam Adani joined him. While India Inc. stalwarts joined Modi much later, Modi never forgets those who stood by his side.

Controversies and accidents

The Adani Group faced stiff opposition from the trading rivals of the West Coast. But still, it managed to build enough critical monetary standards to list its companies on the stock exchange in 1992. Economic liberalisation and relaxation in trade policies helped the Adani Group a lot. His business benefitted from his proximity to powerful politicians like Narendra Modi, the then chief minister of Gujarat.

Adani also faced many controversies and events throughout his life. Gautam Adani was accused of supporting Narendra Modi during the 2014 Lok Sabha elections. He was accused of providing special benefits to Modi by providing Adani Group's chartered aircraft to travel for rallies across India. Speaking on the allegation in an interview, Adani said that the BJP paid market value to the group of companies for using the aviation services.

By the mid-1990s, his commercial successes began to attract attention, which included unwanted attention. His wealth and success also invited the envy of others.

In 1997, some criminals allegedly tried to extort money by kidnapping Adani. The billionaire was reportedly asked for a ransom of $1.5 million. According to the charge sheet filed by the police, on 1st January 1998, Adani and Shantilal Patel were abducted at gunpoint when they left the Karnavati Club in a car and headed towards Mohammadpura Road. It is alleged that a scooter forcefully stopped the car and then some people arrived in a van and kidnapped both of them. The charge sheet states that before being released, he was taken to an undisclosed location in a car.

Adani has been reluctant to speak publicly about this horrific incident. When asked about the incident by London's *Financial Times*, Adani only said, "It is one of two or three very unfortunate incidents in my life." Adani was allegedly kidnapped by underworld don Fazal-ur-Rehman alias 'Fazlu Rehman'.

In 2018, the Ahmedabad court acquitted the two main accused—former gangster Fazlu Rehman and Bhogilal Darji alias Mama. Rehman, facing several other criminal charges, was lodged in the Sabarmati Central Jail at the time, while Darji was out on bail. Kunal N Shah, counsel for both the accused, said that the judge acquitted his clients as the prosecution failed to establish the case of kidnapping and their role in it. As per reports, while Rehman was arrested on the Indo-Nepal border in 2006, Darji was arrested in Dubai in 2012.

Rescue during the 2008 Mumbai terror attack

The kidnapping was not the only unfortunate incident in Adani's life. On 26th November 2008, terrorists attacked the iconic Taj Hotel in Mumbai while Adani was dining there. Adani hid in the basement as terrorists killed over 160 people. When the commandos took control of the situation and fought with the terrorists, he managed to escape safely.

According to reports, Adani was having dinner with Dubai port CEO Mohammad Sharaf at the Weather Craft restaurant that night when he saw terrorists entering the hotel, firing indiscriminately and hurling grenades. Since he was seated at a height, he could clearly see the terrorists firing in the direction of the route to the swimming pool and so he ran towards the old wing. Soon after, the hotel staff helped the guests, including Adani, to the basement. A few hours later, when they started suffocating in the basement, they were taken to the Taj Chamber Hall on the upper floor.

Earlier, Adani was quoted in a report, "We were more than 100 people and everyone was praying for their lives. Some hid under the sofa, while others hid in other places. Sitting on a sofa, I told them to trust God. I also talked to my distressed family in Ahmedabad and my driver and commando who were in my car outside the hotel."

Adani spent the entire night of 26th November (Wednesday) in the basement of the Taj Hotel and then in a hall. He was then rescued by security personnel at 8:45 am on Thursday. He was taken out through the back door of the hotel and then taken in a police van. After landing at Ahmedabad airport by his private plane on November 27, Adani said, "I saw death just 15 feet away."

In 2002, he was detained by the Delhi police on charges of cheating on the complaint of a rival.

In the late 1990s, he was investigated for alleged invoicing irregularities and money laundering. He was also accused of possible collusion with the accused businessman Ketan Parekh.

❑

Adani's Social Work: Adani Foundation

In 1996, the Adani Foundation was established in Ahmedabad to take care of the corporate social responsibilities of the Adani Group. Simultaneously, work was started with some rural communities around the Adani port in Mundra. The foundation comprises a team of committed professionals whose job is to plan and implement growth and development programmes for rural communities. The team works together on multiple issues in each community to enable holistic development.

The foundation follows a participatory approach to ensure a sense of ownership for the services and community assets it provides. The foundation has brought tangible changes in the lives of people in rural communities through institutional and individual grants for education and medical relief. Today, the foundation works as a registered NGO in Gujarat, Himachal Pradesh, Maharashtra and Rajasthan.

The foundation is active in four key areas for society:

- ✓ Education
- ✓ Medical assistance
- ✓ Rural development
- ✓ Charitable initiatives

Gautam Adani has been responsive to the concerns of employees, society and stakeholders since its inception. He has always been a responsible citizen and implements all the activities of his companies in harmony with the global environment and works actively to reduce their burden on the environment.

Donated 100 crores to PM's Fund

Gautam Adani contributed ₹ 100 crore to the Prime Minister's Fund through the philanthropic wing of his group to fight the coronavirus outbreak. Adani joined Tata Group, Reliance Industries and other corporates who have come forward to contribute towards fighting the unprecedented crisis.

Adani said that the group's employees contributed around ₹ 4 crore towards the Covid-19 relief efforts and the Adani Foundation taking up relief projects in India contributed ₹ 4 crore totalling ₹ 8 crore.

He said, "We will continue to live by our legacy. I would like to reiterate that the Adani Group will continue to support governments and fellow citizens in this difficult time."

Gautam Adani committed his infrastructure group to support the government and citizens in the fight against the coronavirus outbreak by putting resources together.

The chairman of the Adani Group said that we are foreshadowing a time that will divide human history into two eras—the world before the outbreak of Covid-19 and the world that survived it. Despite decisive global actions and disciplined lockdowns of nations, the pandemic continues to threaten human well-being.

He said, "History will know about the pandemic, which has already taken thousands of lives across the world. Many decades or centuries later, when our children look back, they should be proud of our compassion as citizens of the world's most populous democracy, who did not give up. They should know that all Indians fought well and united with the government in the fight for India.

"Governments, both at the centre and in the states, have taken the lead against Covid and I am sure this assistance will help activate immediate support at the grassroots level."

Adani said, "The compassion and values of our people restore our faith in nation-building inspired by our core philosophy of good development. I also salute our heroes working sincerely in our ports, power plants, transmission sites, distribution stations, edible oil refineries, and gas business to ensure efficient delivery of essential commodities to Indian homes."

Along with this, Adani Foundation contributed ₹ 5 crore to Gujarat CM Relief Fund and ₹ 1 crore to Maharashtra CM Relief Fund during Covid.

It also immediately provided 100 ventilators along with PPE (Personal Protective Equipment) and N-95 masks to the Ahmedabad Municipal Corporation. He said that in collaboration with the Adani Foundation, the women's cooperatives produced more than 1.2 lakh masks.

While commercial canteens prepared healthy food for truck drivers and labourers, essential commodities were being delivered through Adani gas-powered CNG autos across Ahmedabad.

"Our businesses ensure uninterrupted supply of essential gas and electricity to Indian homes. Additionally, as a responsible corporate, we will stand by the nation in various capacities.

In the last three decades, whatever goals the Adani Group has achieved have been in the national interest. We will continue to live by our legacy."

To counter the growing spread of Covid-19, Adani Group imported cryogenic tanks and medical-grade oxygen cylinders from Saudi Arabia. This will go a long way in the fight against Covid.

❑

This is Just the Beginning: Chairman's Speech (2009)

We have been continuously expanding our capacity and businesses since our inception and the past year has been no exception despite significant challenges in the economic conditions in the market. Last year, I informed you about the infrastructure, material handling equipment and construction of the new terminal.

In addition, I am happy to state that mechanisation of handling of fertiliser/FRM, steel and coal has been achieved. Online bagging of fertilisers, Goliath crane handling of steel plates and pipes, as well as fully mechanised coal handling systems are the right steps towards better efficiency, making the port one of its kind in the private sector. Under the total port range, Mundra port has four ports—North, South, East and West Ports. West Port is on the way to completion as planned for full coal operations. The railway line has been extended closer to the new coal terminal, thus completing rail connectivity to the port and the entire SEZ area. The receipt and dispatch yard has expanded from 5 to 10 lines.

A master plan is being prepared and a business proposal for adding new capabilities is being studied for the full development of the unique and only port with a 40 km waterfront. Environment clearance has been received for the first phase of the entire 40 km waterfront. Plans are underway for a bunker terminal, edible oil terminal, godowns, two berths for dry cargo, and a doubling of the rail line between Adipur and Mundra, which will increase the carrying capacity and consequently lead to an increase in trade.

The external focus that I mentioned last year has enabled all three business verticals to show significant growth. There has been significant growth in the port business. During the year, three notified areas have been merged into a multi-product SEZ. During the year, nine units have been permitted to set up their manufacturing and service facilities in SEZs. On the infrastructure development front, several entities have been approved as co-developers for setting up hotels, hospitals, schools and other infrastructure facilities. In addition, water treatment plants and water and electricity distribution networks have been set up. The logistics business has carved a niche for itself as a provider of quality logistics solutions.

On the performance front, I am happy to state that the revenue has increased by 38.73 per cent and the total revenue is more than ₹ 1,135 crores. Profit after tax is up by 116 per cent at ₹ 461.08 crore and EPS is at ₹ 11.51. Cargo volumes have improved across all commercial sectors—it has gone up from 28.80 million tonnes in 2007-08 to 35.72 million tonnes in 2008-09, showing a year-on-year growth of 24.03 per cent.

We have seen slowdowns all over the world not only in economies but also in matters of corporate governance equally. However, I believe that the high standards of corporate governance and transparency that we follow and our adherence to the best industry practices set us apart.

We are moving towards the expected target and Mundra port is already handling 36 million tonnes. The Dahej port is operative and should be operational by the middle of next year. Development of Goa port is on the horizon. With this, the presence of the West Coast will be important. Strategic steps are being taken to develop existing ports along with green sector projects on the East Coast and next year should be an important year in that aspect.

We have also taken several quality, health safety and environment (QHSE) initiatives, which are at the core of the port business.

The group is very conscious of its values. Our value-driven processes along with our commitment to achieve goals are our core strengths. The group always acts as a responsible corporate citizen. Adani Foundation plays a vital role in bringing about sustainable development in and around its area of operation. The group aims to enhance the quality of life of the surrounding communities. We have started the process of the rural underground drainage system, free health check-ups, initiative for the development of the girl child, better sanitation, and upgradation of ITI in Mundra.

The group also strives to create institutions of excellence in various fields of higher education and has undertaken to set up a medical college in Bhuj as a public-private partnership project. I am happy to inform you that we have obtained necessary government approval to start a medical college from August 2009 with admission of total 150 students in first year MBBS for the academic year 2009-10 and all necessary formalities have been completed. Adani Institute of Infrastructure Management (AIIM) will also start this year.

The management is committed to the high standards of operations and hence has further strengthened the management set-up and appointed a whole time director with vast experience to lead the operations and plan the future strategy. The hunt for the right talent is on and I am proud to say that we have some of the best talents in the industry, who are committed and dedicated to the work and goals that will help achieve the vision.

I would like to express my gratitude to this vast family of shareholders, bankers and investors for their continued support, reinforcing our commitment to creating a sustainable long-term value for all stakeholders. I am also grateful to the state and central governments, who have also made plans for development.

Our core values—trust, courage and innovation—are well integrated into everything that we do. We believe that tough times don't last long, but tough people do. I feel very happy when I get testimonials from our dear members and when they assure us of their continued support in all circumstances.

And even now, I say that this is just the beginning!

❑

Practical Optimism: Chairman's Speech (2019)

"It is hard to believe that the 100-year-old Keynesian statement was made at a time when the views on telecommunications and global e-commerce were not even vague.

"At the time of his morning tea, he could order by telephone the various products on the whole earth in such quantity as he thought necessary and could expect their quick delivery at his doorstep. He could at the same time and in the same way boldly invest his money in the natural resources and new ventures in any part of the world."

This was first published in John Maynard Keynes's influential best-seller *The Economic Consequences of the Peace* in 1919 when the term globalisation had not even been coined (it first appeared in its modern sense in 1930). The fact is that globalisation existed even then, except that its pace was much slower compared to today's world.

Some things never change

If Keynes's time is remembered for the gradual globalisation of social and economic life, ours will be remembered for the unbridled speed at which globalisation is engulfing our lives driven by the ubiquitous access to the Internet. The consequences are still emerging as the political, cultural and economic barriers of our world dissolve faster than ever in the double solvent of global interdependence and hyper-interconnectivity, creating unprecedented new opportunities, new business models and many new challenges.

However, of all the challenges, one of the most significant consequences of globalisation has been the pandemic and the most difficult of them has been Covid-19. While it is no surprise that a pandemic like the 1957 Asian Flu spread through trade and travel routes, it is clear that the world was not prepared for the explosive rate of spread of a pandemic of the scale of Covid-19. It exposed several vulnerabilities of global interdependence that would need to be corrected and each country is expected to do so differently.

Curiously, the cure for this disease is being found through the process of globalisation, as evidenced by the worldwide collaboration on accelerated genome sequencing vaccine development and vaccine manufacturing. So, paradoxically both the problem and its solution lie in our embracing globalisation.

Lesson during crisis

It cannot be denied that while Covid-19 posed a challenge to every country, India's size and population density made it a formidable challenge. In fact, the pandemic made a dent in economic priorities and forced the world to use time and resources to deal with the crisis as India did.

There is no denying that India could have done much better and that every loss of life is a tragedy. However, as the world rushes to vaccinate its people, we see India being criticised time and again for not doing enough to protect itself. It is sometimes worth noting that India has more population than Europe, North America and Oceania combined. In other words, our country is facing a bigger challenge than the other three continents at a time when every country is optimising what it can do for its people and improved healthcare infrastructure is in place over several decades. Given that our vaccination effort is larger than the combined efforts of 87 countries, it is only appropriate to take a step back and quantify the scale of the challenge faced by our country.

In this context, I believe that the initiative of self-reliance launched by the government is a transformative and right step in the journey of our country.

The Covid-19 pandemic has demonstrated to most countries around the world that free market economies cannot exist at the cost of self-reliance. We must believe in our capabilities and be able to depend on them for economic construction, especially in times of crisis. Therefore, the five pillars of *'Atmanirbhar Bharat'*—Economy, Infrastructure, System, Vibrant Demography and Demand—are essential to ensure that our economy builds internal strength to manage disruptive events like Covid-19. The definition of a free market economy will undergo a change in the Covid-19 world and we must write our own definition without hesitation. After all, India is not only the world's largest democracy, but it is also the world's most unique and bold experiment with democracy.

One size does not fit all and it is clear that the phenomenon of hyper-globalisation, which created unrealistic hopes of being a panacea for efficient manufacturing and services around the world, has been one of the most significant reasons for the inequalities we see today. Therefore, only when we are able to fully mobilise the efforts of our people, will we be able to develop our economy in such a way that we can take advantage of the demographic dividend of our country, which we have not yet been able to do fully. Covid-19 is a wake-up call for all of us to transform ourselves. There can be no better time for us to embark on the journey of true self-reliance to accelerate our nation-building in the post-Covid-19 world.

Organisational value as a platform of numbers

The last one year has been one which has further strengthened my belief in the values of an organisation. Nearly a decade ago we chose courage, faith and commitment as the guiding values that would determine our actions, and today I attribute the resilience that we have displayed to the steadfastness of these values. This reinforces my belief in the perseverance of our organisation and it has been demonstrated in our group's results. The Adani Group has not only emerged as India's benchmark during tough times for market leadership, but we have also channelled our organisational capability to pivot rapidly in the right market direction. An exciting example of this agility is our expanded partnership with Total (now Total Energies), who are strategically growing their renewable portfolio.

These developments exemplify the flexibility of our diverse business across industries and geographies. Despite the pandemic-induced massive disruption in economic activity, all six of our listed entities posted results well above market expectations, and some of these record highlights are seen below:

- ✓ Increase in asset capacity and operational excellence and efficiency ensured that the EBITDA of our listed portfolio registered a year-on-year growth of 22 per cent (32337 crores in FY 2020-21).
- ✓ Return on Equity Shareholders ROE registered a significant growth of 166 per cent on a year-on-year basis (9415 crores in FY 2020-21).

- ✓ All the portfolio stocks of Adani have delivered more than 100 per cent returns and outperformed by a significant margin (Nifty-50 gave 71 per cent returns).
- ✓ Adani Green Energy Limited (AGEL) added 925 MW of operating capacity, achieving a high consistent solar CUF of 22.5 per cent and wind CUF of 26.8 per cent.
- ✓ Adani Transmission Limited (ATL) added 3931 circuit km to its network reaching 18,801 circuit km and sold a record 7,169 million units during the year.
- ✓ Adani Ports and Special Economic Zone Limited (APSEZ) achieved a 'cargo volume' of 247 MMT (up to 11 per cent) and gained 4 percentage points to reach a market share of 25 per cent.
- ✓ Adani Total Gas Limited (ATGL) added 102 CNG stations. 500 commercial and 40,939 domestic customers are receiving a combined quantity of 515 MMSCM (CNG+PNG).

Strategical highlights

- ✓ APSEZ announced four acquisitions–KPCL, GPL, Dighi Ports and SRCPL–thus improving East Coast-West Coast parity. It also announced the setting up of a container terminal at Colombo port in partnership with John Keels and SLPA.
- ✓ Adani Enterprises Limited (AEL) handles airport operations at Ahmedabad, Lucknow and Mangaluru; it signed concession agreements for Guwahati, Jaipur and Thiruvananthapuram and is in the process of acquiring Mumbai International Airports Limited (MIAL) and Navi Mumbai International Airport Limited (NMIAL) airports.
- ✓ AGEL strengthened its partnership with Total Energy, which acquired a 50 per cent stake in its 2.35 GW portfolio of operating solar assets and a 20 per cent equity stake in AGEL from the founders for an investment of US$2.5 billion.

While we look back, we feel satisfied with our results.

I believe that the real phase of the Adani Group's accelerated growth as an entity that benefits from a portfolio of companies with multiple strategic closeness is now gaining momentum. It helps us bridge the B2B to B2C gap in unique ways and will encompass our new businesses, such as airports.

Data centre security and others

What we have built over the past two decades is India's largest integrated and yet diversified infrastructure business, which is now manifesting itself as an integrated 'Platform' and getting us closer to unprecedented access to the Indian end consumer. I don't see any business model like ours with unlimited B2B and B2C market access over the next several decades.

Creating a blueprint to capitalise on trends

While we are known to be an organisation that takes quick decisions in the space of renewable energy and clean energy, it has also allowed us to improve our expansion process further and has given us the confidence to explore many new areas as has become increasingly evident with our diversified business portfolio. As an example, it is worth noting that the thought process of accelerating our clean energy footprint was started as recently as 2020 (January 2020 at the Davos World Economic Forum). Two things became clear from my meetings in Davos:

- ✓ First, climate change had become the defining issue of our times and climate change action must be acknowledged as a global, national and individual responsibility.
- ✓ Second, our country will have a defining role to play in driving one of India's biggest consumption growths as it balances the need to accelerate its renewable energy ambitions while simultaneously providing affordable electricity to its citizens.

It was in Davos that I decided that we should align with our country's vision on renewable energy and set ourselves the goal of becoming the world's largest solar power producer. I also decided that a significant part of our group's future investments should be focused on sustainable and renewable energy.

I wrote my thoughts and the group's ambitions in an article. I wrote, "Our vision is to become the world's largest solar power company by 2025, and then the world's largest renewable energy company by 2030." I also said, "We will create 25 GW by 2025 and also be the largest solar player in the world." At that time, our existing portfolio of renewable energy was only 2.5 GW.

We have grown rapidly since January 2020 and my focus has been on building an organisation that can add an unmatched 5 GW of generation capacity each year over the next decade and foster a clean energy future. So far, we are on target. I will highlight a few key points:

- ✓ We won the world's largest solar tender five months after the promise in Davos in the second quarter of 2020 when SECI awarded us 8 GW through a competitive bidding process.
- ✓ After this, in the third quarter of 2020, Mercom said that we have become the world's largest solar energy developer. We went from No. 6 in 2019 to No. 1 in 2020—in just nine months.
- ✓ Simultaneously, we formed a game-changing partnership in energy to begin laying the groundwork for a global partnership. The inclusion of Total Energy as a 20 per cent partner in the renewable energy business seals a strategic alliance, which includes investments in LNG terminals and renewable assets across India, apart from the gas utility business. The partnership in the renewable energy sector in India will be a significant contributor to Total Energy's aim to transform itself into a clean energy leader.

- ✓ The value of our renewable energy business has grown over 600 times since January 2020, delivering the best returns in all stock exchanges.
- ✓ After that, in May 2021, we acquired SoftBank and Bharti.

The 5 GW portfolio of renewable assets allows us to leapfrog and reach our target of 25 GW four years ahead of our schedule.

This is what templatisation means to us and it gives us the confidence to expand rapidly in many adjacent areas. This success is also an expression of the value of our three organisational values—courage, trust and commitment—that fundamentally define our group.

Adani Foundation: Growth with goodness

As a group, carrying out business in places where some of the poorest sections of our population live, we are deeply aware of our responsibility to help marginalised and disadvantaged communities.

Over and over—just creating jobs. Through a range of initiatives led by the Adani Foundation, we have touched the lives of lakhs of people in thousands of villages, bringing about beneficial changes in education, health, infrastructure development and sustainable livelihood development. We expect to expand our work and double these numbers over the next five years.

In line with the rest of the world, the primary focus of the Adani Foundation over the past year was guided by the fight against Covid-19. One of the issues in the national spotlight of the widespread nature of this pandemic was the severe disparity in access to relief and care in our scattered communities. As the virus continued to spread, we mapped out the urgency of the moment and studied how we could mitigate the crisis across India. We quickly realised that fighting required more than a standard assortment of medical items like protective gear and diagnostic kits. Additional means were most needed to quickly distribute medical oxygen throughout the country.

The solution was linked to a number of items that were in short supply locally. We needed more cryogenic tanks capable of transporting oxygen in supercooled liquid form. More medical oxygen cylinders for hospitalised patients, more oxygen generator plants for healthcare facilities that were unable to rely on transportation supplies and higher oxygen concentrations for people managing their infections on their own were needed.

It was a formidable challenge, but a challenge that we could achieve quickly and efficiently. Working with our business partners and Indian missions around the world, we were able to secure a huge life-saving inventory of these critical items, the largest of which we brought in with the help of the Indian Air Force. Our tireless logistics teams ensured that oxygen tanks and cylinders were refilled frequently and sent to all corners of the country.

I am also proud that the foundation has gone beyond just procuring essential supplies. Within days, our engineering and medical teams transformed our Adani Vidya Mandir School and Noida Indoor Stadium in Ahmedabad into emergency Covid-19 care facilities with hundreds of beds, oxygen support and catered food. Our hospitals in Mundra, which serve as a general medical oasis for the neighbouring districts, were swiftly converted into 100 per cent Covid care hospitals.

Never before was the work of the Adani Foundation as important and relevant as it is today. I am deeply impressed by the efforts made by our foundation's team members, often ignoring the risks to their own health.

Long-term trust

In the past few months, many voices have been heard wondering whether India's goal of becoming a five trillion dollar economy in the next four years can be achieved. I personally see this as an unimportant question. History has clearly demonstrated that there are many lessons to be learnt from the crises brought over by every pandemic and I believe that India and the world will become wiser as we go through this pandemic. India will be a five trillion dollar economy and then it will become a fifteen trillion dollar economy.

Over the next two decades, the dollar-plus economy is emerging as one of the largest global markets in terms of consumption, size and market capitalisation. However, there can be no doubt that the largest middle class that will always exist, working age and increasing consumption share of the population will have a positive impact on India's growth rate, commensurate with the demographic dividend that India has. The most essential factor will be a better-trained workforce and I have no reason to believe that in the next two decades, we will not be able to adequately address this challenge. It is a virtuous cycle, driven by an increase in the middle class population, and today India has a longer runway than any other country in the world.

❑

Goal to Make the Country Self-Reliant: Chairman's Speech (2020)

Webster's definition of resilience is 'the ability of a strained body to recover its shape and size after deformation, especially due to compressive stress'. It is hard to believe that less than 3 months ago, on 11th March 2020, the World Health Organisation declared the outbreak of Covid-19 as a pandemic, meaning that Covid-19 is spread across the globe. If ever there has been a time when the need for global resilience has been important, it is now.

Power to overcome

In times like these, one looks for inspiration. In this context, the famous author Wayne Mueller writes that for thousands of years, mankind has endured famine, war, plague, hunger, and countless injustices; it has experienced countless births and deaths. Every community of people has had to find some way of talking about what has sustained or brought them graciousness—even in the midst of terrible sorrow! We have struggled to name this human characteristic. The universal force that makes the grass imperceptibly make its way through concrete, the power that makes the earth move, the energy that possesses and blesses all life, is the essential presence in our deepest nature that ever cannot be expressed with absolute accuracy. But that still makes us who we are. History is a great story of overpowering humans. This is what we were born to do.

Decisive government

We must realise that there are no absolutely right or wrong ideas. An unprecedented, difficult model, what is needed during a crisis like Covid-19, is a government that is ready to make decisions based on the best available information at a given point in time and continuously adapts as new information becomes available. For this, the government of India and the bureaucracy should be applauded. Countries with more resources than us have struggled and while our battle with the virus is far from over, I have no hesitation in saying that had there been a delay in decision-making, we could have faced a calamity that would have affected not only the world but also India. Yes, businesses have suffered greatly, lives and jobs have been lost and the migrant labour crisis has saddened the entire nation, but the consequences of unknown choices would be dire. What our nation's leaders, doctors, healthcare workers, police, military, small roadside vendors and citizens have done to support each other is what really defines India and its resilience. Add to this the fact that the government is now able to do direct benefit transfers as a result of the integrated approach created through Jan Dhan, Aadhar and mobile linking systems and we are starting to see the benefits of the government which had the foresight. To set up the infrastructure, we need to be able to handle a crisis.

Possibilities

Where we are sitting today, I can say that history is in the process of being written. I will be the first one to admit that I have no way of predicting the likely short or medium-term economic consequences as a result of Covid-19. However, there is no denying the fact that India will be a consistently upward market over the next several decades and this cannot be ignored easily. It will be one of the world's top consumption, manufacturing and service centres, and a beacon of stable democratic governance. If there ever was a time to bet on India, it could be no better than now. What I can predict is that on the other side of this crisis, there will be massive new opportunities, great new leaders, great businesses and some strong nations. Those who succeed will be the ones who understand that resilience is built on the other side of the tunnel of crisis and we are already preparing for it.

Resilient group performance

I am pleased to share that each of our six publicly traded companies has performed well, even as we begin to face tough conditions after the first few weeks of 2020. However, we may have to revamp the need-based course in our strategies. The roadmap is clear in view of the challenge we are facing. Our businesses are closely linked to the lifeline of the economy, providing essential services to enhance the quality of life of citizens and addressing critical national infrastructure priorities. We view our group companies as personal growth drivers, complementing each other's strengths.

Any blow to the system always helps to take home some key points and this is what Indian businesses have learnt over the years. Certainly, there is a value of optimum post-Covid-19 and perhaps a conservative capital structure for some sectors has significance as well. Establish systematic risk mitigation plans. Optimal capital structure and risk mitigation are both a part of maturing business philosophy as they grow in size and lay the foundation for consistent value-creation along with stability.

At the group level, our focus is on optimising capital utilisation, redesigning the organisational structure to reduce risk in our businesses and financing operations in phases. I am happy to share that during the year, the group has been able to bring in strategic global equity partners in Adani Gas, Adani Green Energy Limited and Adani Mumbai Electricity Limited. The total investment is $1.6 billion, and it will help drive the future growth of our businesses. It is also pertinent to mention that AEML (part of Adani Transmission) has recently issued an investment grade $1 billion bond, the first by a private integrated utility from India. The issue garnered considerable interest from international investors and was subscribed 5.9 times. I should also mention here that APSEZ raised $750 million by selling off foreign bonds, the proceeds of which will be used for fund expansion, further reducing the cost of debt and progressively moving the balance sheet. Over the past 12 months, the group has successfully placed seven bonds totalling $4.26 billion in international markets.

Over the years, Adani Enterprises has focused on building emerging infrastructure businesses, contributing to nation-building and segmenting them into separate listed entities. Having successfully built unicorns like Adani Transmission, Adani Power, Adani Ports and SEZs, Adani Green Energy, and the recently formed Adani Gas, we have set our sights on making the country self-reliant with our existing portfolio of strong businesses. The next generation of our strategic business investments will be centred around the areas of solar PV manufacturing, airport management, technology parks and water infrastructure.

Business review

This has been another year of resilient performance and operations in our business segments. We continue to be the largest resource player in the country in the resource segment, delivering industry-leading performance with a growth of 17 per cent over the previous year.

In our mining services business, we have achieved a capacity of 100 million metric tonnes per annum with an enhanced project pipeline. We have also forayed into the washery service business and obtained LOI for 10 MMT for Hingula Washery project. We delivered strong performance while working on our three coal blocks in Parsa East and Kanta Basin (PEKB), Gare Palma-3 (GP-3) and Talabira-2 and 3A. PEKB has continued production at a peak rated capacity of 15 MMT, while GPIII and Talabira-2 and Talabira-3 have been commissioned during the current year.

During the year under review, we registered a significant increase in the volume of our solar modules, and the capacity increased by 55 per cent to 990 MW. As a result, EBITDA increased to ₹ 301 crore, i.e., to ₹ 37 crores in FY19 as against the marginal rupee. As the government pushes for economic reforms and encourages green energy, we expect this segment to continue its growth.

Group's journey towards sustainability

Our journey towards sustainability has accelerated over the past 12 months. We are now leading the clean energy transformation not only in India but also globally, and our group is building one of the largest integrated energy portfolios. We aim to be the world's largest solar power company by FY25 and the largest renewable energy company by FY30. I should mention here that our group and 'total' signed definitive agreements to deepen our existing partnership and commitment to developing multiple energy offerings for the Indian energy market. We are fully committed to supporting our nation in diversifying our energy combination through partnerships in natural gas and solar energy.

Growth with good

We are fighting the Covid-19 battle unitedly in the Adani family. Our foundation has contributed funds. We have contributed 100 crores to the Prime Minister's Citizen Assistance and Emergency Situation Relief Fund (PM Cares Fund). I am equally grateful to our workforce in India for their financial contribution. They have contributed 4 crores to the fight against Covid-19. It is because of the solidarity displayed by this workforce of over 17,000 people that our foundation can add more funds. We have contributed 4 crores collectively and 8 crores for Covid-19 relief projects in India. As a responsible corporate, we will stand by the nation in various capacities in this hour of need. I would like to take this opportunity to thank our teams for the following measures:

- ✓ Adani Foundation has contributed ₹ 5 crore to Gujarat CM Relief Fund and ₹ 1 crore to Maharashtra Chief Minister Relief Fund. We have also contributed to Kattupalli District Collector's Covid-19 Fund and Bhadra District Administration.

- ✓ The foundation is also contributing to the Chief Minister's Relief Fund in several other states, such as Kerala, Jharkhand, Andhra Pradesh.

- ✓ Women's cooperative societies aided by the Adani Group produced over 1.2 lakh masks to help the economically disadvantaged sections of the population.

- ✓ Gujarat Adani Institute of Medical Sciences (GAIMS) is the only hospital equipped to deal with Covid-19 cases in Kutch, India's largest district.

The spirit and compassion of our people at such times restore my faith in our core philosophy of development with goodness. Let us all contribute to lifting our nation above this crisis. It may take time, but there is enough optimism to show that it is possible. Together, we will remain resilient and hopeful in these testing times.

❑

Adani Group's Entry into Bengal for Business

The Adani Group is going to invest more than ₹ 10,000 crore in West Bengal over the next decade. Adani Group Chairman Gautam Adani congratulated West Bengal Chief Minister Mamata Banerjee and Governor Jagdeep Dhankhar during the inauguration of the 'Sixth Bengal Global Business Summit' (BGBS) in Kolkata on 20th April 2022.

Speaking on the occasion, Gautam Adani said that the Adani Group's investments in Bengal would extend to world-class port infrastructure, state-of-the-art data centres and under-sea cables which would connect them to oceans, centres of excellence in digital innovation and supply centres, warehouses and logistics on a large scale.

Adani Group Chairman Gautam Adani said, "Thank you for inviting me to the '2022 Bengal Global Business Summit'. It is my honour to be here in Kolkata and to talk to you for the first time. Bengal has always fascinated me. Perhaps it is my love for rivers and oceans that the infrastructure journey of the Adani Group began from a port on the shores of the Arabian Sea.

"I am also impressed by the fact that some great civilisations have emerged on the banks of rivers. Be it the Egyptians on the Nile, or the Chinese on the Yellow River—or our own civilisations—one on the banks of the Indus and the other on the Bengal delta—all were inspired by the rivers flowing through these civilisations. So, I don't have to look further than Bengal to get inspiration. A hundred years ago, the great social reformer Gopalkrishna Gokhale gave us the unforgettable line—'What Bengal thinks today, India thinks tomorrow'. Bengal really helped shape India.

"It is the land of many great souls—Ramakrishna Paramhansa, Rabindranath Tagore, Swami Vivekananda, Raja Ram Mohan Roy, Subhash Chandra Bose, Ishwar Chandra Vidyasagar, Sri Aurobindo Ghosh, Kazi Nazrul Islam, Sarat Chandra Chatterjee, Sarat Chandra Bose, Bankim Chandra Chatterjee—I could go on and on—the list is as amazing as it is endless. No single state has produced as many great men of nationalism as Bengal has.

"However, one thing that is even more surprising, but perhaps less known outside Bengal, is that no state in India has given us as many women freedom fighters as Bengal has. Kalpana Dutta, Pritilata Waddedar, Suhasini Ganguly, Bina Das, Kamala Das Gupta, Sucheta Kripalani, Matangini Hazra, and Sarojini Naidu are some of the women from Bengal whose courage has no parallel in our history. These women empowered themselves to define their own destiny— which was the ultimate sacrifice for a free India.

"That is why it is not surprising to me that the greatest worship performed by the people of Bengal is mainly that of Devi. In fact, no state represents women's empowerment as Bengal does.

"Honourable Chief Minister, you have carried forward the legacy of these great women. From the social point of view, your flagship scheme 'Kanya Shree' focusing on the girl child has been an astonishing success. It is not surprising that the scheme was awarded the 'Highest Public Service Honour' by the United Nations. Similarly, the UN award-winning 'Utkarsh Bangla' programme for skill development and the 'Shobooz Sathi' scheme for children to cycle to school demonstrate your deep understanding of the needs of the youth of our society, whom you have now given a platform to succeed.

"No wonder your popularity is unmatched, your charisma is remarkable and your people's trust in you is unshakeable.

"Bengal is not only a delta of the Ganges and the Brahmaputra, but it is also a delta of art, science and thought—and Didi, you are the true expression of this great delta of thinkers, poets, writers, designers and painters.

"That is why what I am determined to bring to Bengal is the best of the Adani Group—our expertise in infrastructure, our pace of execution, our experience, and our focus on building bigger and better. The technology and scale that I am committed to bringing will help in reorganising the infrastructure in Bengal. What I am committed to bringing is the promise that I will live up to the expectations of the people of Bengal. Let me explain what I mean.

"The Adani Group's investments in Bengal will extend to world-class ports, infrastructure, state-of-the-art data centres and under-sea cables that will connect them to the oceans. We will bring centres of excellence in digital innovation, supply centres, warehouses and logistics parks on a large scale and the continued expansion of the Fortune products of Adani Wilmar, which is already a household name in the state.

"Overall, we expect our total investment in Bengal to exceed ₹ 10,000 crore over the next decade. We estimate that this investment will create 25,000 or more direct and indirect jobs for the people of Bengal. Thereafter, as we continue to expand here, we will bring our world-class expertise in the green energy value chain to Bengal.

"In conclusion, I would like to state that we are all born to be free souls and nothing has inspired me more than two meaningful lines from the Nobel laureate Guru Rabindranath Tagore's 'Gitanjali':

Where the mind is without fear and the head is held high
Into that heaven of freedom, my father, let my country awake!

"Though we can debate whether Tagore defined the bold Bengali spirit or Bengal defined the bold spirit of Tagore, what is undeniable is the bold spirit which is present in every Bengali.

"No wonder the most ferocious yet beautiful tigers in the world decided to make Bengal their home. Honourable Chief Minister, Adani Group is honoured to be here—to bring a change—and to work with the people of Bengal."

❑

Largest Infrastructure Developer

Adani Group is on its way to becoming the world's largest renewable energy generation company by 2030. Speaking at a JP Morgan event, Adani said that the group is already the largest solar energy player in the world where they are responsible for production and under construction and contracted projects.

"We have achieved this in just two years and our renewable portfolio has reached our initial target of 25 GW a full four years ahead of schedule. This puts us on the path to becoming the world's largest renewable energy generation company by 2030. There are many new avenues for us, including establishing ourselves as one of the largest green hydrogen producers in the world."

Adani declared that by 2025, more than 75 per cent of their planned capital expenditure would be on green technologies. He said, "We will increase our renewable energy generation capacity from 21 per cent to 63 per cent in the next four years. No company is manufacturing on this scale.

"Over the next 10 years, we will invest more than $20 billion in renewable energy generation, component manufacturing, transmission and distribution. We are now India's largest private sector electricity producer, largest private port operator, largest private airport operator, largest private consumer of gas and electricity utility business, and the developers of the largest private electric transmission company and largest renewable energy infrastructure company.

"In the last eight years alone, we have acquired over 50 assets worth about $12 billion. Each one of these has been a success and we keep getting better at integrating the acquisitions we have made. This is a rare ability that we have shaped.

"Adani Group's plans for airport-centric growth include metropolitan development which spans entertainment facilities, e-commerce and logistics capabilities, aviation dependent industries, smart city development and other innovative business concepts. The best example is our Mumbai airport.

"We will not only expand the existing airport but will also operate the Navi Mumbai International Airport by 2024. This airport will handle 80 million additional passengers. This coincides with India becoming the third largest aviation market in the world."

Digital business

"Upcoming new businesses will include all of our digital-related enterprises, which now span data centres, industrial clouds and Adani Digital Labs.

"Earlier this year (2022), we established 'Adani Digital Labs' as a part of Adani Enterprises to be able to provide a unified experience to all our end consumers. Today our end consumer base is growing at the rate of 15 per cent. With our digital platform Adani Consumer, we will potentially have over one billion consumers by 2030.

"I have little doubt that every one of our B2C businesses will operate on a mobile platform. So, the consumer insights we gain through a unified platform will set us on the path to building our own super app platform.

"Adani Group has become the third conglomerate in India to cross the $200 billion market capitalisation. The current focus of the company is on various sectors like solar manufacturing, defence, airports, roads and green business. The Adani Group stock has gained over 120 per cent in just one month, while Adani Wilmar has gained over 87 per cent in the same period."

> *"If India becomes a $30 trillion economy by 2050, no one in India will sleep hungry."*
>
> **—Gautam Adani**

Gautam Adani says that if the country becomes an estimated $30 trillion economy by 2050, then it will also be home to a nation where no one will sleep on an empty stomach.

"We are about 10,000 days away from the year 2050. During this period, I hope to add about US$25 trillion to our economy. This translates to an additional US$2.5 billion in GDP every day. I also estimate that during this period, we will eradicate all kinds of poverty.

"It could also mean that the stock market would add about US$40 trillion to market capitalisation during these 10,000 days, which translates to an additional US$4 billion every day by 2050.

"The uplifting of the lives of 1.4 billion people due to this may seem like a marathon in the short run, but it is a sprint in the long run. The World Bank in its latest report on poverty in the country has said that India saw a steep decline of 12.3 percentage points in extreme poverty between 2011 and 2019—from 22.5 per cent in 2011 to 10.2 per cent in 2019."

❑

Message on Labour Day

Every year, May 1 is also acknowledged as 'May Day' because of its universal celebration. 'International Workers' Day' celebrates the dedication, courage, hard work, sacrifice and leadership of the workforce and employees all over the world. India is home to some of the largest corporations in the world and with over 500 million people, has the second largest workforce globally. It is surprising that the occasion of International Workers' Day is not celebrated as enthusiastically as Diwali or Holi or even Independence Day in India.

For Gautam Adani, Adani Group Chairman, 'International Workers' Day' has always been a day to express his appreciation and gratitude towards the more than 11,000 people who make their dreams of nation-building come true. Employees remember gratitude and appreciation from employers and companies on 'International Workers' Day' for the rest of their lives. This is why it is such an important day for companies like the Adani Group to applaud their employees.

To make the occasion special for everyone associated with the Adani Group, Gautam Adani shares a special message with his colleagues, associates and employees through 'May Day'. On one such occasion, Gautam Adani paid tribute to the commitment and sacrifice of the employees of the Adani Group. He praised them for helping the group realise the dream of transforming India into a superpower. He also expressed his confidence in the workforce to help the group maintain its position as the 'driving force behind India's infrastructure industry'. His message:

"A different factor that defines the Adani Group is its ability to execute the last mile better than all other companies. My dear friends! That last mile is you and it is your contribution and sacrifice that has taken us from strength to strength. On this 'Labour Day', let me thank all of you and your families and salute you for everything you do.

"These spirits, backed by the humanitarian approach, actions and policies of our company (under your guidance), have given Adani Group a unique competitive edge over our competitors. We will continue this successful march towards the long-term goals of our states."

The Adani Group has always appreciated the commitment and perseverance of the people working under its banner and their families, who play the best supporting roles. Chairman Gautam Adani has always considered the workforce as the custodian of his vision and not as a group of individuals working for an organisation.

❑

Not 'Lecture', but 'Conversation'

In the backdrop of the ongoing '26th United Nations Climate Change Conference' in Glasgow, Gautam Adani, founder and chairman of Adani Industries, said that the world needs a 'conversation' and not a 'lecture' on climate.

Faced with agitation by climate change activists in India over coal shortages, Adani said that some people call for a complete halt on thermal power generation, but they do not consider discussing alternatives for balancing people's energy needs while fighting climate change.

Currently, there is a coal shortage across the world due to skyrocketing demand since the economy is back on track. The electricity demand grew by 20 per cent in India itself, but at the same time, coal imports have declined by 40 per cent due to rise in international prices. This volatility is being recognised for the post-pandemic growth in power demand, which was accelerated by lower-than-normal stocks of domestically produced coal due to the heavy monsoon.

Adani also addressed the role of social media and mainstream media in spreading chaos over the energy crisis and said that none of them has taken the responsibility of stopping the spread of fake news.

Instead of a constructive public dialogue, we were fighting amongst ourselves. A large section of mainstream media opted to cover the abuse being exchanged on social media, demonstrating that the speed of news distribution clearly outweighed the quality of research and content.

With regard to the climate summit, expressing his opinion, Adani said that world leaders would not be able to reach a binding agreement to deal with the climate crisis as the summit was about a 'broad statement' about transformative emissions reduction. According to Adani, this applied even to the strongest global economies as they were also unable to meet their energy requirement using green sources.

Lectures are being given about our emissions that are lower than the global per capita average and historically negligible even as developed economies failed to keep their pledge to provide $100 billion a year to help the world transition to green technologies.

Responding to a question whether his group has taken steps towards becoming net-zero, Adani pointed out that 70 per cent of his company's energy-related capital expenditure is in green technologies. Taking a jibe at rich countries, he said that this percentage would amount to an investment of $50 billion to $70 billion for renewable energy for the coming decade.

He said, "Our investments in renewable energy are being made with a view to producing the world's cheapest green electricity within the next decade. We hope to make green hydrogen production cheap enough to help India become the net exporter of green energy rather than an importer of fossil fuels."

❑

Motivational Speech at AGM 2021

Dear shareholders, as much as I wanted to welcome you all personally, the current security measures have made these virtual meetings unusual. However, I am optimistic that our 2022 AGM will be an in-person meeting and I will actually have the opportunity to shake hands with some of you.

Today, I want to share with you all some reflections from the past 12 months—a period that has been exceptionally difficult due to a fierce pandemic that will leave its mark on the world for many decades to come. The statistics—sadly—are startling. With close to 190 million cases worldwide, the Covid-19 pandemic is already the most widespread threat to global health in recorded history. It is also one of the deadliest. The virus has already killed over 40 lakh people in its deadly march across the world. No continent, no country and no community have been spared.

We must accept that every life lost is a tragedy. Undoubtedly, our country should have done much better, especially during the deadly second wave. However, as the nations of the world marshal their resources to fight the pandemic, India is being targeted by many critics for not doing more to protect its citizens, especially with regard to vaccination. We must acknowledge that given the sheer size of our population and the densely populated metropolises, the challenge before India is far greater than that of most other countries. To put this perspective in numbers, India has more people than the combined population of all countries on three continents—Europe, North America, and Oceania. In other words, our vaccination effort must be larger than the combined efforts of 87 countries. The fact is that out of 320 crore vaccine doses given worldwide, 35 crore doses were given in India. While I agree that the criticism is justified, we should not fall prey to voices that demoralise our country or demoralise the frontline workers who make extraordinary sacrifices. And it is the frontline workers who have been our inspiration. Helping the nation during a crisis is not about deciding the number of corporates like us. Instead, it is about stepping up to make sure we do our part, it is about helping everyone we can reach out to, and it is about taking the nation forward.

First of all, in everything we do, no one has inspired or reminded us more about our duty to serve the nation than the frontline workers who exemplified the great Indian ideal of *'Seva Paramo Dharma'* through the agony of the pandemic. The Adani Group went around the world to find vital essentials like liquid medical oxygen, cryogenic tanks and oxygen cylinders, but our contribution is fuelled by the enormity of the efforts put in by our women and men.

The Indian Air Force flew countless missions day and night to help us with essential supplies, both near and far. Yes, we promoted PM Cares Fund without any contribution, but money cannot match the personal selflessness of the people on the street who rose above their needs to help their fellow Indians whom they did not know and may never see again.

Yes, we have provided logistics support by air, sea, rail and road across the country and carried thousands of tonnes of essential supplies. But this is nothing compared to the unfathomable great work of our doctors and nurses who risked their lives to serve their fellow citizens.

There have been different stories of humanity. The sacrifices we have made are humble. Through it all, we have done our best to support oxygen delivery and patient care as the people of our Adani Foundation brought together resources and experts to help. For example, in a matter of days, our engineering and medical teams turned Ahmedabad's Adani Vidya Mandir School into an emergency care facility with hundreds of beds, oxygen support and catered food. It was literally '*Vidya-daan se Jeevan-daan*' as the learning halls of our school became the halls of life. Similarly, our general hospitals in Bhuj and Mundra were converted into 100 per cent Covid care hospitals.

This would not have been possible without the coordinated efforts of thousands of my fellow Adanians who ignored risks to their own health to help carry out this mission. An exceptional example of this is the length to which our logistics department went to deliver refrigerated vaccines to all parts of India, from east to west and north to south. As an interesting statistic—the distance they covered is equivalent to travelling the earth twice.

❑

India: An Incredible Nation

More than three decades after the group's inception, Gautam Adani's vision and belief in nation-building and unprecedented business opportunities in India have grown exponentially. Speaking to the distinguished audience at the 'TIE Global Summit', the 'Optimistic Entrepreneur' said:

"India is still incredible, considering the plethora of opportunities it offers to the world. In my view, India is at a dramatic juncture today. I believe that in the next few decades, India will be firmly established as the biggest opportunity of the 21st century and will be even stronger after 2050.

"Amid the diverse challenges expected in a large democracy of its size and periodic economic downturn, the unique opportunities presented by our home country has made it significantly different from its global peers.

"The structural reforms that have strengthened the Indian economy in recent times have laid the foundation for accelerating growth. By 2050, Indian GDP will be US$28 trillion, which will be 15 per cent of the global GDP. Given India's population growth, by that time, one in every three middle class consumers in the world will be Indian, and India will become the largest global middle class.

"This middle class will secure India and drive an unmatched rate of internal consumption—no country has ever produced such a vast middle class. The retail segment alone would be worth $10 trillion. India will be the target investment of every global company.

"Taking a 30-year stock market CAGR of 9 per cent in a developed country, the Indian market index would have risen by a factor of 13, keeping the Sensex in the range of 600000. By the year 2050, India will have built its own trillion dollar companies."

Digitisation and renewable energy

"Today the two—energy sector and the technology sector—are competing increasingly. I see this technology-energy crossroads as the most defining factor in lifting India's population balance—not just out of poverty—but actually.

"Affordable green power combining digital technologies—including sensors and the Internet of Things, artificial intelligence and machine learning, 5G and cloud infrastructure—will all empower India economically in a number of micro-sized processes and will transform each one.

"Micro-farming, micro-water, micro-health care, micro-housing, micro-education, micro-manufacturing... the list is endless and the impacts of renewable energy and technology being able to shape current processes are profound for both urban and rural India, and even more so for rural India.

"The pandemic has taught us that the traditional need for close proximity can be irrelevant and risk-prone. India had already made a major debut in this area through the development of its digital services. It is now positioned as a significant beneficiary of this change. More companies are planning to split execution and control operations in the coming days. Both these sectors were transformative and could help create millions of new local jobs in the manufacturing, supply chain and technical services sectors.

"Let people be bullish and reflect on India's soft power, including its political values, cultural alignment and foreign policy approach. Combine this soft power, which India has demonstrated strongly, with the hard power of $28 trillion GDP and a stock market worth $30 trillion—and you have an incredible nation, which is on its way to becoming the biggest opportunity of the 21st century."

❑

Adani Group: Mining Business

Electricity is an essential tool to empower humanity in a rapidly growing world. While developed conglomerates like the Adani Group have taken a leap to promote eco-friendly solar and wind power, coal remains the main fuel for India's 1.25 billion strong population.

It is well established that the average electricity consumption of people in India is very low as compared to our global peers. With increasing urbanization and changing lifestyles, the demand for electricity is likely to increase in the future. According to industry estimates, the demand for electricity in India is expected to grow to 1600 billion units in 2022 and 2100 billion units over the next decade. This will be met by diverse energy sources including coal.

Adani Enterprises Limited Group bridges the gap between the demand and supply of coal through a combination of imports and responsible mining. Apart from contributing to domestic coal production with the help of eco-friendly practices, it has also developed a strong supplier base in—South Africa, Australia, USA and Russia—among other coal-rich geographies.

India is one of the world's best-rich mineral deposits, with the largest global reserves of various minerals. At a time when the world is moving from globalization to self-reliance, the need to mine these reserves and present the country's downstream manufacturing capabilities with a domestic head-start advantage is a premium, which is manifested in logical proximity, cost advantage and timely resource availability.

This reality places India's mining sector at the heart of the self-reliance India initiative, which emphasizes the need to generate natural resources for national needs and create significant domestic advantage in the value chain for finished products, infrastructure and national competitiveness.

Given this, mining is not incidental to India's development, but represents a building block of national prosperity.

India's consumption outlook for various mineral resources remains optimistic over the long term. Based on a 7.4 per cent GDP growth rate between 2022 and 2024, India's coal consumption is projected to grow by 3.9 per cent annually to 1.18 billion tonnes in 2024, a growth partly catalysed by the timely availability of coal within the country.

India's iron ore production grew by 20 per cent to 246 million tonnes in 2021, meeting needs within and outside India. This availability sustained the growing build-up of downstream steel capacities, facilitated exports of value-added end products on the resource, and strengthened India's foreign exchange earnings.

Although electricity is largely generated through coal, thermal power plants account for about 75 per cent of the country's electricity generation. India's total electricity generation in December 2021 was 203.190 giga watts from coal and 24.9 giga watts from gas-fired power plants, indicating dominance of the former.

The Indian thermal power plant market is expected to register a CAGR of around 2.3 per cent between 2022 and 2027, which is higher than most developed countries.

The Indian government allowed the coal mining sector to open up for commercial use, creating opportunities for private players. The government is in process to start operations in about 100 previously closed / abandoned mines. It plans to use around 100 metric tonnes of coal for gasification purposes to domestically secure the energy needs of India and reduce its dependence on import.

The government is offering more than 500 mines of various minerals for auction through the state governments and increasing industrialization. Strengthening thermal demand is intended to monetize over ₹ 28,000 crore in mining, profitable, first-mile connectivity by over 160 mining sector projects.

These realities have created an unprecedented growth target for India's private sector, providing a multi-year business opportunity.

- ✓ The National Steel Policy aims to increase per capita steel consumption to 160 kg by financial year 30-31. The government aims to increase per capita rural steel consumption from 19.6 kg to 38 kg by financial year 30-31.
- ✓ In July 2021, India sent its first coal export consignment to Rampal Power Plant in Bangladesh, strengthening coal exports. Iron ore exports reached 1.7 billion US dollar in the financial year 21-22, a growth of 168 per cent over the previous year due to a lower base effect.
- ✓ The Ministry of Mines notified the Mineral Conservation and Development (Amendment) Rules in November 2021 to provide guidelines for conservation of minerals, systematic

and scientific mining and development of minerals for the protection of the environment in the country.

- ✓ To unlock India's mineral potential, the Ministry of Mines submitted 152 mineral block reports to the State Governments during the year under review.
- ✓ The government allocated ₹ 393.24 crore to the Union Coal Ministry for financial year 22-23 in the Union Budget as against the Revised Estimates of 644.09 crore in financial year 21-22. (Approved by the Geological Survey of India) 15 were handed over to the State Governments.
- ✓ In September 2021, India and Australia participated in a Joint Working Group meeting on Coal and Mines to strengthen bilateral cooperation in the coal sector. In September 2021, the government approved the Memorandum of Understanding between the Geological Survey of India (GSI) and Joint Stock Company Rosgeologia, Russia in the field of Geology.
- ✓ The government took initiatives including mining and mineral policy reforms to accelerate production and capacity utilization of iron ore deposits by state-owned mining companies.
- ✓ In the Union Budget 2021, the government reduced customs duty on semi, flat and long products of non-alloy, alloy and stainless steel to 7.5 per cent to enhance MSME competitiveness. The Government of India reduced the import duty on copper scrap from 5 per cent to 2.5 per cent.
- ✓ The expenditure budget of financial year 22-23 includes ₹ 314.54 crore for Central Sector Schemes / Projects and ₹ 393.24 crore for Coal Mines Pension Scheme.

Adani Enterprises expanded into mine development and operations in 2008. The company bridges the gap between demand and supply of coal through responsible mining and imports from South Africa, Australia, USA and Russia, among other coal-rich geographies.

The company's growing industry presence has been marked by a string of positive achievements.

Within just a decade, the company emerged as one of the largest developers and operators of coal mines in India, apart from international footprints in Indonesia and Australia. The company's mining projects are located in Chhattisgarh, Madhya Pradesh, Odisha and Jharkhand. The company's book size of 131 MTPA (101 MTPA coal block and 16 MTPA iron ore block) includes MDO and commercial coal mining capacity of 14 MTPA.

The Parsa East Kente Basan project commenced production in a record 3.5 years, which is a benchmark for the coal mining industry in India. Thereafter, the project reached peak capacity. The company dispatched its first rake from PEKB mine to Rajasthan Rajya Vidyut Utpadan Nigam Limited power stations in March 2013. In addition, the company's GP III, Talabira II and III mines became operational in less than three years.

The company's outperformance was derived from proprietary capabilities across the value chain, which included capabilities in exploration, mine development, construction, ore extraction, beneficiation and transportation. The company has unique financial, contractual and project management insight to manage these projects.

As India's largest resource management company, mine developer and operator (with domestic and global presence), the company continues to add coal production capacity at its mines. With imports still not meeting coal demand, the company is optimistic about leveraging its integrated presence across the supply chain with embedded technologies to drive operational efficiencies.

The company leverages synergies across various group verticals, spanning the trading, logistics, power generation, transmission, distribution, ports (sea, air), road, rail and water sectors. The company provides complete support for setting up a production complex, i.e. land, transportation and utilities such as electricity, water, etc. The company is also setting up one of the largest copper refinery complexes in India.

Parsa East and Kente Basan Coal Block

The Parsa East and Kente Basan coal blocks (PEKB) in Chhattisgarh have been allocated to the Rajasthan Rajya Vidyut Utpadan Nigam Limited (RRVUNL).

RRVUNL has entered into a coal mining and distribution agreement with Parsa Kente Collieries Limited (PKCL), a joint venture company of RRVUNL and Adani Enterprises Limited and has appointed PKCL as the sole mining contractor.

PKCL - As the mine developer and operator of PEKB, is engaged in development, mining, transportation and dispatch of washed coal for the power projects of RRVUNL. The project started mining operations and transmitting coal to thermal power stations of RRVUNL in March 2013. Raw coal production was 15 MMT and washed coal dispatch to Thermal Power Plants of RRVUNL was 12.34 MMT in the financial year 21-22.

Kente Extension Coal Block

Kente Extension Coal Block has been allotted to RRVUNL in Chhattisgarh. Rajasthan Collieries Limited (RCL) and RRVUNL (a joint venture company of RRVUNL and Adani Enterprises Limited) entered into a coal mining and distribution agreement appointing RCL as the sole mining contractor.

RCL is the mine developer and operator of Kente Extension Coal Block and will focus on development of the coal block, mining, beneficiation and scheduling of coal for transportation and dispatch of coal to recipient power projects of RRVUNL. Kente Extension is under development.

Parsa Coal Block

Parsa Coal Block has been allotted to RRVUNL in Chhattisgarh. Rajasthan Collieries Limited (RCL) and RRVUNL (a joint venture company of RRVUNL and Adani Enterprises Limited) entered into a coal mining and distribution agreement appointing RCL as the sole mining contractor. RCL, the mine developer and operator of the Parsa Coal Block, will focus on development of the coal block, mining, beneficiation of coal and scheduling for haulage and dispatch of coal for power projects of RRVUNL. Parsa Coal Block is under development.

Gare Pelma Sector III Coal Block

The Gare Pelma Sector III Coal Block in Chhattisgarh was allocated to the Chhattisgarh State Power Generation Company Limited (CSPGCL) for limited use in its thermal power plant in Chhattisgarh. Gare Pelma III Collieries Limited, a 100 per cent subsidiary of Adani Enterprises Limited, was appointed by CSPGCL as Mine Developer and Operator for development, operation, mining and dispatch of coal for power projects of CSPGCL. On November 16, 2017, CSPGCL and GPIIICL entered into a Coal Mine Services Agreement.

GPIIICL, as Mine Development and Operation of Gare Pelma Sector III Coal Block, is undertaking development, mining of coal block and arranging transportation and dispatch of coal for recipient power projects of CSPGCL. On March 26, 2019 the permission was granted to open the Coal Block. Coal production started on December 6, 2019 and in financial year 21-22 the coal production was 3.27 MMT. Coal deliveries commenced from March 16, 2020 and the total coal deliveries in financial year 21-22 was 3.52 MMT.

Talabira II and III Coal Blocks

Talabira II and III Coal Blocks in Odisha have been allocated to NLC India Limited (NLCIL) for limited use in their thermal power plant. Talabira (Odisha) Mining Private Limited (TOMPL), a subsidiary of Adani Enterprises Limited, was appointed by NLCIL as Mine Developer and Operator (MDO) for development, operation, mining and dispatch of coal to NLCIL. NLCIL and TOMPL entered into a coal mining agreement on March 23, 2018. TOMPL as mine development and operator of Talabira II and III coal blocks is undertaking development, mining, loading, transportation and despatch of coal to the points of delivery. On March 29, 2019 the permission was granted to open the coal block. TOMPL started operations in the financial year 20-21 and the coal production volume was 6.35 MMT in the financial year 21-22.

Suliyari Coal Block

The Suliyari Coal Block in Madhya Pradesh was allotted to Andhra Pradesh Mineral Development Corporation Limited (APMDC) for commercial mining of coal. Adani Enterprises Limited (AEL) was appointed by APMDC as the Mine Developer and Operator (MDO) for upgradation, operation, mining and delivery of coal to APMDC. APMDC and AEL entered into a coal mining agreement on March 8, 2018. AEL, as mine development and operator of Suliyari Coal Block, will be engaged in development and distribution of the coal block in place of development, extraction, loading, transportation and dispatch of coal. Suliyari Coal Block is operational from April 2022.

Bailadila Deposit-13 Iron Ore Mine

The mining lease of Bailadila Deposit-13 Iron Ore Mine in Chhattisgarh is held by NCL (NMDC - CMDC Ltd.). The NCL has appointed the Adani Enterprises, as the Mine Developer and Operator (MDO), for refurbishing, operation, extraction and dispatch of iron ore.

AEL is a sub-contractor to Bailadila Iron Ore Mining Private Limited (BIOMPL), a 100 per cent subsidiary of Adani Enterprises Limited, for development of iron ore blocks, extraction, loading and carriage. This iron ore mine is under development.

Gare Pelma Sector I Coal Block

Gare Pelma sector one coal block in Chhattisgarh has been allocated to Gujarat State Electricity Corporation Limited (GSECL) to ensure proper utilization in their thermal power plants in Gujarat. On December 15, 2018, GSECL granted and issued a conditional approval letter (LOA) to Adani Enterprises Limited (AEL, 74 per cent) and Sainik Mining and Allied Services Limited (SMASL, 26 per cent) for expansion, operation, mining and dispatch of coal for end-use.

Gare Pelma Sector II Coal Block

Gare Pelma Sector II Coal Block in Chhattisgarh have been allocated to the Maharashtra State Power Generation Company Limited for captive use in its thermal power plants in Maharashtra. The Maharashtra State Power Generation Company Limited issued the final acceptance letter to AEL on November 5, 2019 for development, operation, mining and loading into wagons of the power projects of Maharashtra State Power Generation Company Limited. AEL formed an SPV named Gare Pelma II Collieries Private Limited. An agreement on Coal Mine Service Agreement was signed between Gare Pelma II Collieries Private Limited and Maharashtra State Power Generation Company Limited. Production is expected to begin by the year 2024.

Gidhmuri Paturia Coal Block

The Gidhmuri Paturia Coal Block in Chhattisgarh has been allocated to the Chhattisgarh State Power Generation Company Limited for use in its thermal power plants in Chhattisgarh. Gidhamuri Paturia Collieries Private Limited (GPCPL), an SPV of the mine developer of Adani Enterprises Limited (AEL, 74 per cent) and Sainik Mining and Allied Services Limited (SMASL, 26 per cent), was appointed by CSPGCL as the Mine Developer and Operator for development, operation, extraction and dispatch of coal. CSPGCL and GPCPL entered into coal mining and the agreement was signed on May 2, 2019.

GPCPL, as the Mine Development and Operator (MDO) of Gidhmuri Paturia coal block, will be engaged in renewal of the coal block, mining, transportation facilities and dispatch of coal. The coal block is being developed.

Kurmitar Iron Ore Mine

The mining lease of Kurmitar Iron Ore Mining Private Limited in Sundergarh district of Odisha is held by Odisha Mining Corporation Limited. Odisha Mining Corporation Limited has appointed Kurmitar Iron Ore Mining Private Limited (KIOMPL), a 100 per cent subsidiary of Adani Enterprises, as the mine developer and operator that will do the work for beneficiation, working, extraction, transportation and dispatch of iron ore to the point of delivery. OMCL, AEL and KIOMPL signed an iron ore mining agreement on October 31, 2019. The production and delivery volume of coal in the financial year 21-22 was 3 MMT respectively.

- ✓ The company operated the Kurmitar Iron Ore mine.
- ✓ The company signed an agreement with the Ministry of Coal for Jhigador, Khargaon and Gondkhari coal mines.
- ✓ The company emerged as the successful bidder for the Bijhan coal mine. The company was also the sole successful bidder for the Gondbahera Uzheni East coal mine.
- ✓ The company focused on digital transformation, taking various initiatives ranging from efficiency improvement to data-driven.

- ✓ The company is focused on 'Green Mining' (Renewable Energy) for mining and washing as a part of its Environmental, Social and Governance (ESG) commitment.
- ✓ The company's business units were mandated with Environmental, Social and Governance (ESG) metrics and MAP techniques.
- ✓ The company was focused on reducing its carbon and water footprint.
- ✓ Social accounting, as measured by social return on investment, was aligned with people's needs and capacity building initiatives.
- ✓ Adani's mining initiative was driven by digitization, aimed at strengthening the decarbonize.
- ✓ The company entered into new sectors—copper, aluminium and cement to reduce the dependence on coal, reducing the sustainability credit of the company.

While the company's sustainability personality is inspired by the SDG Millennium Goals, they have been customized to local needs and ongoing sustainability.

The company is committed to promoting talent diversity and inclusion (individuals of different genders, religions, castes, ethnicities and education), enriching its workplace through diverse approaches.

The company's policies are woven around sustainability, biodiversity, re-forestation, holistic and inclusive growth to balance the objectives of business, environment and society.

There is scope for additional potential in iron ore, bauxite and coal mining based on proven deposits in addition to potential sub-surface deposit exploration opportunities. Various infrastructure projects undertaken across the country continue to provide lucrative business opportunities for the company. The company is focused on mine portfolio development and diversification in a socially sustainable manner.

Adani Australia

Adani Australia is a multifaceted energy and infrastructure company dedicated to providing energy solutions. By providing energy solutions to Australia and the Asia-Pacific from thermal and renewable energy, it contributes billions of dollars in taxes and royalties to the Australian economy, creating jobs and helping to upgrade key infrastructure such as hospitals, schools and roads.

Adani Australia owns and operates the Abbot Point Terminal, responsibly 'exporting' coal from Queensland for over 35 years. It is Australia's northernmost coal port and is located 25 kilometres north-west of Bowen in North Queensland. The port is a modern, high volume, fast turnaround port complex with natural deep water and a multi-user port facility (with a capacity of 50 MTPA).

Adani Renewables, Australia's first solar farm was commissioned in October 2019 near Rugby Run Moranbah, supplying 65 megawatts of renewable energy, powering around 23,000 Queensland homes. A power purchase agreement was signed to sell 80 per cent of the power produced in the market. More than 247,000 solar panels were installed, generating 185,000 megawatt hours of electricity every year. Adani Renewables Australia is also involved in commercial talks for its second solar farm in Whyalla, Australia.

Adani Mining Private Limited

Adani Australia owns and operates the Abbot Point Terminal. It has responsibly exported Queensland coal for over 35 years. It is Australia's northernmost coal port and is located 25 kilometres north-west of Bowen in North Queensland. The port is a modern, high volume, fast turnaround port complex with natural deep water and a multi-user port facility with a current capacity of up to 50 MTPA.

Adani Renewables Australia's first solar farm near Rugby Run Moranbah officially opened in October 2019, supplying 65 megawatts of renewable energy to approximately 23,000 Queensland homes. A power purchase agreement was signed to sell 80 per cent of the energy produced. More than 247,000 solar panels have been installed, generating 185,000 mega watt hours of electricity every year. Adani Renewables Australia is also currently in commercial talks for its second solar farm in Whyalla, Australia.

Adani Mining Private Ltd is an Australian mining company operating out of regional Queensland. The flagship of Adani Mining is the Carmichael mine and rail project. The Carmichael Project, located more than 300 kilometres west of the Queensland coast, is in the ideal position to maximize the opportunities presented by the Galilee Basin.

The Carmichael Project is a thermal coal mine and rail project that will transport coal from the Galilee Basin to countries in Asia, including India, providing thousands of jobs for Queenslanders in the process.

Delivering 10 million tonnes of mining per year, coupled with a 200 kilometre narrow gauge rail line that links to existing rail infrastructure through the Port of Abbott Point, Townsville, Rock Hampton, Mackay, Bowen, Gladstone, Central Highlands and Isaac regions. Communities like these are ideally positioned to find new jobs and contracting opportunities for local workers and businesses.

The company also provides door-to-door resource delivery model. This includes responsibility and accountability for sourcing resources from suppliers, managing ocean-borne logistics, providing intermediate holding facilities at discharge ports, and providing resources to customers.

This unique approach has helped the business garner over 600 satisfied customers across various downstream industries (power, cement, iron and steel, among others).

The company ventured into Coal Management in 1999 to bridge the gap between the requirement of coal in thermal power plants and the coal requirement of the nation.

During the last few decades, AEL maintained its position as the largest coal supplier in India and a leading supplier of critical minerals across the world. The company is the largest coal importer in Indonesia. It is one of the leading revenue earners for Indian Railways.

The company is India's largest non-coking coal off-taker in Indonesia, South Africa and the United States, serving private and PSU customers in India.

Its project in Indonesia was Adani Group's first overseas project in coal mining and operations. The move was in line with its long-term resolve to support the growing demand for coal in energy-starved India.

This journey led to the creation of PT Adani Global, a subsidiary of Adani Enterprises Limited, with a focus on coal mining, logistics and business operations in Indonesia. The company then obtained an exploration license from the Indonesian government in the year 2007.

Based in the island of Kalimantan, alternatively known as Borneo, the company built a coal terminal to service its mining operations. The present capacity is 2500 TPH and is to be upgraded to 5000 TPH.

Since its incorporation, a highly experienced in-house team was entrusted with exploration responsibilities. Among others, the company is using Multi Seam, Shallow Dip and Open Cut Mining, mechanized mining methods for coal production with 45-50 T class excavators, 25-30 T class dumpers, 160-190 HP class dozers, etc. It has also built a coal terminal to service mining operations. Mine coal is crushed to produce a thermal coal product for export and domestic markets.

Cape Vessels usually come about 8 to 10 nautical miles from the jetty. Chartered vessels transport coal from the jetty to the main vessels. Coal is trans-shipped to the mother vessel by floating crane 'Surya Pratama Karya', which is equipped with a material handling system (designed and manufactured in-house). 'Surya Pratma Karya' has transported more than 20 MMT of coal so far.

Lamindo has over 90 per cent of its workforce from Benue. With a total population of over 10,000 in Benue, PT Lamindo Inter Multicon contributes significantly to the economy of Benue. PT Lamindo Inter Multicon employs a number of contractors on various projects. It also provides employment to more than 1500 people.

The company imports coal through all foremost Indian ports, reducing logistics cost and ensuring timely delivery.

The company's complement of 10 marketing offices (four international), 18 branch centres and 20 operational ports has led to irresistible leadership in the market. The company is present in the growing coal markets of Sri Lanka, Thailand, Vietnam, China and Dubai.

❑

Adani Defence and Aerospace

India accounts for 3.7 per cent of global military spending, making it the third largest military spender in the world. The country stands at an inflection point as far as this sector is concerned. Even as the defence sector continues to grow, there is likely to be a decisive change in the spending pattern. The Government of India has stressed the need for self-reliance in defence equipment manufacturing in line with the 'Make in India' initiative, which is a definite change from the past when a major part of India's defence equipment was imported from other countries. In addition, the proposed corporatization of the Ordnance Factory Board (OFB) may help in induction of state-of-the-art technologies and enhance operational efficiency. Further in addition, various opportunities have been created for India's defence sector, encouraging private sector participation through articulation of long-term policies. The Government of India has increased the Foreign Direct Investment (FDI) in India's defence sector to 74 per cent and up to 100 per cent through the automatic route and through the government route for companies seeking new defence industrial licenses.

The time is ideal for the sustainable development of this sector. The technologies are developing, emphasizing the need for modern equipment and weapons. With many countries increasing their defence spending, it has become imperative for India to increase its defence budget. These realities will make room for replacement of equipment on one hand addressing the need for rising costs.

✓ To support the modernization of the defence sector, capital outlay increased by 18.75 per cent in the Union Budget for the financial year 2021-22 over the previous year, the highest increase in 15 years. In this Union Budget, 68 per cent of capital procurement was earmarked for domestic industry and 25 per cent of the R&D budget was earmarked for industry, start-ups and academia.

The Defence Ministry prepared a draft of Defence Production and Export Promotion Policy (DPEPP) 2020 to position India among the leading exporters in the defence and aerospace sectors. The pillars of DPEPP 2020 include the following –

✓ Improvement in procurement ecosystem, indigenization and support to MSMEs and start-ups, optimization of the resources.

This ability is reflected in the numbers. India's defence and aerospace manufacturing market was valued at ₹ 85,000 crore in the year 2021, which is expected to reach ₹ 1 lakh crore by the year 2022 and may increase to 70 billion American dollars by the year 2030. Furthermore, the Indian defence market represents an accessible cumulative revenue generation opportunity of 306.95 American dollars.

The development of India's defence sector from import to self-reliance is expected to change the global status of this sector as well. According to the Stockholm International

Peace Research Institute Report 2020, India is among the top 25 allocations, and is on top for promoting investment, FDI and ease of doing business, promoting innovation and R&D, encouraging and improving DPSUs and OFBs, quality assurance and testing infrastructure and in providing and promoting exports.

✓ The government released the Defence Acquisition Procedure 2020 (DAP) to transform India into a global manufacturing hub with a focus on indigenously designed, developed and manufactured weapon systems. The DAP 2020 offset guidelines were revised to encourage Indian defence equipment manufacturing companies to manufacture complete defence products (on components or sub-parts) with priority for discharge of offsets to defence product exporting countries. The government set a target of ₹ 35,000 crore in exports in aerospace and defence goods services by the year 2024-25, which can propel India towards the global defence supply chain.

The government aims to ensure transparency, predictability and ease of doing business by building a robust ecosystem and supportive government policies. In this direction, the government has taken initiatives such as de-licensing, de-regulation, promotion of exports and liberalization of foreign investment.

✓ Under the Atmanirbhar Bharat initiative of the Government of India, the country's Ministry of Defence prepared a list of 209 items (Positive Indigenization List) for which import will be prohibited beyond the time limit indicated against them, so that a wide opportunity area could be made available in the country for the manufacturing for these items.

In the defence sector, the Strategic Partnership (SP) model envisages the establishment of long-term strategic partnerships with defence manufacturing companies in India through a transparent and competitive process, wherein they will partner with the global Original Equipment Manufacturers (OEMs) to set up domestic manufacturing infrastructure and tie up for technology transfer to set up a supply chain. For the manufacture of indigenous defence equipment in three years (financial year 2018-19 to financial year 2020-21), the government approved the requirement for 119 proposals worth approximately ₹ 214,255 crore.

The Adani Group ventured into defence and aerospace in the year 2017 with a vision to help transform India into a world-class high-tech defence manufacturing destination. Within a short span of time, the company built a comprehensive ecosystem of defence products including small arms, precision guided munitions, unmanned aerial systems, structures, electronics, radars, EW systems and simulators, among others. The company focuses on building proprietary technologies through complementary collaborations.

The Defence Ministry has set a target of 70 per cent self-reliance in the arms sector by the year 2027, thereby creating attractive prospects for industry players. The company's portfolio may expand with the introduction of a green channel positioning policy to encourage private sector investment in defence production.

The company bagged contracts worth over ₹ 1000 crore from the Indian Armed Forces, including the first small arms contract awarded to a private sector small arms manufacturer.

The company formally signed the first development-cum-production partner contract with the Defence Research and Development Organization (DRDO) for long-range guided bombs for the Indian Air Force. The company will undertake the design and development of the Smart Guided Bomb System with DRDO and will be appointed as the sole supplier to the Indian Air Force.

The company began by providing an Air Defence Fire Control Radar to the Indian Army, which included a contract worth over ₹ 900 crore.

The lockdown due to the pandemic in various states of the country has disrupted the operations of the company. However, the company continued to operate safely while protecting the employees.

Despite manufacturing challenges, the company continued to ramp up production of the Hermes 900 fuselage, maintaining its culture of zero defects, zero rework and zero safety record for three consecutive years. The continued success testifies to the company's excellence in continuous industrialization, engineering and quality systems, and its ability to deliver products with zero-concessions. The company is expected to receive an additional contract for 22 shipsets of Hermes 900 fuselages to be delivered over 36 months.

The company commenced operation of the MiG 29 simulator at Adampur under a 20-year Build Operate Maintenance contract with the Indian Air Force.

Small Arms and Ammunition

The company forayed into small arms manufacturing by acquiring a majority stake in PLR Systems in the year 2021. In line with its vision to build unique capabilities with an aim to enhance indigenization capabilities in India, the company commissioned the first private sector barrel manufacturing facility. It also had the privilege of being the first private sector company in India to be awarded a small arms supply contract by the Indian Armed Forces. With the commissioning of the barrel line in the third quarter of the financial year 21-22, the company expanded its manufacturing capacity to over 100,000 small arms per annum and emerged as the only facility in the space to achieve 100 per cent indigenization.

The company proposes to deepen its presence in the personnel protection sector with the establishment of a state-of-the-art small calibre ammunition manufacturing facility in Hyderabad. The manufacturing facility is expected to be commissioned by the third quarter of the year 2023 with an installed capacity to produce 100 million rounds per year for all major small arms.

Counter Drone System

With the growing threat of lethal drones to India's borders and critical infrastructure, the company emphasized its presence in the counter-drone domain with successful live demonstrations of Rudrav Counter Drone Systems at customer locations. Rudrav Systems has been the most sought after system among various customers. It will be deployed across multiple airports under a unique availability-based model, which will provide 24x7 security to airports against rogue drone threats. The company intends to strengthen its traction in providing proven security solutions. The company was selected as the development cum production partner for the indigenously designed counter drone solution.

Missiles

Building on a firm powerful foundation for an indigenous missile system, the company was selected as a development partner by DRDO for the first project under the development-cum-production partner model. Under the DCPP model, the company will undertake the design and development of a smart guided bomb system with DRDO and will be appointed as the sole system supplier to the Indian Air Force. Enhancing the company's missile portfolio, another DCPP contract was awarded for UAV Launched Precision Guided Missiles for the Indian Armed Forces. The company was selected to develop an ensemble drone system around a unique algorithm that enables these drones to operate in no GPS environment.

Airlines and MRO

The Maintenance, Repair and Overhaul (MRO) sector, which ensures the availability and airworthiness of aircraft, is of vital importance to the Indian and global aerospace and defence industry. The size of the Indian MRO industry is expected to grow from 1.7 billion US dollars in 2021 to 4.0 billion US dollars by 2031 – at a Compound Annual Growth Rate (CAGR) of 8.9 per cent against an expected global CAGR of 5.6 per cent. The company continues to build a one-stop solution for all aircraft related services in India and South Asia focusing on multiple areas such as aircraft maintenance, overhaul and repair, component services, training, simulators, digital solutions and airport services.

As per a report published by the Stockholm International Peace Research Institute (SIPRI), India is the world's fourth largest spender in the military segment. At USD 81.4 billion, India lags behind only the United States, China, and Russia in its military expenditure.

However, despite its rank in the top five military spenders, in terms of percentage, India's defence budget for GDP. This is reported to be grossly inadequate with the adequate level pegged at least 2.5%.

Even though our defence expenditure has risen from 6% from 2021 and by 47% from 2013, our armed forces continue to struggle with critical equipment shortages, right from fighter aircrafts, submarines and helicopters to modern infantry weapons, antitank guided missiles and night-fighting capabilities.

India's defence capabilities have historically been fulfilled by Russia, post the weapons embargo imposed by the US during the Cold War2. Given the strategic importance of the sector, the defence sector was under the stringent controls that govern Public Sector undertakings till 2001. The Vajpayee government in an effort to boost indigenous defence manufacturing then, first allowed 100% private sector participation and allowed FDI up to 26%. However, during the tenure of the Modi government, FDI is gradually increased to 49% in 2014, then 74% in 2020, and 100% under the approval route.

India has allocated INR 5.25 lakh crore for military expenses in the union budget of 2022-2023. The share of the defence budget stands at 13.3% of the total government expenditure.

To encourage indigenisation, the government has initiated an import ban on 411 weapons, platforms and systems that will be indigenised gradually from 2022 to 2030. These include high value imports such as artillery guns, lightweight tanks, missiles, destroyers as well as lower-value imports such as spare parts, small components and sub-systems for fighters, ships, submarines and tanks, providing a much needed boost to local defence production.

Defence exports have risen nearly tenfold between 2016-17 and 2022-23 to reach approximately INR 16,000 crore. India now exports to nearly 85 countries. Major platforms like Dornier-228, Brahmos missiles, Advanced Towed Artillery Guns (ATAGs), radars, simulators, mine protected vehicles, armoured vehicles, ammunitions, thermal imagers, body armours, besides systems, line replaceable units and parts from the bulk of the exports portfolio.

The country hopes to achieve an annual export target of INR 35,000 crore by 2025 and has launched a slew of measures to support domestic production. The government has simplified export procedures and has initiated measures like end-to-end online export authorisation, notification of three Open General Export License (OGEL) for the export of parts and components. The government has also released three positive indigenisation lists of 3,000+ components imported by Defence Public Sector Undertakings (DPSUs). Private organisations like Tata, L&T, Mahindra, Godrej, Bharat Forge are some of the peers of Adani in this segment.

Adani was looking for a market entry strategy in the aviation segment. The Group has identified the following pillars for their defence manufacturing: collaboration with global partners, developing platforms and technologies of critical importance, setting up a capability based ecosystem and international grade facilities.

Trying to identify the most productive and profitable option while exploring the countless opportunities available in defence production.

The government has further facilitated the growth of the MRO market by easing taxation norms, and lowered the GST on domestic MRO services from 18% to 5%.

Let us have a further look at the MRO market: India's aircraft maintenance market is dominated by three players— GMR Aero Technic, Air Works, and AI Engineering Services Limited (AIESL). India's MRO market is small, heavily fragmented, with a lot of scope for capacity utilisation. Despite the growth opportunities in the Indian aviation market, around 85% of the USD 1.4 billion maintenance work of Indian airlines is carried out in other countries, such as Singapore, Malaysia and Turkey.

Adani correctly prioritised the ground-handling business as a market entry strategy. This contributes significantly to the revenue of airport operators. Currently, there are revenue sharing arrangements between the third-party ground-handling agents and eight airports. Adani Airport plans to control ground handling at all its airports by 2026 and also offer services to other domestic and international airports, a strategy that supports Adani's vision of adjacent businesses.

Adani's proposed acquisition of Air Works would have helped the Group immensely as Air Works already handles MRO activities for the Navy P-8I and the Air Force 737 VVIP aircraft out of its EASA and DGCA certified facilities at Mumbai, Delhi,

Hosur and Kochi, giving the Group, an almost ready to execute order book.

Adani Defence is committed to help India achieve self-reliance in defence manufacturing. It has capabilities in small arms, unmanned aerial systems, radars, defence electronics and avionics, tactical communication systems, and electro- optical systems.

Adani's defence portfolio includes strategic acquisitions such as Alpha Design Technologies (ADTL), Comprotech, AutoTech, and Alpha Tocol. In October 2022, it emerged that Adani Defence was in talks for acquiring Air Works, Operations) provider, at an enterprise value of INR 400 crore. It has continuously been identifying and evaluating companies that have the ability to add to its defence portfolio through specialised offerings.

The Adani Group has demonstrated its commitment to build a self-reliant nation in defence production. Right from investing in building India's first Unmanned Aerial Vehicles (UAV) manufacturing facility, to India's first private sector small arms manufacturing facility, followed by India's first comprehensive aircraft MRO facility in Nagpur, the Group has continuously invested in capacity building.

It is also building a holistic ecosystem with Indian MSMEs through investments, incubators, strategic expertise, counsel and R&D.

The Group has cited its intention to collaborate with best-in-class global partners for technology transfer and advancements, which can help achieve India's defence ambitions and give the Group access to international markets.

The Adani Group is also committed to meeting export benchmarks set by the government. India's defence exports touched an all-time high of ₹ 15,920 crore in FY 2022-23. The Group has invested in creating export orientation with world class facilities led by quality control processes. Entrepreneurs are inherent risk takers, and Adani is no exception. The defence industry was a completely new and greenfield opportunity for the Adani Group. The Group had no previous experience in this sector of strategic importance. However, that did not deter Gautam Adani. After identifying the market entry strategy, along with his team, he laid down a path for building a formidable portfolio of companies that would fortify Adani Group's foray in the defence sector.

It is this risk taking ability that has driven the Group's foray into sectors/industries which are completely new.

As per a report cited in Fortune magazine, India is expected to spend an average of INR 1.5 lakh crore annually till 2030 for armed forces modernisation. The opportunity, worth nearly INR 10.5 lakh crore or USD 130 billion over a period of seven years has boosted India's entrepreneurial ambitions in private defence production. The capital outlay for defence modernisation and infrastructure development is INR 1.63 lakh crore for the FY 2024. Out of this outlay, nearly 75%, or approximately INR 1.2 lakh crore, will be allocated to domestic firms for boosting indigenisation.

Adani realised the market opportunity available in this segment and focused on creating a market entry strategy, identifying areas of quick growth through a combination of acquisitions, joint ventures and strategic partnerships.

He realised the growth potential of the Maintenance, Repair and Operations (MRO) market. The current market size for MRO in the civil and defence segment is USD 1.7 billion and USD 2.5 billion, respectively. A large part of the defence MRO is currently undertaken by armed forces and defence PSUs. The market is expected to grow from USD 1.7 billion in 2021 to USD 4 billion by 2031, with a CAGR of 8.9%, underlying the nature of this hyper growth segment.

The government has further facilitated the growth of the MRO market by easing taxation norms, and lowered the GST on domestic MRO services from 18% to 5%.

Let us have a further look at the MRO market: India's aircraft maintenance market is dominated by three players— GMR Aero Technic, Air Works, and AI Engineering Services Limited (AIESL). India's MRO market is small, heavily fragmented, with a lot of scope for capacity utilisation. Despite the growth opportunities in the Indian aviation market, around 85% of the USD 1.4 billion maintenance work of Indian airlines is carried out in other countries, such as Singapore, Malaysia and Turkey.

Adani correctly prioritised the ground-handling business as a market entry strategy. This contributes significantly to the revenue of airport operators. Currently, there are revenue sharing arrangements between the third-party ground-handling agents and eight airports. Adani Airport plans to control ground handling at all its airports by 2026 and also offer services to other domestic and international airports, a strategy that supports Adani's vision of adjacent businesses.

Adani's proposed acquisition of Air Works would have helped the Group immensely as Air Works already handles MRO activities for the Navy P-8I and the Air Force 737 VVIP aircraft out of its EASA and DGCA certified facilities at Mumbai, Delhi, Hosur and Kochi, giving the Group, an almost ready to execute order book.

Air Works has been in existence for nearly 70+ years, founded in 1951 by P.S. Menon and B.G. Menon. Its' portfolio of services include line maintenance, cabin and interior refurbishment, exterior finishing and painting, avionics upgrades, retrofits, maintenance training, and redelivery checks.

The acquisition of Air Works would have provided Adani with the right start for a sustainable revenue stream in the military aircraft overhaul and repair market.

Strategic Vision

As a nation, dependence on other countries for defence equipment procurement is not conducive to strategic autonomy. Having a defence production strategy which is dependent on other economies leaves our foreign policy vulnerable. The government, over the past many years, has encouraged privatisation and instituted the necessary changes. The government has boosted private participation under Make in India framework and encouraged creation of domestic expertise in key areas, specifically, fighter aircraft, helicopters, submarines, and armoured vehicles and battle tanks.

To encourage private participation, export procedures have been simplified and made industry friendly. Through a slew of measures, such as end-to-end online export authorisation, notification of three Open General Export License (OGEL) for export of spare parts and components, the government has tried to facilitate private participation in defence.

Under the Industries (Development & Regulation) Act, the validity of the industrial license has also been increased from 3 years to 15 years. This has provided companies the right platform to kickstart operations without delays.

Adani has rightfully contributed to the government's vision of an Atmanirbhar Bharat, where we are looking a roadmap for not just amping up defence production, but also indigenisation to meet domestic requirements and boost defence exports. Adani Defence and Aerospace reflects the energy and the entrepreneurial zeal of its founder. The Group ventured into the defence space in 2017 and through a combination of organic and inorganic growth methods, it has crafted a versatile and strong portfolio of defence companies. Within a span of five years, the company has acquired segment specific capabilities by a string of acquisitions and partnerships: acquisition of Alpha Design Technologies (defence electronics, aero structures for helicopters and fighter aircraft), General Aeronautics (for drones), Comprotech (a partnership between Comprotech Engineering and Adani), AutoTech, and Alpha Tocol (fabrication of aircraft parts and machined components).

In areas where acquisitions are not possible, the Group has gone ahead with joint ventures and strategic partnerships for rapid capability build up. One such Joint Venture is with the Israeli firm, Elbit Systems, in 2016, for manufacturing.

Unmanned Aerial Vehicles (UAVs)

The Group has also partnered with Public Sector Undertakings and strategic institutions in Indian defence. The company was tasked with developing missile products under Development-cum-Production Partner (DCPP) policy, resulting in the successful testing of the Very Short Range Air Defence (VSHORAD) missile.

The Adani Group has invested considerably in building operational capabilities in more than 20 locations, including the Adani Aerospace Park in Bangalore, an Unmanned Aerial Vehicles (UAV) facility in Hyderabad, a defence cluster in Mundra, and a large integrated ammunition complex near Kanpur in Uttar Pradesh. The group is working with Defence Research and Development Organisation (DRDO) to industrialise general purpose bombs, missiles and precision- guided munitions. It has successfully tested very short-range air defence and unmanned precision guided missiles.

Adani is the first private company to have invested in end-to-end development and manufacturing ecosystem for small arms. The Uttar Pradesh Defence corridor that the Adanis are developing is South Asia's largest ammunition hub that will have a first-of-its-kind facility for strategic loitering kamikaze drones.

The strategic vision of the Founder is supported by actual operational readiness that is driven by sector specific specialists.

Being a late entrant into the defence segment it has not been easy for Adani to build a niche for himself. There have been numerous challenges but the founder has always responded with his trademark zeal for performance.

In the course of setting up a competitive defence manufacturing business, Adani ran into multiple delays and obstacles. One of which is the delayed acquisition of Air Works.

Adani's Defence arm had agreed to acquire Air Works for INR 400 crore in 2022. However, the acquisition ran into trouble, due to the liquidation of the major shareholder in the target company, Punj Lloyd Group, which holds 23% stake. The MoU between the two organisations has already expired twice, with the last extension scheduled to run out in Q4 of FY 23.

However, under the leadership of Gautam Adani, the Group has not given up their ambitions in the MRO (Maintenance, Repair, and Operations) market and is in the process of chalking out alternate strategies for continued growth.

Adani Defence Capabilities

Adani Defence is building state-of-the-art capabilities ensuring Swa Raksha (Swa means 'Self' in Sanskrit and Raksha means 'Protection'). Its principal defence products includes –

1. Medium Altitude Long Range – UAV – Unmanned Aerial Vehicle – Hermes 900

- ✓ Highly autonomous and mission effective
- ✓ Multiple hard points and 250 kg modular internal installation bay.
- ✓ Value chain for high level of indigenization.
- ✓ Certified to fly in civilian airspace.
- ✓ Multi-payload and continuous wide area surveillance capabilities.

2. Tactical UAS – Medium Range, High Performance – Hermes 450

- ✓ Mature and battle proven system.
- ✓ Over 300,000 operational flight hours.
- ✓ Leading safety and reliability record over the years.
- ✓ Carries 180 kg payload with an endurance of 17+ hours.

3. Modular Payload Configuration – Hermes 450 – Sky Striker

- ✓ Tactical Loitering Munitions.
- ✓ Sky Striker.
- ✓ Fully Autonomous Loitering Munitions.
- ✓ Operator – can locate, acquire and engage designated targets.
- ✓ Versatile armament with 360 degree attack capability.
- ✓ Optional recovery capability and proven high speed performance.
- ✓ Locally designed and assembled platforms are exported to various countries.

4. Tactical Mini UAV – Skylark

- ✓ Biological airborne ISTAR capabilities.
- ✓ Dual payload capabilities with 5+ hours of endurance.
- ✓ Electric driven with ultra-low noise and visibility feature.
- ✓ Fully autonomous for landing operations.
- ✓ Rapid deployment with take-off.

5. Skylark – Thor – Multi Rotor Low Altitude VTOL UAV (Vertical Take-off and Landing)

- ✓ Specifically designed for military applications.
- ✓ Can be deployed even in adverse weather and terrain conditions.
- ✓ Fully foldable, clear 360 degree view.
- ✓ Advanced real-time navigation mode with programmable flight patterns.
- ✓ Widely used by various armies across the world.

6. AI based Swarm Technology

- ✓ Quad copter that lasts for longer duration.
- ✓ Long range and long endurance capability, gasoline powered.
- ✓ Open architecture-based scalable swarm capability.
- ✓ Equipped with BVLOS and day / night surveillance capability.
- ✓ GPS Design Navigation Capability.
- ✓ On-board intelligence for human recognition.
- ✓ Long lasting quad copter.

In partnership with Elbit Systems - Elbit Systems is a defence and homeland security technology company. It is engaged in several global air, land and naval systems programmes.

Major technologies include aircraft, helicopters, unmanned and land vehicle systems. Elbit also specializes in munitions, cyber systems and electronic warfare, etc.

7. Light Machine Gun – Negev 5.56 x 45 mm / 7.62 x 51 mm

- ✓ Rugged and reliable LMG with powerful target acquisition.

- ✓ The only LMG in the world with semi-automatic mode.
- ✓ Special features enabling safe use in CQB operations.
- ✓ Battle proven for adverse and rough conditions.

8. Carbine / Assault Rifle - ACE 5.56 x 45mm / 7.62 x 51mm

- ✓ Excellent weapon for modern warfare scenario.
- ✓ Proven reliability in adverse and extreme conditions.
- ✓ Modern streamlined ergonomic design.
- ✓ Amphibian with 360 degree Picatinny Rails.

9. Assault Rifle / Carbine / SMG - Tavor X-95 5.56 x 45 mm / 19 x 19 mm

- ✓ Modular and versatile weapon system that can be modified for various operations and scenarios.
- ✓ Small arms with a long barrel, bullpup configuration.
- ✓ Gravity concentrated to the rear.
- ✓ Law-recoil, tight stability while firing.

10. Masada 9 x 19 mm - Striker Fire Pistol

- ✓ Cold Hammer - Fjord Polygonal Rifled Barrel.
- ✓ Cold Hammer - Forged polygonal rifled barrel.
- ✓ Clean and crisp trigger reset with built-in trigger protection.
- ✓ Law barrel reduces perceived recoil.

11. Submachine Gun - UZI Pro 9 x 19 mm

- ✓ Made using most advanced firearms technology.
- ✓ Small and compact design easily concealable.

- ✓ Ideal weapon for VIP security, CQB and personal protection.
- ✓ Closed bolt operation for maximum accuracy.

12. Assault Rifle - Tavor 5.56 x 45 mm

- ✓ Versatile, innovative and technologically advanced weapons.
- ✓ Optimized ergonomic design.
- ✓ Bullpup configuration and gravity to the rear.
- ✓ Full bipedal.

13. Sniper Rifle – Galil Sniper 7.62 x 51 mm

- ✓ Two-stage trigger, foldable bipod and butt stock with adjustable cheek rest
- ✓ Reliable Scope Mount
- ✓ No deviation after dismounting and remounting.
- ✓ X 10 Day Telescope.
- ✓ Back-up with Tritium for night fighting.

14. Sniper Rifle – Dan .338 / 0.338 Bolt Action

- ✓ Incomparably accurate high precision sniper rifle.
- ✓ Bolt action using LAPUA Magnum .338 ammunition.
- ✓ Quick interchangeable barrel.
- ✓ Ambidextrous safety and magazine release.
- ✓ In partnership with Israel Weapon Industries (IWI). IWI is a member of the SK Group.
- ✓ IWI has been a world leader in the development and production of small arms for more than 85 years.

- ✓ All IWI weapons are battle-tested under adverse conditions across the globe.
- ✓ They adhere to even the most stringent military standards.
- ✓ Comprehensive and smart.
- ✓ Enhanced and automated detection, classification and neutralization capabilities.
- ✓ Instant identification, classification of drones and operators.
- ✓ Precise direction, location, tracking of drones/operators.
- ✓ Quick Installation and Easy Operation – Auto or Manual
- ✓ Detection of friend and foe with the ability to locate.
- ✓ Reliable, scalable and modular.
- ✓ Ensures multi-layer detection.
- ✓ Customizable to meet user defined requirements.
- ✓ Premium and fully automated C2 platform.
- ✓ Day and night operational capability in urban, semi-urban and rural environments.
- ✓ Various installation configurations (mobile, stationary, portable, vehicle, hand-held, etc.).
- ✓ Extended coverage range.

15. Radar Systems - Advanced 3D (X & S Band)

- ✓ 360 degree coverage with a detection range of 10+ kilometres
- ✓ Detects up to 100+ targets at once.
- ✓ Automatic classification between drones and other aerial objects.

16. SIGINT

- ✓ Long range passive system for automatic detection and classification.
- ✓ Direction Finding (DF) and Drone Geo-location.
- ✓ Software - Defined Radio (SDR) wideband scanning and detection.
- ✓ Full Band Coverage 400 MHz - 6000 MHz.
- ✓ RF / GNSS Jamming System.
- ✓ Smart Jamming covers all operating bands.
- ✓ Clean spectrum jamming – not affecting other frequencies.
- ✓ Long range, omnidirectional and directional antennas supported with advanced waveforms.
- ✓ Expandable for take-over and spoofing operations.

17. EO / IR (Electro-Optical / Infra - Red) System

- ✓ Aids in visual detection, tracking and assessment.
- ✓ Available in both Cooled / Uncooled configuration.
- ✓ Automatic locking and tracking of a target that has slipped from the radar.

18. Hard Kill

- ✓ High power microwave to neutralize swarm of drones.
- ✓ High power laser offers long range neutralization.
- ✓ Hunting drone that can navigate in environments devoid of GPS.
- ✓ Pre-planned autonomous patrol missions that can operate at speeds in excess of 140 km/h.
- ✓ Integration with air defence systems and small arms.

- ✓ Globally acclaimed proven system.
- ✓ Currently deployed in India, Israel, Northern Europe, America and Africa.
- ✓ Field certified TRL 9 system MIL - STD - G adapted to work in harsh environments.
- ✓ Developed local ecosystem to ensure local support for local manufacturing and seamless service and operations.
- ✓ Multiple applications on critical infrastructure, sensitive sites and national borders.

Indamer

Indamer is one of the oldest and leading corporate aviation organizations in India. Established in 1939, Indamer is approved by DGCA under both CAR 145 and CAMO. It provides 'one stop shop' solutions in airframes, components, Defence MRO etc. Indamer also provides a number of other aircraft and aviation-related services.

Adani Defence and Aerospace, the defence manufacturing branch of the Adani Group, entered into an agreement to acquire Air Works, the country's largest aircraft Maintenance, Repair and Overhaul (MRO) organization for an enterprise value of ₹ 400 crore. The acquisition strengthens the civil aviation portfolio of Gautam Adani-led Adani Group, which operates seven airports in the country—Mumbai, Ahmedabad, Lucknow, Thiruvananthapuram, Jaipur, Guwahati and Mangaluru.

Adani Defence & Aerospace has a significant role in the Indian MRO market, both in the defence and civil aerospace sectors, and is expected to grow threefold from 1.7 billion dollars to 5 billion dollars by the year 2030.

Established in 1951, Air Works Group is India's largest and highly diversified independent MRO, with the largest pan-India network presence across 27 cities. From business and executive jets to airlines and defence platforms, Air Works provides aviation services to most domestic airlines such as IndiGo, GoAir, SpiceJet and Vistara. It also serves international airlines such as Qatar, Lufthansa, Turkish Airlines, Fly Dubai, Etihad and Virgin Atlantis.

In addition, Air Works has developed a comprehensive operational capability within the country for major defence and aerospace platforms. From testing to MRO of the Indian Air Force's 737 VVIP aircraft, it provides certified facilities and base maintenance at Mumbai, Delhi, Hosur and Kochi for its EASA and DGCA ATR 42/72, A320 and B737 fleet of aircraft.

Commenting on the deal, Ashish Rajvanshi, CEO, Adani Defence & Aerospace, said, "Given India's growth trajectory and the government's focus on building the country's network through a vast network of air connectivity, it is imminent that the primary growth of India's airline and the airport should be inevitably done. Therefore, the Maintenance, Repair and Overhaul sector has an important and key role to play in the defence and civil aerospace sectors. Add to this the ongoing modernization programme to make India a major market for defence aircraft, and what emerges is one of the most exciting, comprehensive, large-scale and digital MRO services within the nation's borders".

"Air Works Group has impeccable proven capabilities and its 70 years of aviation heritage has successfully delivered several India-first and industry-first projects. Combine this with the capabilities of the Adani Group and what we get is an entity that truly represents what self-respecting India should look like in one important sector".

Anand Bhaskar, MD & CEO, Air Works Group, says, "India has the potential to become an MRO hub for the defence and civil aircraft sector. This is a great opportunity for Air Works and its employees to come under the Adani Defence &

Aerospace platform. The policy measures and initiatives of the government including convergence of civil and defence MRO will create economies of scale and employment opportunities on a large scale".

As of March 31, 2021, GTI Capital Group, an India-focused investment company, was the largest shareholder in Air Works Group with 25.75 per cent stake, followed by Punj Lloyd's subsidiary Punj Lloyd Aviation (23.24 per cent) and the Menon family (15 per cent), who founded the company in 1951.

Over the years, the Adani group signed several deals in the defence sectors, including the acquisition of Bengaluru-based Alpha Design, a firm that also caters to the aerospace sector, and is a joint venture with Israeli firm Elbit Systems. It also acquired a 51 per cent stake in the small arms business of Gwalior-based PLR Systems in an all-cash transaction.

In continuation of Adani Group's vision of nation building, Adani Defence Aerospace is committed to playing a pivotal and seminal role in helping India transform into a destination for world-class, high-tech defence manufacturing in line with the Make in India initiative.

Adani Defence & Aerospace leads Adani Enterprises Limited to foray into defence and aerospace and its vision is to help transform India into a destination for world-class high-tech defence manufacturing aligned to the 'Make in India' initiative.

❑

Adani Enterprises Limited

Currently the Adani Enterprises Limited is focused on businesses related to airports, roads, network management, data centres, solar manufacturing, defence and aerospace, edible oils and foodstuff, mining, integrated resource solutions and integrated agricultural products. Below is the message from Managing Director Rajesh S. Adani:

"At AEL (Adani Enterprises Limited), we have established ourselves as a responsible incubator today for the businesses of tomorrow, which may or may not be there today. However, the complementarity of businesses is designed to generate positive returns regardless of the state of the markets and there is enough cash from some businesses to satisfy the capital appetite of others. In this way, it is possible to develop all businesses within our desired overall risk and capital appetite.

The highlight of the company's performance during the year under review (2022) was the incorporation of a new subsidiary, Adani New Industries Limited. This is one of the most exciting developments at AEL as it will address the production of green hydrogen, associated downstream products and manufacturing of wind turbines, batteries and electrolysers. We believe that they represent the businesses of tomorrow, which take mankind to a world that is cleaner and 'greener'.

Adani New Industries serves as the holding company for the end-to-end supply chain of frontier energy and technologies within AEL to meet India's long-term energy security needs. We believe that this business, viewed from a focused perspective within the Adani Group, has resulted in AEL emerging as the largest listed incubator of futuristic businesses that require patience and nurturing. It has been our experience that this responsible incubation has helped our individual companies grow rapidly on listing, validating the strength of our incubation process.

The financial year 2021-22 proved to be a landmark for AEL's incubation journey and preparation for the coming decade.

Despite challenges in the external environment—pandemic, war, rising freight and low container availability, AEL has achieved attractive growth in its existing businesses on the one hand, and invested in new growing businesses on the other.

The attractive growth was the result of a prudent portfolio-based approach. This approach involved a variety of businesses and we recognize that over a given period of time, there will be some businesses that can do better in a limited perspective. This is a dynamic example of an initiative in a new and exciting sector. When viewed from a larger perspective, we believe such initiatives can help shift India's energy needle from imports to captive production which can have downstream effects on the country's balance of payments, currency strength and competitiveness.

Coming to our operational performance during the year, the company's solar module manufacturing ecosystem, which will be an integral part of Adani New Industries, maintained a volume of 1.1 gigawatts despite rising input costs.

With the data centre business in Chennai set to be completed in the first half of the financial year 22-23, the company completed land acquisition for data centre projects in other states, laying the foundation for multi-locational growth within a compressed period.

In the airports infrastructure business, the company completed the acquisition of Mumbai Airport, one of the largest airports in India, together with the development rights for a green field airport in Navi Mumbai. The company also took over the airports of Jaipur, Guwahati and Thiruvananthapuram during the third quarter of financial year 21-22.

After these acquisitions, Adani Airports now serves every fifth passenger in the country. We believe this represents an achievement to be proud of, given that the company only entered this business in the year 2019, despite going through an expansion phase when air passenger throughput was absent or impacted. We are optimistic that our airport network, structured around a hub-and-spoke approach, will change the paradigm of the airport business in India.

During financial year 21-22, our road portfolio grew to 5000 lane kilometres through 14 projects in 10 states. The company's business was significantly strengthened through a concession agreement for the 464 kilometre Ganga Expressway project in Uttar Pradesh, involving an investment of 171 billion dollars.

We believe the scale of this project represents validation of the company's ability to win large contracts. The project win places it in the high table within the sector and should bring attractive returns given the respective economies of scale.

Bids won in the past were converted into projects and some of them are nearing completion – a successful demonstration of competence across the entire project lifecycle. Construction of the Bilaspur - Pathrapalli road project is nearing completion. The company intends to complete two or three projects in financial year 22-23. The company was also awarded the Bhagalpur Waste Water Project (as a part of our water business portfolio) in Bihar under the Hybrid Annuity Model.

The company's commitment towards successful incubation and subsequent independence was validated during the year under review. The company completed a successful initial public offering of its joint venture Adani Wilmar Limited in the Indian capital market. The issue was enthusiastically received by investors with 17 times subscription.

The success of the offering validates the faith placed in the Adani Group. The issue ended the year under review with a gain of 125 per cent on its offer price, which is a validation of the company's commitment to reward investors.

The company also embarked on its digital journey with the launch of Adani Digital Labs, which integrates all consumer businesses on a single platform. The platform is expected to enhance consumer interaction across Adani Group's portfolio companies. This journey has been fuelled by investments in digital and new-age start-ups including Cleartrip.

As far as traditional businesses are concerned, the company's Parsa East and Kente Basan (PEKB) mine, the first and only captive open cast coal mine with washery in the country, continued to operate at a peak capacity of 15 MMT per annum. Apart from other operational mines at Talabira II and III, Gare Pelma III and Kurmitar, the company also started operations at its Suliyari coal mine with a peak capacity of 5 MMT.

The sum of these performances is that AEL registered a 75 per cent increase in consolidated total income at ₹ 70,433 crore in financial year 21-22; Consolidated EBTDA increased by 45 per cent to ₹ 4,726 crore. A judicious mix of established and growing businesses will continue to deliver strong numbers, protect the present and build investment into the future.

It is relevant to mention that the company continued to play the seminal role of a responsible corporate citizen during the year under review.

During the initial months of the financial year 21-22, the company leveraged its sourcing and logistics capabilities to procure oxygen plants and concentrators as a part of its Covid relief initiative for public welfare. Through the Adani Foundation, the company continues to make a positive impact in the areas of education, health, sustainable livelihood generation and community infrastructure development.

I must thank our stakeholders – employees, lenders, shareholders, government and society at large – for their continued support and license to operate, which has smoothly transitioned into a multi-business operation in various sectors.

The success of the Adani Wilmar IPO presents yet another example of the growing number of post-listing successes of AEL-incubated companies. At AEL, our portfolio includes mature and nascent businesses.

Performance

In a portfolio of businesses affected by diverse market pulls and pressures, the paramount validation of our strategic direction is our capital management.

After the development of the balance sheet date, by 2022, AEL will strengthen its net worth by issuing primary preference equity of UAD 1 billion to International Holding Company, Abu Dhabi. This fund raising reflects the confidence of global marquee investors in the long-term stability and prospects of the country in general and AEL's business plan in particular.

AEL's consolidated total for the financial year 21-22 grew by 75 per cent to ₹ 70,433 crore. Even though many of AEL's businesses are still in the development stage, they have started contributing to EBITDA. The airports and roads business of the company generated a healthy EBITDA during the financial year 21-22, validating the strength of the AEL incubation story.

One of the company's achievements was the financial closure for its green field Navi Mumbai International Airport project. The company arranged the entire loan amount of ₹ 12,770 crore from the State Bank of India, bringing Mumbai closer to the launch of another infrastructure landmark.

A reliable feature of the company's operations was that the significant investment in new growth businesses did not compromise its financial discipline.

During the year under review, the company strengthened its governance structure and assurance practices through creation of Audit Committee and Nomination and Remuneration Committee (100 per cent independent).

The company also constituted a Corporate Responsibility Committee consisting of 100 per cent independent directors with the objective of providing an ESG roadmap and assurance to the Board. AEL also overhauled its board-level review mechanism to reduce risk.

The main message one wants to send is that AEL is prepared to embark on an exciting journey with investments in the future energy value chain, airports, roads, data centres and materials like copper and petrochemicals. We believe these businesses represent the building blocks of India's next 25 years leading up to the year 2047—the first century of the nation, and we are optimistic that as these businesses grow, they will also generate substantial returns and will increase the value for our shareholders.

During this period, I expect India to add around 25 trillion US dollars to its economy. This represents a growth of 4 billion US dollars in the market every day by the year 2050. During this period, India would have eliminated all forms of poverty. We have a real shot at getting it done – in just 10,000 days".

Headlines

- ✓ Adani Enterprises, in its capacity as a focused incubator, is unlike any listed company in India.
- ✓ We have built an entire company around the incubation theme, which is unlike any other listed company in the country.
- ✓ We have exclusively focused on incubation for more than two and a half decades in fast growing post-liberalization India.
- ✓ We combine the roles of venture capitalist, private equity investor and advisor.
- ✓ We give Adani Group the courage to venture into newer and newer areas.
- ✓ We invest with the foresight that our business will bridge the national gap in a few years.
- ✓ We bring a responsible composure to our commitments – as opposed to being pressured into short-term decisions by the debt on our books.
- ✓ We incubate businesses with an aspiration to create industry leaders and sectorial transformers.
- ✓ We leverage the power of deep pockets, multi-year patience, group knowledge, visibility to recruit talent and availability of adequate capital.
- ✓ We provide shock absorbers to our incubating companies to tide them over challenging market cycles and regional upheavals.

- ✓ We have shown the courage to invest extensively in start-ups, turning an early handicap into a competitive advantage.
- ✓ We have successfully combined the spirit of a start-up with the competitiveness of a mature organization—a rare foundation around which to build a modern business.
- ✓ We have responded with a portfolio approach—a collection of businesses—that enhances business sustainability.
- ✓ We grow our business through strategic business units, which are accountable to the Board of Directors for their sustainable development.
- ✓ We work with the objective of building strong businesses that drive profitability within our system and enhance shareholder value upon separation.
- ✓ We believe that our incubation pedigree is measured and evaluated by how we drive value for all our stakeholders.
- ✓ Adani Enterprises Limited is more than a company. It is a snapshot of the world as it is likely to be in the future.
- ✓ Adani Enterprises connects today's space with relevant businesses that will be increasingly relevant in tomorrow's world.
- ✓ **Solar Manufacturing** is engaged in the manufacturing of photovoltaic cells and modules that represent the building blocks of the solar energy revolution.
- ✓ **Airports**: Engaged in the management of premier airports to deliver a world class experience.
- ✓ **Road, Metro and Rail**: Engaged in the development of infrastructure projects facilitating mass mobility.
- ✓ **Data Centres**: Engaged in the development of data centres to help India maintain the most responsible ESG propositions at the most competitive costs in the most attractive locations within the country's Internet-derived data. We are a profitable

and sustainable business competently prepared to make the relevant changes. These businesses are not built just to make a presence in their respective sectors, they are built to lead their sectors, offering a superior value—value proposition to customers.

✓ **Defence and Aerospace**: Engaged in manufacturing strategic military and defence products that enhance India's self-reliance.

✓ **Edible Oils and Foodstuffs**: Engaged in the manufacturing, marketing and branding of food processing products that enhance health, hygiene, safety and well-being.

✓ **Agricultural Products**: Engaged in increasing India's agricultural produce with the aim of feeding a growing nation.

✓ **Water**: Engaged in the development of infrastructure projects that enhance water transportation and use efficiency.

✓ **Mining Services**: Engaging in the responsible extraction of resources and consumption, increasing safety and reducing logistics costs, lowers their break-even point and expands their markets. As a result, the businesses that constitute Adani Enterprises are not built solely to serve existing markets. They are built to enhance markets, enhance lives, secure national interests and strengthen prosperity—the most effective means by which we can take India forward.

✓ **Integrated Resource Management**: Access to energy resources from various global regions and timely delivery to Indian customers, engaged in strengthening working capital efficiency.

✓ **Petrochemicals**: Engaged in the production of a range of green fuels and green energy that help India decarbonize rapidly.

✓ **Copper**: To engage in the production of copper and downstream products that meet the growing needs of the country's consumer durables revolution.

Economic Development

The GDP growth achieved by the country in the first 60 years has only been repeated and compressed in the next seven years. We believe that India will return to an aggressive growth phase from the current year.

Demographic Advantage

Not only is India adding more people to its population every year, India's average age of 29 is also lower than the comparable average age of China (38) and the United States (38). This indicates that India's youth will remain economically active for a long time, a strong foundation on which to build a consumption-driven economy.

Our optimism stems from the fact that India has two consumption curves running simultaneously. In the first stage, there is a catch-up curve where India with low consumption (in virtually every product or commodity) that is below the global average, plays catch-up. There is a second curve where average per capita consumption aligns with economic growth for that year. When you put these consumption drivers together you get a sustainable consumption appetite for the long term, the scale of which, if anywhere, is unmatched.

Aspirations

Modern Indians are different from their predecessors. The modern Indian aspires to live better, consume more, is less price-sensitive, open to buying on credit, smartphone influenced and aware of trends globally more than ever before. The result is that we see a gradual decline in savings and an increase in spending. Why it matters is because it is spreading across the world's second largest population, creating an opportunity for unprecedented economic transformation.

Government Policy

The main driver of economic change is the top-down. The Government of India has embarked on an unprecedented package of economic reforms, giving the country a long-term vision. The core of this direction is centred around the concept of self-reliance—*Atmanirbhar Bharat*—which ensures that India produces most of its needs within itself and uses critical mass to meet the needs of other countries.

In addition, the Government of India announced a production-linked incentive scheme, stimulating capital expenditure in several large industries. We are optimistic that these policies will give the country a decisive push towards manufacturing-led growth, accelerating the creation of jobs, income and prosperity.

Privatization

The last two Union Budgets have underlined the need for monetization of national economic assets through responsible privatization. An important privatization that took place during the last financial year was that of Air India, the national carrier of India. We expect this trend to extend to other assets and sectors attracting private sector capital and enterprise resulting in increased national productivity. We also see the government's demonetization plan as a decisive economic trigger.

India and Adani Enterprises

At Adani Enterprises, we believe that we are a growing part of the emerging India story. We are not just a collection of a few businesses (as on March 31, 2022) but we are also the largest organized listed business incubator in the country focused on Make for India and Make in India.

The main message we want to convey is that if India grows faster than in the past and faster than global economic growth, Adani Enterprises has the potential to ascend to the next level.

Adani Enterprises' business is built around a single idea: invest today in what India needs tomorrow. These businesses address large—and relatively under-penetrated—spaces with respect to consumption appetites today or in the near future.

By setting up large capacity with some of the most genealogically Green Hydrogen: Engaging in the production of Green Hydrogen with the aim of creating a cleaner world and providing affordable energy to users.

❑

Adani Data Centre Business

With the government planning to triple the country's installed power capacity for data centres, India's digital economy is expected to reach 1 trillion US dollars by the year 2025. This indicates an investment opportunity of 4.5 billion US dollars for setting up data centre infrastructure by that year.

Adani Connex has a vision to build data centres of 1 gigawatt capacity by the year 2030, supported by ongoing land acquisition and construction activities in Chennai, Noida, Navi Mumbai, Hyderabad, Vizag, Pune, Kolkata and Bengaluru. The first data centre is already operational in Chennai.

Macro

India is projected to emerge as the world's third largest economy by the year 2030, with 776 million internet users, 75 million small and medium businesses (SMBs), 5 million+ developers,

59,000 start-ups, 1,200 listed enterprises, including 1,300 global development centres. Indian SaaS ecosystem (SaaS as an ecosystem is not just a partnership, but it is a special way in which apps fit together and work together) is now the third largest in the world and is expected to become the global SaaS by the year 2025. It is expected to serve 11 per cent of the demand. In line with these technology trends, McKinsey predicts a 1 trillion US dollar digital economy by the year 2025.

Digitization

There are about 830 million smartphone users in India. Digital distribution of goods and services is on the rise, along with entertainment, healthcare, and education. In addition, the pandemic has had an enormous impact on remote and hybrid work, requiring greater investment in cloud-based services and mobile technologies. This could significantly increase the demand for data centres in the country.

Data Sovereignty

The proliferation of cloud computing highlights the importance of data sovereignty. With massive amounts of data crossing borders and public cloud regions, the Indian government encouraged local development of data centres to protect India's consumers. The government's proposal to recognize the data centre sector along with critical infrastructure sectors such as power, railways and roads has added to its importance.

Support

The government is targeting an investment of ₹ 3 lakh crore over the next five years as part of the hyper-scale data centre plan and has been planning to provide around 4 per cent capital investment as incentives to companies with real estate support and faster approvals.

5G

Fifth Generation Long Term Evolution is the latest upgrade in mobile broadband networks. While 4G was a leap forward, allowing people to stream music and videos on the go, 5G is designed to connect more devices beyond smartphones with higher speeds and capacity.

E-commerce

The Indian e-commerce market is expected to grow to 111.40 billion US dollars by the year 2025 from 56.6 billion US dollars in the year 2021. Furthermore, the online retail market is estimated to account for 25 per cent of the total organized retail market and is expected to reach 37 per cent by the year 2030. Therefore, it is expected to reach 350 billion US dollars by the year 2030. Every month, India adds around 10 million daily active internet users—the highest in the world. 100 per cent FDI is permitted in B2B e-commerce. 100 per cent FDI is permitted under the automatic route in the marketplace model of e-commerce. Nearly 100 per cent pin codes in India have adopted e-commerce. More than 60 per cent of transactions and orders in India come from tier two cities and smaller towns. E-commerce payments in India are expected to grow at a compound annual growth rate of 18.2 per cent between the year 2021 and 2025 to reach 120.3 billion US dollars.

Smart Phone

Indian smartphone users rank third in the list of 'Maximum time spent on device' globally (2021) behind Indonesia and Brazil. Third on the list is India, where the average smartphone usage time is 4.6 hours per day, which is close to 40 per cent year-on-year growth.

The Adani Group's expansion into B2B businesses makes data gathering critical, leading to a deeper understanding of consumers and their potential actions. The result is that the data centre business is not just another standalone business, but is positioned to take advantage of the vast data generated by the group's consumer-facing businesses—airports, edible oils, etc., can interface with 500 million users by the year 2025 (a population equal to the number of the United States).

The result is that data management and storage at Adani Company represents the frontier of digitally driven research, driven by the need to gain advanced knowledge of consumer preferences that can accelerate strategy and competitiveness.

AdaniConneX

According to a research study, in 2021, the data Centre market in India was valued at USD 4.35 billion and is expected to reach USD 10.09 billion by 2027. It is not at all surprising then that data Centres are now suddenly in the spotlight.

As per a report by the ratings agency ICRA, Indian data Centre's capacity is expected to witness a five-fold increase as it is expected to add overall 3,900-4,100 MW of capacity involving investments of INR 1.05-1.20 lakh crore in the next five years. During FY 2023-24, the industry is expected to have a CAGR of around 18-19%. The corresponding growth during FY 2018-21 was 24% which was led by rack capacity utilisation and ramp up of new data Centres. Industry observers are expecting that with increased revenue and better absorption of fixed costs, bottom lines for data Centre operations will improve and operating margins will be in the 40-42% range. Since data Centres are capital intensive projects, Return On Capital Employed (ROCE) is expected to remain modest as and when ramp-up of the data Centres takes place over a period of time. The rise of data Centres has been driven by the government's push on creating digital infrastructure, such as the Digital India initiative. A further push was received when data Centres were classified as infrastructure assets. By providing infrastructure status to data Centres, government has enabled data Centre players to get longer tenured debt at competitive rates and access to foreign funding through the External Commercial Borrowing (ECB) route.

The key challenges for the sector are, increasing competitive intensity which is expected to exert pressure on margins for incremental business and large-debt funded apex plans could exert pressure on credit metrics of the players.

AdaniConneX is a joint venture between the Adani Group and EdgeConneX, the largest private data Centre operator in the world. It was set up with the objective of developing a 1 GW national data Centre platform to support the goals of Digital India. AdaniConneX has built a network of 100% renewable energy led data Centres across the country, in sites like Chennai, Navi Mumbai, Noida, and Hyderabad. EdgeConneX has technical expertise in data Centre design and operations and Adani has strong capabilities in full-stack renewable power management helping the group offer new standards of accountability, safety, and sustainability.

Some of the peers of AdaniConneX in the data Centre market are Amazon, Microsoft, CapitaLand, Mantra Group, NTT, CtrlS, Nxtra and STT. These groups had significant presence in the data Centre space and with the rise of favourable regulations, they have further increased and fortified their investments.

Post pandemic, the demand for hyperscale data centres has accelerated as more businesses realise the value of digital transformation, driven increasingly by digital-first consumers who are demanding app-based services, 24x7 customer support, personalised communication and performance at scale. Hyperscale data Centres have over 5000 servers and are spread over 10,000 square feet.

Over the next 5-10 years, India's data Centre industry is expected to attract investments of INR 70-72K crores, as per a report by India Ratings and Research (Ind-Ra). These are expected to be driven by either large conglomerates (around 40%) or cloud service providers (around 30%).

Adani knew that the demand for data Centres will explode, given the support from policy and regulatory stakeholders. It is known that co-location services account for around 62-65% of revenues as compared to managed services which account for 28-30% of revenues. As a result, the strategy of AdaniConneX is to focus on meeting the demand in the co-location segment. These services have higher operating margins due to shared resources compared to managed services clients.

Power expenses account for 55-60% of total costs towards maintenance of multiple cooling paths and redundancy. Considering ESG guidelines, data Centres are also expected to invest in green power to meet their power requirements. It is here that Adani Group's core strength in the infrastructure market comes into play - right from power generation to distribution, making it again one adjacency that the Group can dominate due to backward and forward integrations. State governments in Maharashtra, Telangana, Karnataka, and Uttar Pradesh have provided special incentives like exemption on stamp and electricity duty, power subsidies, land at subsidised cost and other concessions to boost data Centre development. Adani data Centres have been built in Chennai, Hyderabad, Mumbai, Noida, Pune, Vizag, taking advantage of these incentives and subsidies.

The ministry of information technology has crafted plans to offer incentives worth up to ₹ 15,000 crore under a national policy framework for data Centres. Incentives ranging from 4-6% are available if the components including IT hardware and power are procured from Indian manufacturing units and incentives up to 3% can be availed for use of renewable energy. Adani already has a substantial footprint in the renewable energy segment. The Group is placed favourably as compared to some of its competitors to ensure it meets the benchmarks for availing these incentives, while contributing positively to the environment as well.

Adani once again placed bets in a growing market, assessed the Groups' current capabilities and wisely chose an area that had synergies with the existing businesses.

Adani realised that the demand for hyperscale data Centres will grow as more and more organisations demand digital transformation services. This demand will also be backed by the rising data usage by retail customers, and ease-of-use optimisations, security, and reliability requirements for enterprise users. The government has also supported the rise of data Centres with favourable policy regulations such as Digital India, the draft data localisation bill, and accordance of infrastructure status to data Centres. the value drivers for the other businesses. He also knew that the key challenges for the sector were increasing competitive intensity, margin pressures for securing incremental business. He was also aware that these are large debt-funded capex projects and could jeopardise the credit worthiness of these organisations. The Adani Groups' expertise in large-scale, capital-intensive projects and their credit worthiness came in handy during the execution of the data Centre strategy. EdgeConneX is the world's largest private data Centre operator; and their operational expertise was complimentary with the core competencies of the Adani Group, priming the venture for success.

In true Adani style, the Group is preparing for the future by planning to build 1000 MW data Centres, almost twice the present size of the industry, over the next decade.

Enterprise

Digital transformation initiatives by enterprises are widening the market. Enterprises move their workloads from captive data centres to third-party co-location data centres and public / hybrid clouds.

Large Cloud Players

India's cloud market is growing in double digit percentage. The country's public cloud services market is expected to be valued at 10.8 billion dollars by the year 2025, growing at a CAGR of 24.1 per cent between the year 2020 and 2025. Due to high customer demand, requiring a greater number of cloud regions, each with 3-4 subcontracted regions, building significant data centre capacity to meet captive requirements is essential.

Government

India is witnessing digitization of government processes, including Smart Cities, Digital India, Meghraj and Aadhaar.

Tech Native Business

About 65 per cent of India's population is under the age of 35, which is reflected in a strong bond with digital technologies. The country's average internet data usage is set to increase from 1.24 GB per month in the year 2018 to 14.1 GB in June 2021.

Government Initiatives

Some of the Indian reforms and global developments driving data centre capacity growth include –

- ✓ The Government of India's flagship 'Digital India' programme intends to transform the country into a digitally empowered society and knowledge waste ecosystem.
- ✓ Giving infrastructure status to data centres will boost the digital ecosystem through low capital cost, thereby attracting large investments.
- ✓ More than 1.2 billion Indians have enrolled in the world's largest biometric digital identity programme called Aadhaar, creating an accessible data foundation.

- ✓ The focus of the Meghraj Project initiative is to accelerate e-service delivery in India while optimizing ICT spending of the government.
- ✓ The Government of India has formulated a policy to provide 'infrastructure status' to the data centre sector, raising it at par with industries such as railways, roadways and power.
- ✓ The central government proposes to turn India into a data centre hub with an ambitious ₹ 12,000 crore incentive plan to encourage investment.
- ✓ Government's investment target of ₹ 3 lakh crore over five years as a part of hyper-scale data centre plan, plans to provide 3-4 per cent capital investment as incentives for investment companies, real estate support and faster regulatory approvals.

Adani Group has vast experience in delivering critical and large infrastructure projects across sectors. This will be leveraged to commission the Adani Connex data centre infrastructure around global standards.

One of the most important factors for Adani Group to be successful as a data centre operator is its leadership in energy management including generation of green energy. As a result, the company is attractively positioned to provide customers with differentiated offerings such as building cutting edge data centres in the primary and secondary markets as well as data centres with green energy.

Adani Group has rich experience in completing large projects with unique flower-stack capabilities in power generation, transmission and distribution including renewable energy. EdgeConX, on the other hand, brings unique capabilities in the design and operation of more than 50 global data centres in more than 40 markets. As a validation of this capability, the joint venture won the trust of leading hyper-scalers and Fortune 50 companies.

The company has technical expertise and a customer-centric approach that translates into customized and specialized solutions.

The company's sustainability commitment is visible through the adoption of emerging technology and sustainability practices, resulting in green data centres.

Environment Protection

The company takes the following initiatives to maintain environmental sustainability -

Renewable Energy

✓ The company is engaged in collaborative efforts to reduce its carbon footprint through the use of renewable energy.

✓ The company is committed to providing 100 per cent renewable energy to its data centres.

✓ The company hopes to leverage state-of-the-art technologies (solar, wind, hybrid storage).

✓ The company intends to integrate green hydrogen as a backup power solution for data centres (feasibility study completed).

✓ The company will provide energy at competitive cost under an integrated approach towards renewable energy development.

Energy Efficiency

✓ The company leveraged state-of-the-art technology and design best practices to reduce Power Use Effectiveness (PUC).

✓ Company designed facilities to increase mechanical and electrical efficiency.

✓ The company will continuously strive to moderate the carbon footprint and power intensity.

Water Resource Management

- ✓ Treated water is used for rain water harvesting.
- ✓ The company will reduce water and energy intensity through technology-driven innovation.
- ✓ The company uses air-cooled chillers instead of water-cooled chillers.
- ✓ The company uses water-efficient, free cooling technologies and taps into reclaimed water supplies.

Green Building

- ✓ The company's data centre facility will be set up as a 'Green Building' certified by industry-recognized institutions such as IGBC.
- ✓ The Green Data Centre Rating System will facilitate construction and operation of data centres with improved resource efficiency, reducing operating costs.

Social Diversity and Inclusion

- ✓ The company aims to create aspirational and sustainable workplaces by promoting diversity and inclusion.
- ✓ Adani Connex Culture – Mixed ethnicity, regional affiliation, physical ability, age, education. Domicile and merit-based recruitment is reflected.

Training and Development

- ✓ The company supports employee development through online and digital learning platforms, on-the-job training and leadership development opportunities.

- ✓ Adani Connex (in partnership with EdgeConX) provides onsite employee training at overseas facilities for global exposure and access to best practices.

Community Development

- ✓ Adani community-led programmes are run through the Adani Foundation.

Health and Safety

- ✓ The company is committed to 'Zero Harm and Zero Leakage' which safeguards the health and safety of employees, associates and partners.
- ✓ The Company has engaged HSE Management with HSE experts to closely monitor the development and implementation of the EHS Policy, KPI-based implementation, structured review and feedback mechanism, regular assurance, reporting and monitoring.
- ✓ The company partnered with a world class consulting firm to enhance its security outcomes.

Governance, Business Ethics and Compliance

- ✓ The company strikes a balance between economic, social and environmental performance while meeting stakeholder needs.
- ✓ The company conducts trainings and workshops from time to time (periodically) on awareness of its code and conduct.

Data Security

- ✓ The company implements stringent industry-recognized security controls on its data centre infrastructure.

✓ The company has invested extensively in security of data and its physical premises from any compromise of confidentiality, integrity and information, data and intellectual property.

The Indian data centre industry is expected to double and exceed 1 gigawatt by the year 2023, given the increased data consumption driven by laws related to data localization within India. The data boom in India is being driven by significant use of social media and messaging services, increasing use of smart devices (smartphones, tablets, smart home solutions, etc.), adoption of IoT (Internet of Things) and cloud services by corporates. Make in India and China+1 structural changes will attract companies to set up facilities in India, which is expected to spur demand for IoT and cloud services. Although India has emerged as one of the world's largest data consumers, the number of data centres and their capacity is far less than that of the US and China. AEL will leverage the vast amount of data generated by its various consumer-related businesses (airports, power distribution, edible oil, domestic gas connections etc.) that interface with millions of customers every day and can cover an estimated 500 million consumers by the year 2025.

India's digital infrastructure is expected to be driven by the adoption of ICT technologies such as telemedicine, telepresence, digital payments and remote learning, migration to cloud and off-premises environments, as well as other government initiatives including Smart Cities, Digital India and Meghraj.

The result is that an increase in demand can be anticipated, helping the Indian data centre industry to double from 499 Mega Watt in the first half of 2021 to 1 gigawatt in the year 2023.

❑

Airport and Road Construction Business

India is the fifth largest global aviation market and is poised to emerge as the third largest by the year 2025. The country's aviation sector potential is marked by a population that is the world's second largest, and a land mass that is the world's seventh-largest.

Within this large market, the democratization of air travel has been one of the defining developments in recent times, marked by affordable airfares, connectivity to a large number of cities, and the convenience of internet ticketing. This increase in passenger growth has created the need for large service-operated airports, transforming them from mere connectivity hubs to nodes of urban development (aerotroplis).

Adani Enterprises ventured into the airport development sector in the year 2019 not only to participate in the ongoing regional development but also to transform it.

Adani's journey into the airports business through Adani Airports Holding Limited (AAHL) began when the Group won the mandate to develop and operate six airports in Guwahati, Ahmedabad, Lucknow, Mangaluru, Jaipur, and Thiruvananthapuram for a period of 50 years.

The fact that it was a greenfield opportunity for the company did not deter it from approaching this area. The Group proceeded with the vision of the Chairman of finding strategic adjacencies and expanding in areas that contribute to the Group's overall strengths. The global aviation industry was widely affected by the lockdown imposed following the outbreak of the pandemic. By early April 2020, the number of international flights had dropped by nearly 80 per cent while domestic flights had dropped by 70 per cent worldwide. The Indian aviation sector recovered markedly after the vaccine roll-out and the global easing of travel restrictions.

The COVID-19 pandemic dealt a debilitating blow to the travel and hospitality sector - but this did not deter the company from executing its plans - this is again a trait that have observed Gautam Adani has demonstrated repeatedly, of conviction, commitment and courage.

Expansion into airports helped the Group expand multi modal logistics further, building out its port and logistics business. The airports are spread across several states, generating employment, supporting local communities and enterprises, contributing positively to the GDP. Given its expertise in other areas, the company has invested in Operations and Maintenance (O&M) excellence, with a focus on sustainability and capital management.

Let us now look at the principles of business that we can learn from AAHL.

The company focused on complementing the development of airports for further transformation—expanded infrastructure, enhanced service and a complement of air and non-air revenue aimed at attracting 'non-passenger airport visitors' to do and to transform into development.

The company intends to design airports of the future, offer seamless processes that facilitate touch-less operations.

To value this place, Adani Enterprises developed its airport business. The company won bids to complement 8 airports and acquired operational interests.

The vision of Adani Airports is to be the most admired enterprise in the aviation sector while creating lifestyle destinations for people to experience the world.

Adani realised that airports were a synergistic fit in the Group's infrastructure business. It offered the right complementary capabilities alongside the port business, which benefits from operational excellence, efficiency and seamless multi-modal integration both with rail and road transport. Airports are a long term investment with RoI coming in later than most businesses. Adani knew that along with the ports and SEZ business, airports were the next logical expansion for the Group.

However, entry into that sector was not easy. For many years, the airports management sector was dominated by two companies - GMR and GVK group. At one point of time, the two groups controlled almost 70% of the traffic in the domestic market. Post the first wave of privatisation, GMR and GVK controlled major airports in India. GMR controlled Delhi and Hyderabad, and the GVK Group managed Mumbai and Bengaluru. To ensure more equitable participation in a critical infrastructure sector, the government allowed companies with no prior experience to bid for the project. Let us understand the business model of airport operations – airports in India work on a model with a revenue sharing model between the concessionaire and the Airports

Authority of India, the revenues including both airport as well as commercial properties around the airport.

Entry of other private companies, such as Reliance, was not successful in this segment. In 2009, Reliance Airport Developers Private Ltd was awarded 95 year lease rights to develop and operate five small airports in Maharashtra. The venture was not successful and the airports today fly private jets only. Despite the fact that a big Indian business house did not have a successful entry into this segment, Adani remained unfazed.

The monopoly of GMR and GVR in this sector was immense; GMR agreed to share 45.99% of revenue with AAI for the development of the Delhi airport, while the GVK group offered 38.7% for the Mumbai airport. The rising power of the duopoly and the monopolistic environment forced AAI to look at alternative revenue models as the present revenue model allowed operators to conceal revenue from airport operations, leading to lesser revenue shared.

It is important to mention here that most of the revenue however comes from non-core verticals, mostly resulting from monetising real estate and retail operations. This non- core revenue is crucial as even though aviation has been hit by demands imposed during and post COVID, passenger traffic across India is set to hit 50 crore by 2037. a rigorous analysis and was certain that the business would yield assured annuities of hybrid revenue from airport-related activities such as cargo and ground handling, aircraft parking and fuelling, and also non-aero functions such as income from retail shops and licences, advertising, and development rights on land alongside the airports.

After evaluating the sector, and trying to create a level playing field for other companies as well, in February 2019, the government decided to open operations and management of six airports to the private sector. The Adani Group found a perfect opportunity to step up their expansion. The Adani Group outbid all its peers and gained the contracts to manage the six airports. In March 2019, the group finally won the rights to develop and operate the six airports in Lucknow, Jaipur, Thiruvananthapuram, Mangaluru, Guwahati, and Ahmedabad. The government had made some changes to the contract. Unlike the previous years, when operators worked under a revenue sharing model, the government this time asked bidders to offer a fixed revenue per passenger and the Adani Group won after the requisite due diligence, having offered the highest per-passenger fees to AAI in its bids.

The Group has a vision to join India's biggest cities through the aviation sector in a hub-and-spoke model. It is part of the Group's strategy to enter areas that enable it to add economic value to sectors that bridge the rural-urban divide. Even COVID-19 pandemic, which drove most infrastructure, logistics and transportation companies in the red, did not deter the Group. Under the guidance of its chairman, AAHL continued to acquire and plan for expansion for the next phase of growth.

The Group now has eight airports in its kitty, making it India's largest airport infrastructure company, accounting for 25% airport footfalls.

Adani's ambitious vision is supported by the team across the organisation. The leadership of the organisation has acknowledged that Indian passenger traffic will hit 1 billion domestic and international travellers. This surge in demand would need at least 200 additional airports. The Group is investing heavily in the Mumbai and Navi Mumbai airport, anticipating that these would become the aviation hot spots in India. The company also envisions building airports as hubs of aviation linked businesses, creating employment, and development of surrounding regions.

In the year 2021, the Indian government calibrated the opening of the first domestic airspace to address a quarter of India's air traffic user base of 200 million people. The company intends to provide end-to-end service integration, which is renowned for achieving the best ASQ ratings across categories. In addition, the business will represent a convergence of the company's B2B and B2C interests, representing proximity to other businesses of the Adani Group.

The company started operations at Ahmedabad, Lucknow and Mangaluru airports in the financial year 20-21, with operations at Jaipur, Guwahati and Thiruvananthapuram starting October 2021. The government also strengthened the aviation sector by expanding airports and promoting maintenance, repair and overhaul operations within the country in line with Air India's disinvestment, modernization and regional connectivity plan. Following the completion of this transaction, the company's portfolio consisted of seven operational airports and one green field airport.

The pride of the company's portfolio is Navi Mumbai International Airport Limited, a subsidiary of MIAL. The proposed state-of-the-art airport is expected to commence commercial operations by December 2024, manifested in a capacity to handle 20 MPPA of traffic (Phase 1).

- ✓ The Airports Authority of India (AAI) proposes to develop over 20 airports in tier-two and tier-three cities in five years.
- ✓ It is proposed to develop AAI Guwahati as an Inter-Regional Centre and Agartala, Imphal and Dibrugarh as Intra-Regional Centres.
- ✓ AAI has proposed to invest ₹ 25,000 crore over five years to enhance facilities and infrastructure at existing airports.
- ✓ The Government of India plans to invest 1.83 billion US dollars for the development of airport infrastructure and aviation navigation services by the year 2026.

✓ In the Union Budget 2022, the Government of India allocated ₹ 10,667 crore for the Ministry of Civil Aviation for the financial year 22-23 (₹ 600.7 crore earmarked for the regional connectivity scheme UDAN and ₹ 9,259 crore for the financial restructuring of Air India).

In the Union Budget for the financial year 21-22, the Government of India expanded the scope of Krishi Udaan in convergence with the Operation Green scheme, providing 50 per cent airspace for agri-business to the North East States and the four Himalayan States / Union Territories. Freight subsidy will be provided. The expansion of product coverage will strengthen the Krishi Udaan scheme and improve air cargo transportation from these states.

The appetite for air travel can be attributed to rise in disposable income, better infrastructure at tier 2 and 3 airports, competitive fares from low cost carriers and supportive governmental policies. India currently has 131 airports out of which around 29 are international airports, 10 are customs and the rest overwhelming majority are domestic airports. Given this huge demand, building airport infrastructure is one of the high growth areas sought by leading corporates. There are plans to increase the number of airports from its present number of 148 airports to 220 airports by 2025. The infrastructure expenditure will be borne by private companies, who will be investing close to USD 9 bn, and the rest will be borne by AAI. The airport infrastructure will span new projects, including terminals and the renovation of present facilities.

Adani, challenged conventional behemoths like GMR and the GVK Group that had been managing airports for more than a decade. Once the privatisation contract for the six airports, Jaipur, Mangaluru, Ahmedabad, Lucknow, Guwahati and Thiruvanthapuram was floated, Adani knew it was the right time to step into the business. These airports controlled around 9% of India's domestic and international traffic, respectively. With the inclusion of Mumbai to the Adani Group's portfolio, its span of influence included ~25% of domestic and international traffic.

A testament to the management and development of the Adani managed airports is the fact that all the seven Adani airports saw an increase of 92% in domestic and 133% in international travellers.

Adani knew the potential of Mumbai airport, which is now the second busiest airport in India in terms of both passenger and cargo traffic. There have been plans to develop the MIAL network further by building it as a hub for aviation in India. Furthering these plans is the development of the Navi Mumbai International Airport Limited (NMIAL) which will be fully operational in 2024 and will provide a huge boost to the West aviation platform. The 2,866-acre airport in Navi Mumbai is expected to handle 90 million passengers by 2036. The Group plans to build transportation connecting Chhatrapati Shivaji Maharaj International Airport (CSMIA) and Navi Mumbai Airport so that they can operate as a single aviation hub with five terminals.

It also provides strategic adjacencies for the Group's other ventures across B2B and B2C models. With the inclusion of of MIAL, AAHL further boosted its participation in other segments of civil aviation, it also controls 33% of India's air cargo traffic. With the next round of privatisation being announced for Amritsar, Varanasi, Bhubaneswar, Tiruchirappalli and Raipur. Except Raipur, all others are international airports. International airports lead to higher revenue generation as they offer higher food, retail and duty free options for passengers. These airports account for approximately 5% each of domestic and international traffic.

Due to the travel restrictions and capital limitations arising post COVID, the Group requested for an extension for the takeover of Guwahati, Thiruvanthapuram, and Jaipur airports. After that period, the airports were successfully taken over and managed.

To drive more operational efficiencies, the Group plans to reduce the operational costs by 30-50%, through workforce interventions, digitisation, and technical collaboration.

To fast track its ambitious growth plans, the Group also instituted several leadership changes at AAHL and Mumbai the company have been shifted from Mumbai to Ahmedabad. All this was done to help speed up the Group's aggressive expansion plans and support the vision of the founder to develop airports as a major business unit.

Management, development, and modernisation of airports is a complex venture. Companies need to establish terms of continuance for contracts and agreements with vendors, suppliers and services providers and need to manage agencies for various outcomes such as security, retail partnerships. Partnerships help an airport operator build sector specific expertise, lends domain experience, and technical knowhow.

GMR has established partnerships with companies like Fraport (which manages the Frankfurt airport), Groupe ADP, Malaysia Airport Holdings Behard, Megawide, Terna. These partnerships gave GMR an unparalleled advantage when it came to airport management experience.

GVK had partnerships with Airports Company South Africa, which owns and operates major airports in South Africa, Bidvest, a freight management company in South Africa, Siemens Project Ventures GmbH and Flughafen Zürich AG, a Swiss airports operator for Bangalore Airport.

The Adani Group was initially able to manage the modernisation, operations and management of the airports due to its vast experience in massive infrastructure project.

Eventually, to gain sectoral management experience, the Group shortlisted FlughafenMunchen GmbH for Operations and Maintenance (O&M) at Ahmedabad, Mangaluru and Lucknow. This partnership would help drive operational efficiencies, help in technical collaboration and help build airport, Germany's second largest airport after Frankfurt.

In 2021, it partnered with April Moon Retail Pvt Ltd (AMRPL) for a strategic partnership to operate duty free outlets at airports by acquiring a majority stake. This strategic partnership will enable AAHL to operate duty paid outlets in airports, and expand the retail footprint and sources of revenue. AAHL has also signed a long term partnership with Uber to offer seamless ride experiences to travellers. As part of its portfolio expansion for Adani One, the Group entered into a partnership with ClearTrip for airport digitisation. With this partnership, AAHL is able to offer an integrated digital platform to its customers for domestic and international flight bookings. This will simplify the travel experience for passengers, allowing them book flights, get updates, access Pranaam Meet and Greet Service, and avail services such as airport parking, cabs and duty-free products.

AAHL has declared its commitment to adhere to the Sustainable Development Goals (SDGs) in order to build a more sustainable business. The aviation business is notoriously fossil fuel heavy, leading to a huge carbon footprint, across airplanes, airports, and other allied facilities. Under the visionary leadership of Gautam Adani, the business has clearly differentiated itself by turning around a fuel guzzling industry into a future ready, sustainable venture.

Sustainable Development Goals (SDGs) are a blueprint for a sustainable future helping tackle global issues such as climate change, environmental balance, inequity. These goals are all interconnected and countries have committed to achieve these by 2030. Out of the 17 goals, AAHL has declared special commitment to a few. These are:

Sustainable Development Goals (SDG 7): Affordable and clean energy, which talks about ensuring access to affordable, reliable, sustainable and modern energy. SDG 7 aims to promote green energy and ensure its universal access by 2030, while making efforts to increase the share of renewable energy in the global energy portfolio, and substantially improving energy efficiency.

Sustainable Development Goals (SDG 11): Sustainable cities and communities. This SDG focuses on making cities inclusive, safe, resilient and sustainable. Its goals are to ensure access to adequate, safe and affordable housing and basic services by planned urbanisation. It also focuses on providing sustainable and accessible transportation while improving road safety, promoting public transportation while protecting vulnerable groups.

Sustainable Development Goals (SDG 13): Climate Action: This SDG focuses on urgent action to combat the crippling effects of climate change and strengthening systems and response mechanisms for climate induced hazards and natural disasters in all countries. It also promotes active planning and citizen education for climate change and incorporating that at the regulatory and policy level. This goal also talks about improving capacity building, warning mechanisms, and education about climate change.

AAHL has demonstrated its intention of SDG compliance through initiatives that include solar energy installation projects, electric vehicle usage, green buildings, conversion to LED lamps etc. The Group aims at reducing fossil fuels consumption as it transitions to greener operational protocols. CSMIA has received 4+ level of accreditation from the Airport Council International due to an effective management of its carbon footprint . This has happened because of proactive steps such as completely switching over to green sources of energy for power consumption needs. CSMIA features an onsite renewable power generation plant of 4.65 MW capacity in tandem with vertical axis wind turbine and solar PV of 10KWp, conversion of higher Global Warming Potential (GWP) refrigerant in ACs to lower GWP refrigerant. These efforts will continue at the Navi Mumbai airports as well, which will have solar power generation, and EVs for on-ground mobility.

Three of the airports in its portfolio - Ahmedabad, Mangaluru and Lucknow have been accredited in the Airports Council International (ACI) Airport Health Accreditation programme. This certification acknowledges the protocols and measures put in place to ensure passenger safety.

The certification has been awarded after thorough evaluation of almost 118 check points. These measures are in compliance with the recommended health measures established in the ACI Aviation Business Restart and Recovery guidelines and ICAO Council Aviation Recovery Task Force Recommendations, along with industry's best practices.

As a major accolade, seven Adani Airports have been honoured with 'The Voice of the Customer' award by the Airports Council International (ACI), as a testament to the passenger friendly experience at these airports. These airports are in Ahmedabad, Guwahati, Jaipur, Lucknow, Mumbai, Mangaluru, and Thiruvananthapuram. The Awards are a testament to the relentless zeal for providing the best-in class passenger experience, and for demonstrating superlative efforts in gathering and adapting to passenger's feedback.

Conducted by the Airports Council International (ACI), the ASQ survey is an internationally recognised benchmarking programme that tracks passenger satisfaction and is a rigorous and evidence based acknowledgment of an airport's performance.

The company will accelerate digital investments leading to proof of services, passenger self-service solutions, centralized airport control centres, airport operations systems, customer relationship management and electronic point-of-sales systems.

Within a few years of entering the business, the company has emerged as a regional outlier. Going forward, the company intends to redefine India's airport infrastructure sector through gateway development, regional footprint growth, focus on consumers and non-passengers, and deep investments in digital technology interventions that enhance consumer broadens one's choice and happiness.

As of April 2024, the US and China continue to be the largest domestic aviation markets. However, India is now surpassing Brazil and Indonesia, becoming the third-largest domestic market with a total airline capacity of 15.6 million seats, according to OAG data, popularising the public-private partnership model with assured returns, transforming India into an MRO hub, Driven by the government's decision to have flexible use of airspace and a mature regulatory framework.

In line with the Chairman's vision of building a transformational airport infrastructure platform, connected across digital and physical, the Group has charted out ambitious plans for tapping new business opportunities.

The Group has outlined plans to develop real estate projects near its airport facilities in tandem with its core airport operations. There are plans to develop almost 70 million square feet on over 500 acres of land across all its airports.

These aero cities or Airport Economic Precints are expected to have variety of options for accommodations, event hosting, convention centres, retail, logistics, healthcare, and commercial operations. The Group initiated discussions with hospitality partners like Marriott International, InterContinental Hotels Group (IHG), and Hilton (India Infoline) for setting up hospitality ventures in the aero adjacent areas.

AAHL is also planning an aggressive expansion and building Mumbai and Ahmedabad as hubs to connect West Asia, Europe and the Far East. The company has also outlined plans to expand both international and domestic traffic from these airports. Mumbai airport already has good connectivity with Europe and West Asia. However, there aren't too many flights operating to the

Far East. Ahmedabad is also underdeveloped as an airport hub. The Group is developing both airside and landside combinations, while simultaneously exploring long-term airline partnerships, optimising slot priorities and minimising turnarounds. Partners are being incentivised through additional retail and rental space, while also finding avenues for non-aero revenue. The company is planning to invest almost INR 10,000 crore in the Ahmedabad Airport over 2023-27 to enhance passenger capacity, while developing it as a hub connecting Bhuj, Kandla, Jamnagar and Bhavnagar.

An important plan is the development of the Navi Mumbai airport. For this, it has outlined a twin airport strategy, through a hub and spoke model.

Mumbai International Airport Ltd., has a maximum passenger handling capacity of 60 million a year. At present, it is handling 45–49 million passengers a year. AAHL estimates the passenger load to double by 2030, hence it is banking on its twin airports strategy. Once fully operational, the Navi Mumbai International Airport Ltd., can handle upto 90 million passengers a year. The airport will become fully operational over a period of four phases, the first of which will be completed by December 2024. The initial capacity that can be handled by the airport will be 20 million.

The model is expected to reduce congestion, drive effective slot allocation, and multiply non-aero revenues. The company is also planning to target foreign airlines with higher imbalances, such as carriers from the U.A.E., and prioritise those part of Star Alliance and One World.

The two airports, less than 50 km apart, are expected to be well connected through a network of land and water transport such as the Mumbai Trans Harbour link. The Group has continuously aligned its business to promoting and developing India and avenues of national growth. Recently, an event was organised by the company at the Guwahati Airport to promote tourism in the northeast area. The event focused on exploring avenues of promotion for tourism, while outlining strategies for execution.

In line with further expansion in allied areas, the Group is also exploring a foray into aircraft services. The aircraft services market is expected to be worth USD 145 B by 2037. The Group has partnered with Airbus to offer a single stop solution for all aircraft related services across India and other countries in South Asia. Airbus is the world's leading civil aviation company and a major innovator in the space of aircraft services. This collaboration will further strengthen technical expertise and on-ground execution capabilities of AAHL.

Road and Highway Construction Business

The road and highway construction business of the Adani Group is engaged in widening and deepening India's arterial transport lifeline.

India is one of the most attractive road and highway construction destinations in the world.

The country stands at a turning point in road construction capacity. India has the second largest road infrastructure in the world, spanning 5.89 million kilometres. This road network transports 64.5 per cent of the country's total cargo as 90 per cent of its total passenger traffic uses the road network. Road transport is on the rise following improvements in connectivity and changes in lifestyle, favouring the use of passenger and commercial vehicles instead of alternatives.

Adani Enterprises entered the business of road and highway construction in January 2018. It is to the credit of the company that within just four years, the company built a portfolio of 14 road projects and three waste water treatment projects in line with one investment.

The Government of India launched the National Infrastructure Plan (NIP) and the National Monitoring Plan (NMP), catalysing the development of the roads and highways sector.

- ✓ The government proposed several mega infrastructure programmes such as the Delhi-Dehradun and Delhi-Amritsar-Katra Expressway projects; The ministry is planning to securitize the Raipur-Visakhapatnam National Highway project, the first highway in the country, to provide timely evacuation of most of the minerals produced in Chhattisgarh, Odisha and Jharkhand to Visakhapatnam port.
- ✓ The government allocated around ₹ 111 lakh crore under the National Infrastructure Pipeline for the financial year 2019-2025, with the road sector likely to account for 18 per cent of this proposed capital expenditure.
- ✓ The Gati-Shakti master plan of the Government of India will be of about ₹ 42,000 crores. As a result, this business has emerged as one of the fastest growing businesses within the company. By the end of the year under review, business enjoyed the convenience of road construction and employment.

In October 2021, the Government of India issued a notice regarding concessions under the vehicle scrapping policy with effect from April 2022, to encourage vehicle owners to discard old vehicles with high fuel consumption costs.

The government launched a conversion project for 15 major roads in Agartala Smart City to make them weather-friendly roads.

The government announced plans to set up charging stations at an interval of 40 to 60 kilometres on national highways to strengthen wayside facilities. In line with the plan, around 700 e-vehicle charging stations are expected to be set up by the year 2023, covering 35,000 to 40,000 kilometres of national highways.

Pan-India presence, covering over 5000 lane kilometres in Andhra Pradesh, Chhattisgarh, Gujarat, Kerala, Madhya Pradesh, Maharashtra, Odisha, Telangana, Uttar Pradesh and West Bengal.

The company plans/proposes to improve upon its already enhanced quality and safety practices. The company wants to tighten the monitoring and control of the project.

- ✓ In the Union Budget for the financial year 22-23, ₹ 68,000 crore more allocation was made for roads, the best increase among all ministries in the financial year 22-23 (with reference to Revised Estimates from the financial year 21-22).
- ✓ The Union Budget for financial year 22-23 allocated ₹ 1,99,107.71 crore to the Ministry of Road Transport and Highways.

The long-term sustainability of the business at Adani Group is built around the need to enhance stakeholder value. Its business is built on environmental, sustainability and governance principles in the following ways –

Its value creation model – environment, sustainability and governance (ESG)—is built around an integrated approach of principles. The company is determined to be the lifeline of India, connecting far flung parts through road, metro and railways.

- ✓ The total budgetary outlay increased by 5.5 times from ₹ 33,414 crore in the financial year 2014-2015 to ₹ 1,83,101 crore in the financial year 2021-2022.

The government proposes to build 25,000 kilometres of highways in the financial year 22-23, taking into account the fastest speed of over 68 kilometres per day as compared to the highest speed of 37 km/day in the financial year 20-21. It is committed to reducing footprint and adopting resource-efficient methods in the following ways ;

- ✓ The company is working towards zero loss of life through its leadership commitment, uniform deployment of safety standards, capacity building, management systems and optimized processes.
- ✓ The company has implemented sound systems to manage environmental impacts, climate-related risks and opportunities.
- ✓ The government has prepared the Gati Shakti Master Plan to develop the expressway to facilitate faster movement of cargo and people.
- ✓ The company has integrated ESG into business operations and integration of ESG aspects for key suppliers by the financial year 23-24.
- ✓ The company integrated systematic materiality assessment into its management system.
- ✓ The company has ensured inclusive growth by undertaking CSR initiatives along with business sustainability to enhance social welfare.

The Roads and Highways construction business takes advantage of the following strengths:

- ✓ The company added experienced and qualified talent.
- ✓ The company implemented Adani Business Excellence Model and ESG Framework.
- ✓ The company acquired the largest green field (Ganga) Expressway in India.
- ✓ The company added ₹ 25000 crore to the order book; The year end order book stood at ₹ 34000 crore.
- ✓ The company appointed competent vendors/contractors to execute the projects. It settled the issues to reduce disputes/ claims.

- ✓ The company achieved project milestones in Suryapet and Mancherial projects within the stipulated time frame.
- ✓ Despite non-availability of labour and skilled manpower restrictions, the company operated the existing sewage treatment plants within the established performance parameters; The company achieved the COD of its packages 2 and 3 within the stipulated time despite the Covid-19 constraints.
- ✓ Adani Road Transport received a Letter of Award from the National Highways Authority of India for Kagal Satara, a road project in Maharashtra worth ₹ 2,008.47 crore. The construction period of the 67 kilometre long road project is estimated to be two years from the date of appointment, with the concession period expected to be 18 years.

The road sector in India is expected to register solid growth as the pandemic subsides with expected frontloaded infrastructure investments.

A total of 1,41,190 kilometres of national highways were completed in the financial year 21-22. The nation intends to develop 22 green field access controlled expressways to reduce travel time. In addition to reducing travel time and fuel costs, fast-track highways will catalyze economic growth. The Ministry of Road Transport and Highways prioritizes reducing the national logistics cost from 14-16 per cent of GDP to 10 per cent of GDP in line with the global average.

❑

Packaged Food Business

One of the largest operators in India's organized edible oil sector that emerged during the pandemic has prioritized food hygiene. There is a higher consumer propensity to buy packaged oil brands than their loose counterparts without packaging, as a result of which India's edible oil sector has registered a significant growth. As a result, the market valued at 3.54 billion US dollars in the year 2020 is expected to grow at a CAGR of 6.82 per cent from the year 2021 to 2027, reaching a potential size of 5.72 billion US dollars in the year 2027.

This a compelling place to be present in this comes from the fact that the import bill for edible oils stood at 13.2 million tonnes in the year 2019-20 worth about ₹ 71,600 crore. Although India imported the same amount of edible oil in the financial year 2020-21, the imports rose to 63 per cent and touched ₹ 1.17 lakh crore due to increase in international prices. India's vegetable oil imports increased from 4 million tonnes to 150,000 tonnes in two decades, reflecting an increase in the country's per capita income and aspirations. In fact, imports are expected to reach 20 million tonnes by the year 2030. India produces less than half of the estimated 24 million tonnes of edible oil.

India's Ministry of Agriculture proposed a five-year Edible Oil Mission plan for an estimated expenditure of ₹ 19,000 crore to reduce the import of edible oils (palm and soybean oil). The Government of India announced a National Edible Oil Mission—Oil Palm to increase oilseed production towards cooking medium self-sufficiency. Also, India will launch an oilseeds mission, with an investment of ₹ 11,000 crore in the 'cooking oil eco-system' for annual consumption. Import of edible oil is the third largest item in India's import bill after crude petroleum oil and gold.

The government took measures to encourage farmers to grow oilseeds with the aim of reducing India's dependence on import of edible oil. As far as staples are concerned, the government is lending and incentivizing channel partners to strengthen supply chain infrastructure and increase adequate storage and processing units for food grains and oilseeds.

Adani Wilmar Limited is one of the largest packaged food FMGC companies in India, offering a range of consumer products under multiple brands. The company has a vibrant basket of edible oils and food staples, has emerged as one of the fastest growing edible FMCG companies in India.

The aim of Adani Wilmar Limited has been –

✓ To become India's largest Food FMCG company in the flagship Packaged Food segment.

✓ Expanding distribution network across rural and urban India with a strong brand, best-in-class infrastructure, wide and deep distribution network and efficient sourcing. The company has over 50 manufacturing facilities (including owned and third-party units) and 85 depots located every 200 kilometres. The result is that Adani Wilmar Limited has a reach of over 90 million households and a retail reach of 1.8 million outlets.

- ✓ Despite the lockdown, the company operated its manufacturing units smoothly to launch sixty new products and brand extensions of ready-to-cook and ready-to-eat facilities. Under the RACE programme, the company intends to cover 8,000 new towns in four to six quarters - while deepening its presence in towns with a population of 20,000, widening its rural footprint.
- ✓ The company strengthened its manufacturing and R&D facilities and seven out of nine palm oil refineries are RSPO-compliant.

Adani Wilmar Limited is consolidating its portfolio of kitchen essentials in line with its vision to emerge as India's largest food FMCG company.

Diversified Product Portfolio

The company is engaged in the production of packaged foods, edible oils, personal care products and industrial essentials (including oleo-chemicals, castor oil and its derivatives and de-oiled cake). Branded products constitute a significant portion of the company's sales for the financial year 2021-22, accounting for around 75 per cent of edible oils and packaged food and FMCG sales volume (excluding industry offered on non-branded basis).

State-of-the-Art Facilities

The company has 22 plants strategically located across ten states in India, comprising 10 crushing units and 18 refineries. Of the 18 refineries, 10 are port-based to facilitate access to imported crude edible oil and reduce transportation costs, while the rest are located in close proximity to crude production bases. The company's refinery at Mundra is one of the largest standalone in India (capacity 5000 MT per day). The company has used 30 leased tolling units by March 31, 2022, adding capacity through an asset-light model.

Deep and Wide Reach

The company has the largest distribution network among all branded edible oil companies in India. As of March 31, 2022, the company was present in one in three Indian households – a household reach of 113 million through its Fortune brand.

Online Ecosystem

Apart from traditional retail distribution channels, the company also serves customers online through Fortune Mart (18 outlets) and Fortune Online (25 cities) which provides home ordering facility. The company's website showcases a basket of the entire Fortune brand products with the option to shop through other major e-commerce platforms. Its B2B app (Fortune Business) for grocery is available in 16 cities.

Brand

The company's flagship 'Fortune' is the largest selling edible oil brand in India. This brand is respected for consistency, values, dependability and superior cooking results.

This brand accounted for a major portion of the company's revenue in the financial year 2021-22. The company's brands address a variety of price points. 'Fortune' addresses premium pricing, and 'Bullet' addresses value pricing.

The company has many popular brands including 'Bullet', 'Kings', 'Aadhar', 'Raag', 'Alpha', 'Jubilee', 'Avasar', 'Golden Chef' and 'Frayola'.

Capacity Enhancement

The company actively anticipates capacity requirements. For example, a major capex was undertaken by AWL in the financial year 2017 to increase refining capacity from about 9,200 TPD to 16,500 TPD now.

Adani Group

Through the presence of Adani Group across India there is a deep understanding of local markets, home market experience, strong logistics and wide distribution presence.

Wilmar Group

The Wilmar Group is the largest supplier of palm oil in the world; global sourcing capabilities; in-depth technical know-how, defined risk management strategy for hedging foreign exchange and commodity risks, rich market intelligence; long term relationship with suppliers.

The company deepened its ESG framework through various initiatives.

Edible Oil / RSPO

Adani Wilmar Limited increased the traceability (to mills) of palm oil sourced to 95 per cent by the financial year 2021-22. It benchmarked operations against Wilmar's sustainability policy; Procured resources from trusted suppliers such as Bunge, Cargill Viterra (formerly - Glencore), Wilmar and ADM.

Reusable Packaging

About 96 per cent of post-use packaging material can be recycled.

Water Resources

Adani Wilmar Limited prudently invests in eco-friendly equipment; The company has installed zero liquid discharge facilities at major plants, recycling all water used in its processes.

Community Upliftment

Adani Wilmar Limited implemented the *Suposhan* Project as part of its Corporate Social Responsibility initiative towards the eradication of malnutrition and anaemia in India, with a focus on children in the age group of 0-5 years, adolescent girls and women of reproductive age.

❑

Adani Digital Labs Business

Adani Digital Labs is one of the most exciting and challenging initiatives of the Adani Group. Adani Digital Labs (ADL) aims to emerge as a digitally empowered group, investing in cutting edge technologies that enhance the future-readiness of traditional businesses on the one hand and deepen the relevance of modern technology-driven ones on the other.

Adani Digital Labs (ADL) was incorporated in September 22, 2021 as a wholly owned subsidiary of Adani Enterprises. ADL's vision is to transform the existing Business Units (BUs) into digital-first BUs by creating an omni-channel, integrated platform to facilitate direct business-customer interactions. Adani Digital's portfolio of services spans strategy and planning, experience design, marketing communications, tech and implementation.

Adani astutely realised that for a conglomerate the size of the parent Adani Enterprises, digital transformation was going to be a unique enabler. Ideas for developing a super app were already afloat, both within the company and outside, amongst competitors. Adani realised the tremendous potential that digital had for scaling up and integrating his large conglomerate. Chasing a trillion dollar valuation for the Group, Adani Digital could very well be the business unit to help unlock latent valuations for the other businesses as well. Keeping this in mind, ADL is positioned as more than just a support function within the Adani Group. ADL is viewed as a strategic catalyst, which is expected to increase the visibility, competitiveness and future orientation of not only a handful of businesses within the Adani Group, but also each of Adani's companies. ADL's existence is not incidental. It is an integral part of it.

Interestingly, ADL's influence will extend from being a back-end technology provider and support system. It will expand the Adani Group's connection with India's millions of consumers through cutting-edge technology, which is the backbone of its vibrant economy. What makes this endorsement work relevant is that the Adani Group (through all its businesses) currently engages 400 million consumers across its businesses of airports, food and beverage.

- ✓ Digitizing and integrating Adani's B2B businesses on a unified platform through 'Super App' that caters to the needs of diverse and demanding stakeholders.
- ✓ Unleashes the power of digital transformation leading to increased productivity, better resource management, better customer engagement, faster product delivery and higher realisation, inter alia.
- ✓ It connects 120 million people through Super Apps by the year 2025 and 300-400 million people by the year 2030 through Adani businesses and partner services across oil, food, gas (industrial and retail), real estate, power and financial services.

Adani Digital Labs aims to future-ready the Adani Group for a time when its business footprint will expand to address over one billion consumers by the year 2030. In view of this, ADL plays key the role of a powerful, dynamic and responsive data with a platform that facilitates consumer engagement, service and enjoyment.

Adani Digital Labs is not only focused on increasing digital engagement between the Adani Group and the consumer, it also intends to on-board every Adani consumer to a digital platform.

- ✓ Its core mission is to expand services through strategic partnerships and acquisitions, providing an ecosystem of services that add consumer value.
- ✓ On-boarding Adani Group's customers or consumers on Super App, engaging them through loyalty and reward programmes, driving greater consumer convenience, enhanced reach and higher sales conversion for partners.
- ✓ Partnering with relevant brands / companies to expand the service spectrum.

Empowered through its Super App to accelerate the growth of the Adani Group with the objective of giving the consumer access to multiple services of the Adani Group, capitalizing on synergies, increasing consumer wallet share and building a stronger India, ADL Expects to grow into a trillion-dollar company (by valuation).

Adani Group, India's fastest growing diversified conglomerate, has acquired a 20 per cent minority stake in Cleartrip Private Limited, an online travel aggregator and part of the Flipkart Group, India's home consumer internet ecosystem.

As a validation of the massive synergies, Cleartrip reported a 10X growth in flight bookings post its acquisition by the Flipkart group. Also, airports owned or managed by Adani indicate an appreciable increase in air passengers (around pre-Covid levels). This partnership will enable Cleartrip to bridge digital boundaries and provide end-to-end online travel services.

This investment will enhance the strategic partnership between the Adani Group and the Flipkart Group. Cleartrip will act as an online travel aggregator partner of the Adani Group. Cleartrip's scalable technology stack, user-friendly interface and industry-first initiatives have made it one of India's most preferred travel brands. The company's seasoned leadership and Flipkart's deep consumer-centric experience helped consolidate the company's leading OTA (Online Travel Agency / Aggregator) position.

By collaborating with the Adani Group in areas such as travel-related products, loyalty programmes and other value-added services, Cleartrip hopes to offer consumers a seamless travel experience. The company's relationship with Flipkart includes multiple dimensions including data centres, fulfilment centres and air travel, raising the possibility of massive job creation in line with the priorities of *Atmanirbhar* Bharat. The Cleartrip platform will go on to become an essential part of the wider Super Ape travel.

The digital world – from social media and GPS systems to artificial intelligence—is accelerating disaster technologies and changing lives. These technologies have the potential to reshape our world. Like making work fluid and flexible, deepening our internet connectivity, working from anywhere, increasing knowledge and taking mankind forward.

In the year 2021, 60.5 per cent of the total population of India will access the internet from their mobile phones. By the year 2025, it is projected to increase to 78.4 per cent. By the year 2030, this is expected to be 89.2 per cent with a corresponding increase in the number of active Indian internet users, which is expected to increase from 776.5 million in the year 2021 to 900 million by the year 2025.

Interestingly, India is expected to have 1.2 billion mobile subscribers in the year 2021, of which around 750 million are smartphone users. The country is set to emerge as the second largest smartphone maker in five years, on the back of rural sector growth clocking a compounded growth of 6 per cent (urban CAGR of 2.5 per cent) from the year 2021 to 2026. The average wireless data usage per wireless data subscriber is expected to reach 40 GB by the year 2026 from 14.6 GB per month in the financial year 2020-21.

What makes Adani's integrated platform relevant is that consumers will increasingly prefer a single application with multiple services. This app-lightness will enhance convenience, speed and responsiveness.

- ✓ Consumers adopt companies that provide services with a clear and intuitive interface, service augmented by other services / functions, encourage other merchants to partner with Super App to provide services.
- ✓ Increased trust (which comes with brand value) and convenience, which increase customer transactions and retention while reducing customer on-boarding costs.
- ✓ Many offline services can be digitized and integrated, the company's digital debut is in line with the government's priority regarding national digitization.

Digital India is a 1,13,000 crore flagship programme of the Government of India with a vision to transform India into a digitally autonomous society and knowledge creation through digital services, digital access and digital inclusion. The Digital India programme has strengthened India's progress in the United Nations e-governance.

- ✓ The company engages with 400 million connections directly and maintains on digital platforms.
- ✓ Airports have easy access to growing passenger traffic through Adani-owned gateways.

- ✓ Digital transformation projects are quite hard to execute, often getting derailed due to executive misalignment, lack of employee support, weak execution and lack of funds. In a survey it was revealed that organisations with a thorough change management strategy are six times more likely to meet or exceed digital transformation objectives. A digital first culture, which embraces change and values innovation are often pre-requisites for implementation of a successful digital transformation. Adani not only drove digital adoption for the businesses as part of their operational strategy, but also drove to modernise the IT architecture of the Group entirely.
- ✓ As part of its IT modernisation strategy, The Adani Group announced a multi-year partnership with Google Cloud, moving more than 250 critical business applications to the Cloud. Strategies like these have ensured that the Group remains agile and digital-first.

❑

Agricultural Products Business

India's agriculture industry is an important part of the Indian economy through Gross Domestic Product (GDP) contribution and livelihood generation. India is the second largest producer of fruits and vegetables in the world and the fourth largest agricultural country.

However, India ranks 103 on the Global Hunger Index (GHI). Owing to fragmented food systems and inefficient supply chains, about 40 per cent of the food produced in India is wasted before it reaches the consumer.

On the other hand, there is an increasing demand for fruits and vegetables, growing population, increased disposable income and higher aspirations. The government is promoting investment in the agriculture sector, especially food processing and cold chain, through schemes and subsidies to increase national capacity, reduce national deficit and increase availability of fresh produce to consumers.

India's domestic apple production in the market year 21-22 was estimated at 2.3 million tonnes, largely unchanged from the previous season. Fruit quality was expected to improve because of favourable weather conditions, general labour availability and improvement in supply chain. The state of Himachal Pradesh contributed 20 per cent to the apple production of the country.

✓ The government announced (Production Linked Incentive) PLI scheme for food processing sector with an incentive outlay of ₹ 10,900 crore in six months starting in the financial year 2021-22.

✓ Schemes like *Paramparagat Krishi Vikas Yojana* helped farmers develop organic clusters and chemical-free inputs. The high proportion of agricultural land (157 million hectares) and diverse agro-climatic conditions encouraged the cultivation of various crops. With 20 agro-climatic zones, all 15 major climates of the world are present in the country and India has 46 out of 60 global soil types.

✓ The Indian Agricultural Export Policy, 2018 was approved by the Government of India in December 2018. The new policy aimed to increase the country's agricultural exports to 60 billion US dollars by the year 2022 and 100 billion US dollars in the next few years with stable trade.

✓ Under the 10th instalment of PM-Kisan, more than 20,000 crore were transferred to over 10 crore beneficiary farmer families. Under the PM-Kisan scheme, over ₹ 1.60 lakh crore has been transferred to over 11.54 crore farmers by the year 2021.

✓ Increased institutional credit provided, increase in MSP, various schemes such as *Paramparagat Krishi Vikas Yojana, Pradhan Mantri Gram, Sinchai Yojana and Sansad Adarsh Gram Yojana* were launched and export of wheat and rice opened up.

- ✓ Initiatives like *Kisan Rath* (mobile app for farmers, FPOs and traders), more than 200 Kisan Rail and Krishi Udaan schemes for transportation of products, and perishable cargo centres, cold storage facilities at airports, inland container depots and cargo terminals.
- ✓ Amazon.com, Microsoft and Cisco Systems were among the specialist giants seeking to use data from India's farmers in a government-led productivity drive aimed at increasing the efficiency of the agriculture sector.
- ✓ With an investment of 272 billion US dollars in aggregate and allied sectors by the year 2030, India can generate revenue of 813 billion US dollars, create 152 million jobs and become the largest private sector player in the country.

Adani Group, with the help of subsidiary Adani Agri Fresh Limited (AAFL), was the first principal player to start business of procurement, storage and marketing of apples in the year 2006. The company operates through state-of-the-art controlled atmosphere storage in the apple belt of Shimla district (Himachal Pradesh).

AAFL has brought a revolution in the apple industry of Himachal Pradesh in 15 years, which is manifested in an exponential growth and awareness among farmers. This approach is to be replicated in other states.

The company enjoys competitive advantage through long-term infrastructure investments and largest built storage capacity in its category (22,500 MT) in Himachal Pradesh.

The company's Farm-Pick brand enjoys leadership, superior quality and a wide pan-India distribution network.

Infrastructure

The biggest strength is the company's state-of-the-art infrastructure, which is the largest fresh produce area in India.

Storage

The company leveraged the latest controlled atmosphere technology to increase the shelf life of the produce.

Experience

The company is engaged in procurement and marketing of fresh produce for more than 16 years, and has significant reputation in the locality.

Kisan Aadhaar

The company works with a large farmer base (around 17,000 registered farmers) to meet the growing demand for fresh produce.

Purchase

The company has a procurement capacity of around 20,000 MT of apples, making it the largest corporate player in infrastructure storage and procurement of fresh produce.

Supply Chain

The company has the capacity to supply fresh apples across the country, empowered by the extended storage facility for the new month.

Technology

The company has invested in cutting edge technologies, extending product life and enhancing quality.

Network

The company's pan-India marketing network makes it possible for products to reach under-served markets.

Partnerships

The company is supported by modern format stores and sales tie-ups with e-commerce players, which is driving its expansion.

The company implemented supply chain changes through the following methods:

- ✓ The traditional procurement model in boxes was replaced by digital sorting and grading (colour, size and weight), thereby increasing farmer revenue.
- ✓ Procurement based on pre-determined prices of different grades of apples, counting market and middleman malpractices, consolidating farmers' income.
- ✓ Farmers served distant markets without the associated recovery risk.
- ✓ Enhanced technical know-how by connecting farmers to global buyers, strengthening productivity.
- ✓ The company reached out to farmers and helped to raise aspirations.

Greater focus on environmental, social and governance standards has helped enhance the company's brand in terms of dependability, responsibility, sustainability, talent recruitment and responsiveness to new opportunities.

The company focuses on enhancing knowledge of products, sharing information about technological innovation and building drive towards sustainability through scientific programmes addressed by subject matter experts.

The company entered into joint ventures with respected companies to develop model orchards at their sites where farmers are taught advanced practices to enhance knowledge to reduce post-harvest losses.

The company marketed improved anti-hail nets to farmers at subsidized cost to reduce losses and protect income.

The company increased livelihoods through recruitment on the basis of merit and experience. The vendors were introducd to various opportunities to grow and extend their business.

The company organizes rural medical camps through the Adani Foundation, marked by free distribution of medicines to the underprivileged; It assisted the rural community and local administration during the pandemic through distribution of free food for migrant labourers apart from distribution of masks and sanitizers. The company organized free vaccination for the employees, contractors and their families.

The company focused on increasing throughput, expanding its product line, and assembling teams in multiple states for each fruit vertical. The company is associated with various service providers to safeguard product quality and shelf life. It seeks to increase its Jammu & Kashmir footprint for procurement and storage of apples through multiple procurement volume driven models. In addition, it seeks to improve the performance of the grading machine to enhance product quality. It seeks to build business relationships with e-commerce and modern-day stores.

The company has played a vital role in increasing farmers' income through responsible intermediation, securing payments and creating a transparent (per gram) payment system in the interest of producers, enhancing systemic integrity.

The company made a significant contribution in improving the technical knowledge of the farmers and contributing towards increasing the productivity and quality through arranging various scientific programmes as per the latest innovations.

The company started pomegranate and mango cultivation.

The company catalysed the business of local transporters especially through off-season dispatch volumes. Employment was provided to the local youth on the basis of their educational qualifications while strengthening rural livelihood.

Farm-Pick expanded its portfolio in Maharashtra, Rajasthan and Gujarat with grapes, pomegranates and mangoes, strengthening its perennial relevance.

The company promoted smaller packaging of fruit ranges to address the affluent masses. The company launched a pilot apple project in Uttarakhand in association with the Directorate of Horticulture, Uttarakhand.

The company outperformed its sector despite tense market conditions owing to a strong farmer base, which helped in large-scale procurement for storage despite poor quality owing to various environmental factors.

Despite widespread pan-India farmer protests, the operations team delivered creditable performance at nine field and plant levels, resulting in achieving the targeted procurement quantities.

The company also started a pilot trading project along with procurement in Shimla district, which was managed credibly.

The company arranges scientific farming programmes in joint ventures with renowned agro-input companies to help farmers increase productivity and quality.

❑

Copper Business

Copper is a fundamental commodity to modern life, with uses ranging from cars to electronics and building blocks alike. For this reason, demand for copper has increased in line with global economic growth, making the metal a reliable commodity to track long-term business cycles. It would be appropriate to communicate that copper represents the building block of the modern world, a proper representative of economic growth and prosperity.

Owing to its properties, either singly or in combination, of high ductility, incorruptibility, and thermal and electrical conductivity as well as resistance to corrosion, copper has become a major industrial metal (third after iron and aluminium by volume of consumption). Major applications of copper include electrical wiring (60 per cent), roofing and plumbing (20 per cent), and industrial machinery (15 per cent).

Copper is used in building construction, power generation and transmission, electronic product manufacturing, and the production of industrial machinery and transportation vehicles. Copper is integral to wiring and plumbing equipment, heating or cooling systems, and telecommunication links. Copper is an essential component in motors, wiring, radiators, connectors, brakes and bearings used in cars and trucks. The average car contains 1.5 kilometres (0.9 miles) of copper wire, and the total amount of copper ranges from 20 kg (44 lb) in small cars to 45 kg (99 lb) in luxury and hybrid vehicles.

Global demand for copper has consistently outstripped supply. The global demand-supply gap has doubled from 0.3 million tonnes in the year 2015 to 0.6 million tonnes in the year 2020. India's long-term copper market appears optimistic with attractive prices. The global copper market was estimated at 255,160 million US dollars in the year 2022 and is expected to grow to an adjusted 343,900 million US dollars by the year 2028 at a CAGR of 5.1 per cent.

Interestingly, 73 per cent of global electricity generation will come from renewable energy sources by the year 2050, and copper will play a key and prominent role in that transition. Solar and wind power farms rely heavily on copper, including cabling and heat exchange in solar and wind farms. For starters, wind farms can contain anywhere between 4 and 15 million pounds of copper; Solar photovoltaic farms require 9000 pounds of copper per megawatt of energy.

Also, copper is important because of the extensive inside-penetration. India's per capita consumption of copper is less than 1 kg, lower than the global average of 3.2 kg and China's 5.4 kg.

The demand outlook for copper for electronic vehicles used in EV batteries, coils, wiring and charging stations is strong for a relevant reason. By the year 2030, more than 250,000 tonnes of copper will be required as part of the windings in electric traction motors in EVs.

India's annual refined copper requirement is estimated to be around 7,00,000 tonnes, with 95 per cent of the country's consumption being met through imports. India's infrastructure expansion along with growth in population, aspirations, urbanization, electric vehicles and renewables are expected to drive the next round of copper demand in the near future.

Demand for electric vehicles will require five times more copper than conventional vehicles. In addition, renewable energy, infrastructure development and electricity demand—emerging as catalysts for strong copper demand.

At Kutch Copper Limited, Adani Group's vision is to emerge as a globally acclaimed copper business committed to building India and enhancing value for stakeholders through trust and courage.

Copper is a key raw material linked to Adani Group's infrastructure portfolio (energy and transport), strengthening national self-reliance and securing its supply chain.

The company is replicating Adani Group's established business model with the objective of maximizing profits, generating free cash flow and enhancing stakeholder value.

✓ In April 2021, the Directorate General of Foreign Trade (DGFT) revised the import policy for copper and aluminium from 'free' to 'free with mandatory registration' under the Non-ferrous Metals Import Monitoring System (NFMIMS), which came into effect from April 12, 2021.

To accelerate copper recycling, the Government of India announced in the Union Budget 2021 to reduce the import duty on copper scrap from 5 per cent to 2.5 per cent.

✓ Industry body ASSOCHAM urged the Government of India to reduce customs duty on copper concentrate from the current level of 2.5 per cent to nil to provide a level playing field and add value to the industry from Free Trade Agreements (FTAs - countries under zero duty) to help compete with the import of copper products.

KCL was incorporated as a 100 per cent subsidiary of Adani Enterprises Limited (AEL). AEL's emphasis on identification and development of profitable and value-creating opportunities has led to successful diversification and growth.

The company will leverage Adani Group's transformational investment arm Modak in the development, operation and post-operational phases.

The company established a best-in-class team with deep domain experience of over 350 person-years in the metal segment.

KCL's scale and inter-business synergies can generate competitive advantages, marked by state-of-the-art technology, resource trading capabilities and energy infrastructure.

The company will enhance value for stakeholders and investors through the creation of valuable metals (gold and silver) and by-products including sulphuric acid, which can be partially converted into phosphoric acid, a by-product for the fertilizer industry. Input is important.

The company has an option to explore value-added downstream opportunities such as copper tubes.

KCL's plant has been designed keeping in mind the sustainability of the environment.

The company will not only adhere to the extant environmental norms, but also establish itself as a global benchmark.

One-third of the company's plant area will be covered by a green belt, investing 15 per cent of its project cost in environmental protection.

Adani's ESG framework is based on the guiding principles of the United Nations Sustainable Development Goals (UNSDGs) and standards under the Global Reporting Index (GRI).

KCL is expected to emerge as the largest prime single-location copper smelting complex in the world by the year 2030, doubling its planned capacity to 1 million tonnes per annum by then.

The demand for copper is expected to strengthen progressively due to continued urbanization resulting in an appreciable demand for air conditioning systems, electric vehicles and renewable energy.

❑

Petrochemicals Business

India is emerging as a global hub for petrochemicals, with the industry within the country valued at 40 billion US dollars. The industry generates a livelihood for over one million people. It provides resources to industries such as pharmaceuticals, construction, agriculture, textiles, and automotive. India ranks sixth in the world in terms of chemical sales and accounts for 3 per cent of the global chemical industry.

The petrochemical sector is expected to emerge as the primary driver of the global oil and gas sector, accounting for more than a third of incremental oil and gas demand by the year 2030.

This is expected to be driven by the growth and profitability of petrochemical products (around 3 per cent CGAR over a decade) and stable global fuel demand (around 1 per cent CGAR).

In this decade, most of the incremental capacity is expected to emerge in Asia (about 65 per cent of green field global capacity), which could help reduce the region's import dependence. This growing Asian capacity, combined with a significant expansion by select US and Middle Eastern companies (driven by feedstock advantages), is likely to create excess supply across various chemicals, which could disrupt traditional petrochemical trade routes and feedstock access. The Indian petrochemicals industry is heavily dependent on imports with over 65 per cent of the installed refining capacity dependent on crude oil.

Amid this volatility, India's petrochemical sector emerged as a growth opportunity. With a significant import dependency and high demand growth, India has emerged as one of the most attractive markets for new petrochemical investments.

Market Access - The current per capita consumption of chemicals in India is low (one-tenth of the world average). Large population base, increasing per capita income and growing demand from end-use sectors make India an attractive market.

Capital Cost: India offers a competitive cost of building infrastructure compared to other demand growth projected at approximately 8 per cent CAGR over 15 years. India could contribute more than 10 per cent of the incremental global petrochemical growth in a decade and more than 15 world requirements - increasing the petrochemical assets by the year 2035 to address the countries domestic demand due to the presence of a large manufacturing market, low cost of labour and a customization space.

Operating cost - Availability of skilled and low-cost labour along with inexpensive power rates has helped keep the operating cost of petrochemical plants competitive.

Strategic location - Surrounded by water on three sides, India's geographical coordinates are uniquely advantageous for trade. In addition, its large market, maritime exports and a flourishing private sector have helped to strengthen the economy. India is located at the centre of the Trans-Indian

Ocean Route connecting the Western continents and East Asia. These coordinates have helped establish close contacts with West Asia, Africa and Europe from the west coast and with Southeast and East Asia from the east coast. India's west and south-west coasts—have been transit landfall points for Middle East crude. India is dependent on crude oil for more than 65 per cent of its feedstock mix. Maritime trade enables the country to meet its feedstock needs.

With major refineries and petrochemical plants located along India's coastline, the country has a unique position in the global chemical sector as it has access to petrochemical feedstock and major demand centres, both of which are met through its ports.

Skilled and Competent Talent - The Government of India has taken proactive initiatives to develop a skilled workforce for the manufacturing and service industry. The Ministry of Skill Development and Entrepreneurship (MSDE) was incorporated in the year 2014 and aims to bridge the gap between demand and supply of skilled manpower, develop vocational and technical training infrastructure for jobs and create new employment opportunities, various Skill India programmes were launched in the year 2015 for training. Specific programmes for the Chemicals and Petrochemicals sector were launched by MSDE. The availability of a competent workforce at a competitive cost contributes to reduction in capex by reducing manufacturing costs and increasing margins.

In the Union Budget 2022, the government reduced customs duty on important chemicals such as methanol, acetic acid and heavy feedstock for petroleum refining. The thrust on infrastructure spending is expected to lead to additional consumption of petrochemicals such as polymers and specialty chemicals. Agriculture-focused measures such as doubling the micro-irrigation outlay to ₹ 10,000 crore could spur demand for polymer-based irrigation products and services.

The new vehicle scrapping policy could boost polymer and elastomer consumption in anticipation of the need for new and additional vehicles.

Increased outlay on healthcare and funding for vaccination, along with requirements for syringes and other polymer-based healthcare products, could boost polymer consumption.

In general, with the increase in government spending, the need for essential petrochemicals and polymers in many regions could increase and boost local demand. The introduction of PLI schemes for key end-use sectors could increase supply and strengthen demand for petrochemical consumption. There are seven sectors in the identified sectors –

- ✓ Mobile phone manufacturing, auto and parts, medical equipment, textile products, etc.
- ✓ The estimated PLI outlay of ₹ 1.41 lakh crore augurs well for the petrochemical industry, using a significant amount of petrochemicals. In the proposed PCPIR (Petroleum, Chemicals and Petrochemicals Investment Sector) Policy 2020-35, the government will undertake related infrastructure projects such as zero liquid discharge-based common effluent treatment plant, integrated solid waste management, real-time environmental monitoring system and emergency response system. Viability gap funding of up to 20 per cent is expected to be provided for sustainable systems and may provide an additional budgetary allocation of 20 per cent.

Adani Group forayed into petrochemical business in the year 2021. It is also exploring opportunities to develop a petrochemical cluster at Mundra. The first proposed project of 2 MMT coal for PVC capacity is likely to be constructed in a phased manner. Phase one will involve development of 1,000 ktpa PVC (2,500 ktpa each sub-stage) and is expected to be commissioned by November 2024.

❑

Discharge of Social Responsibilities

With over 25 years of experience working with communities, Adani Foundation is focused on enhancing integrated development efforts across India. It believes that everyone, whoever they are and wherever they are, deserves equal access to opportunities and a fair reasonable chance for a better quality of life. Over the years, the Foundation has responded to the changing needs of society in alignment with the Sustainable Development Goals—be it sustainable livelihoods, health and nutrition and education for all or addressing environmental concerns or focusing on women's empowerment. Today, the group reaches out to 3.7 million people in 2409 villages across 16 states in India.

In March 2020, the outbreak of the Corona virus marked the beginning of an unprecedented time in modern history. The Foundation's relief efforts continued in the financial year

2021-22 to protect communities amid severe adversity brought by subsequent pandemic waves. As the situation evolved, CSR activities extended their everyday processes to create a more resilient and inclusive society.

During the financial year 2021-22, AEL spent ₹ 12.87 crore towards its CSR initiatives as a part of its commitment to give back to the society. Adani Enterprises Limited spent most of this amount on Covid-19 relief measures.

Out of the above, AEL contributed 13.24 crore to Adani Foundation for implementing various CSR interventions as detailed below.

The first half of the financial year 2021-22 was challenging due to the second phase of the Covid-19 outbreak, whose impact was worse than the first.

In addition to various relief measures for the Adani Group, AEL leveraged its sourcing, logistics and operational capabilities to procure and transport oxygen concentrators from plants across the globe and install and operate them in different parts of the country.

- ✓ Commissioning and operation and maintenance of ten oxygen plants in six states.
- ✓ Import, airlifting and transportation of 250 oxygen concentrates.
- ✓ Importing cryogenic tanks for oxygen supply.

Adani Foundation believes that education is a ladder to a life of dignity, especially for the underprivileged and vulnerable. The core philosophy behind its educational initiatives is to make 'quality' education accessible and affordable to young minds. To reach the most underprivileged populations, Adani Foundation runs cost-free schools and subsidized schools across India. Several smart learning programmes as well as government school adoption projects are being implemented in remote areas. It helps Anganwadis and Balwadis by creating a fun-filled environment for children at an early age.

Adani Vidya Mandir

Adani Vidya Mandir, Surguja was established in the year 2013 with a vision to provide free and quality education to the meritorious children of Surguja district. The school which started its journey eight years ago with 208 students now has 830 students from LKG to Class X.

School provides free study material, uniform, food and transport, is admired as 'temple of knowledge' by all the people in and around the area of Surguja. Serene environment, clean and green campus, competent faculty and student friendly infrastructure are the main attractions of Adani Vidya Mandir.

CBSE Result 2021 - All 35 students who have appeared for Class X CBSE Secondary School Examination 2021 have passed the examination with impressive marks and flying colours. Ms Neelu Yadav and Master Rinku Yadav topped the exam with 92.2 per cent.

Students pursue their higher education in various reputed institutions of Surguja and Bilaspur district. Adani Vidya Mandir illuminates the youth of Surguja with knowledge, insight, wisdom and truthfulness that transform the rural lives of Surguja.

NABET - Accredited - AVMS (Adani Vidya Mandir, Surguja) leaves no stone unturned in imparting quality education. AVMS has applied for accreditation and is setting up each system to meet the conditions under each domain prior to the preparatory journey. Each and every staff member of AVMS is committed to give his/her best to elevate the school to the expected quality set by the Quality Council of India in the areas of school administration, education and support process, performance measurement and improvement based on all the given parameters.

School Website – AVMS has its own school website (Launched in September 2021). The website has been developed by Adani Foundation, a technical and educational vertical, in accordance with the guidelines issued by CBSE for affiliated schools.

Newsletter – AVMS launched its first newsletter in April 2021 entitled *The Trendsetters*. The monthly edition of the newsletter is released on every last day of the month, giving a glimpse of the major academic and non-academic activities of the month. The Newsletter is considered one of the best mediums connect with the stakeholders.

Remedial Classes – AVMS conducts remedial classes in villages as well as after school hours to bridge the learning gap created by the pandemic.

Athletics, Sports and Games – Surguja students studying in Adani Vidya Mandir have business potential in sports. They also display great enthusiasm and enthusiasm in all athletic events. AVMS students have performed brilliantly by securing first, second and third positions in Javelin Throw, Long Jump, High Jump, 100m Run, 200m Run and 400m Run at Heart and Zonal Level Sports Meet. Class X student Master Vijay Yadav qualified for the state level sports competition and brought laurels to the school by securing third position in javelin throw and high jump.

Co-Curricular Activities – Organized by the CCA Department from time to time (periodically) in the session 2021-22 for the spirit of team-building and overall personality development of each student representing the four Houses – Ujjain House, Takshashila House, Nalanda House and Kashi House Inter-house CCA competitions are being organized.

House Masters tick against each student's name in the list of House members, for each opportunity given to them by their teachers in the respective House. Emphasis is placed on reducing discrepancy among students in terms of award of opportunities and thus seeing that no child is left behind and they are duly promoted to upgrade their budding skills.

Objective

- ✓ To support athletes in their quest to excel at the global level and instil pride in the nation.
- ✓ To create a sporting ecosystem that extends from the grassroots to the elite level.
- ✓ Creating a database of promising athletes.

'Garv Hai' - Adani Group's nationwide programme aimed at nurturing India's next generation of sports champions and their journey to represent India at national and worldwide platforms (Commonwealth Games, Asian Games and Olympics, among others) want to support them.

Starting in the year 2016, the project began accepting applications from athletes, coaches, sports academies and others across multiple sports. In the year 2019, a massive exercise spanning 29 states and 100 towns attracted 5000 applicants, out of which 19 potential athletes were selected with the desire to make it big. The campaign received over 3000 entries. Named after the group's pilot initiative designed around the 2016 Rio Olympics - PRIDE - is now a national programme to identify and empower stakeholders in the sports fraternity. Since the 2016 Rio Olympics - PRIDE - has helped over 28 athletes in boxing, wrestling, tennis, javelin throw, shooting, running, shotput, sprinting, archery and more. Proud to have supported six of the 19 athletes who competed for India at the Tokyo Olympics. Wrestlers Ravi Kumar Dahiya and Deepak Punia, boxer Amit Panghal, Indian women's hockey team captain Rani Rampal, tennis player Ankita Raina, javelin thrower Shivpal Singh and race walker KT Irfan were among them. Ravi Dahiya, backed by the Adani Group since 2019, won a silver medal in the 57 kg category at the Tokyo Olympics.

Major Performance

- ✓ Seven Tokyo Olympics qualifiers – out of nine senior athletes.
- ✓ Padma Shri and World Athlete of the Year – Rani Rampal.
- ✓ World Boxing Championship – Amit Panghal – First Indian male boxer to win silver medal.
- ✓ World Wrestling Championship – Two (Deepak Punia – Silver and Ravi Kumar Dahiya – Bronze).
- ✓ Rome Ranking Series (Wrestling) – 3 medals (Ravi Kumar Dahiya – Gold, Deepak Punia and Sajan Bhanwal – Bronze).

❑

Work Culture of Adani Group

The company's business is structured into five buckets -

1. Energy and Utilities
2. Transport and Logistics
3. Consumer Business
4. Natural Resources
5. Metals and Manufacturing

How has the group created a unique incubation umbrella?

Companies manage businesses. Adani Enterprises manages the companies.

Adani Enterprises has transitioned from the development of a single industry (the port) to a collection of several businesses (counting demerges) that have developed completely without any planning. It represents the largest collection of complete business start-ups in any listed company in India or perhaps anywhere in the world. These businesses complement scale, strategic importance and technology sophistication.

The following factors have shaped the incubation history of Adani Enterprises –

Structure – Adani Enterprises operates like a holding company, owning full or significant equity stake in its constituent businesses.

Accountability – Each AEL business vertical or constituent company is headed by a Chief Executive Officer, who periodically reports to the Chairman and the Company's Board of Directors on business growth, profitability, challenges and opportunities.

Financial support – Provides critical cash flow support during the early stages of the company capital expenditure period, which makes it possible to reduce exposure to debt, increases business liquidity and initiates a cycle of responsible reinvestment that drives business growth Helps to mature with speed.

The Playbook – The Adani Group's template of incubation represents a guide to all initiatives that have travelled in the past (and are likely to repeat). Constituent businesses enjoy access to Adani Group competencies which infuse institutional competencies into new businesses, without the need for each of these companies to reinvent the wheel, making it possible to leapfrog capabilities and time frame.

Verticalization – The Company is structured into specific verticals that operate mutually exclusive of each other. In turn, this verticalization increases focus, accountability, and specialization.

Partnership – The AEL corporate team plays the role of a strategic advisor to each of the company's businesses, ensuring that Adani Group Management Bandwidth is always available to assist, support and nurture the businesses.

Governance – Constituent businesses have immediate access to an operating framework (strategic / tactical / controlling / reporting) that makes it possible to capitalize on and build upon the available governance foundation.

At Adani Enterprises, the businesses of its constituent companies are woven around the theme of the broader Adani Group, which drives strategic synergy, direction and results.

India – They believe in India and bet on and actively invest in businesses in which the country's middle-income people will ride the consumption engine (directly or indirectly).

Ownership – The Adani Group comprises a high promoter ownership, which enhances the confidence of other stakeholders.

Futuristic – Invest in a business that is expected to be futuristic or at least prove to be relevant for the next few decades. These limit investment in that business wherever it is likely to lead to a phasing out of the sector due to a wider global direction away from that product or service.

Competitive Advantage—It has invested in a comprehensive culture of excellence—rich field experience, timely project implementation, commissioning projects faster than benchmarks, commissioned assets below industry average, developing markets, establishing leadership and to name a few evolve.

Nascent Locations – It has chosen to enter 'Mature Non-Mature' business locations – 'Mature' based on traditional interpretation of their potential and 'Non-mature' based on their vast emerging market and Adani Group value proposition.

Large-scale – These are large-scale bets in select sectors, which sends a strong message of its long-term seriousness. The unequal starting capacity would have been a drag in a conventional structure; This is an advantage in an incubation structure that quickly establishes economies of scale and potentially prevents competition.

Execution Excellence - It has a culture of expertise in the execution of projects, one of the most challenging sectors in India, marked by its ability to execute projects faster than the regional average by drawing on a recognized group level managerial excellence.

Technology - These invest in state-of-the-art technology standards that generate incremental profitability, helping to recover any additional costs paid. This superior technology pedigree effectively becomes a powerful driver of the company's competitive advantage, positioning the company around technology-driven recalls even as it exists in relatively traditional areas.

Scalable Financial Structure - It has built a strong financial foundation of owned and borrowed funds (lowest cost ever for infrastructure construction companies in India), lowest cost for longest tenure from some of the largest global lenders coherence (semi-equity).

The quality of AEL's incubation has been reflected in the pace at which its various businesses have matured. This has helped the demerged entity mature to emerge as a regional sixty one benchmark with a credible credit rating thereby maximizing stakeholder value. This shows that the influence of AEL is not limited to the incubation period, but helps to create regional leaders.

At the heart of the Adani work culture effectiveness is a strong ESG (Environmental, Social and Corporate Governance) focus that drives value in a responsible manner. Adani Enterprises Ltd. believes that it is business like to do the right thing in the right way.

These are engaged in business for the benefit of all its stakeholders. The customer should be benefited through an enhanced product or service, the employee should get pride, remuneration and career growth. The investor should get a return on capital employed over competitive investment options should generate better returns, the community should benefit from its presence, the government should benefit through taxes and livelihood generation, while its vendors should benefit through outsourcing of products and services.

This commitment to creating integrated value for all its stakeholders represents the bedrock of its long-term existence. This is reflected in increased financial capital, manufactured capital, human capital, intellectual capital, social and relationship capital, and natural capital.

The environmental component addresses the world's priority that businesses consume environmentally responsible resources, consume an optimal amount, recycle waste, consume modest amounts of finite fossil fuels, and resist climate change. Let's build, control the carbon footprint.

Social component - addresses the need to invest in employees, vendor/customer relationships and community well-being.

Governance component - imparts strategic clarity, prioritizes values-cum-codes of conduct, selects a prudent Board of Directors and indicates alignment with UNGC principles, creates a responsible expectation among stakeholders.

The combination—environmental, social and refuge—provides a platform for sustainable development.

At Adani Group, it has centralized the importance of integrity in its operations. People hold the highest standards when it comes to personal and collective integrity, which is reflected in their adherence to standards set by the government, other regulatory agencies and peer global standards. Over the years, its commitment to integrity has been reflected in gender respect, zero tolerance for sexual harassment, impatience for ethical violations, a commitment to fair recruitment and assessment without bias, respect for the dignity of people and the integrity of the environment, and extends to respect and compliance with laws.

The Adani Group has business operations that are driven around a high sense of discipline in terms of compliance, documentation, reporting and transparency on the one hand and operational standards on the other, which is the basis for sustained superior performance.

At Adani Group, the success of its strategic direction is influenced by the Board of Directors. Its directors represent the strategic 'pilots' of its direction, helping the company accelerate or correct course. It has placed a premium on its board composition, which includes prestige achievers. The board has a good proportion of independent directors who can speak their mind and influence the board.

At the core of the group's sustainability lies its ESG (Environment - Social - Governance) commitment. This commitment is formalized through a policy. Furthermore, this ethic is not only documented but alive. Over the years, this commitment has been reflected in active investments in equipment, certifications, people and initiatives directed at moderating the company's carbon footprint. The company's social commitment is reflected in various initiatives to enhance value for employees, vendors, customers and the community.

A company's governance commitment includes an explanation of how it intends to conduct business. In the Adani Group, planning is done for the long term. Its investments are not driven by considerations of short-term arbitrage, but by the sustainable long-term value we can generate.

This is reflected in the verticals of the group's presence. Some locations may be considered relatively nascent, believing that as the lifestyle revolution expands and the consumption market grows, its businesses will progressively mature, its relevance will get deeper.

Adani Group is present in diversified businesses that enrich the overall value of its portfolio. Over the years, this diversity has strengthened its ability to withstand specific regional adversities. Furthermore, its ability to cross-support other businesses has enhanced its corporate stability.

At Adani Group, we believe that growth can best be achieved when the promoter takes a strategic direction, remains engaged in the business at a strategic level but entrusts day-to-day management to professionals.

This arrangement has been catalysed by investment in processes and systems, a scalable foundation that will enable the company to grow profitably and sustainably.

Adani New Industries intends and proposes to build the largest integrated platform with three segments –

1. Manufacturing Supply Chain Products

The company seeks to manufacture key components such as polysilicon, ingots, wafers, solar cell cum modules, wind turbines, generators, electrolyzers, fuel cells and ancillary products for renewable energy generation. The company's solar manufacturing capacity of 3.5 GW (an expansion of the existing 1.5 gigawatts to 2 gigawatts) is a part of the ANIL portfolio.

2. Green Hydrogen Production

The company will focus on integrated renewable energy generation through solar and wind power capabilities. These will power the electrolyzer to produce green hydrogen. The company will build a pipeline to transport green hydrogen from Khavda to Mundra for manufacturing downstream products.

3. Downstream Products

This segment will focus on large downstream products associated with manufacturing of ammonia, urea, methanol/ethanol and other anchor projects.

Mundra Green Hydrogen is the only one in India backed by a player with rich expertise in renewable energy and ports infrastructure. The hub is supported by ongoing investments to increase polysilicon capacity by financial year 2024-25 and a Memorandum of Understanding with POSCO to build an integrated green steel plant.

The Mundra Green Hydrogen Hub will support a number of applications of green hydrogen including substantial use within Adani's portfolio business –

- ✓ Green manure
- ✓ Ammonia Export
- ✓ Marine Dynamics (Ammonia, Methanol)
- ✓ Methanol for Diesel Blending
- ✓ Steel and Petrochemicals
- ✓ Fuel cell mobility at Mundra and other ports
- ✓ Polysilicon, CGD, edible oil and other small scale users of H2
- ✓ Co-firing power generation

Solar Manufacturing

Perhaps the most exciting and challenging development coming from India is the sweeping change in its renewable energy landscape. India not only plays a supporting role in the global renewable energy transition, it plays a leading role in changing its reality within the country and raising its prestige in the global community of nations. The result is an unprecedented growth opportunity for companies across the regional value chain, whether engaged in manufacturing renewable energy products or generating clean energy. The growing scope is reflected in the following details –

India ranked third in the year 2021 Renewable Energy Country Attractiveness Index. India has set an ambitious target of achieving 175 gigawatts of renewable energy capacity by the end of the year 2022 and 500 gigawatts by the year 2030. It is arguably the largest renewable energy expansion programme ever undertaken by any country.

This propounded policy translated into positive ground realities. India has about 63 gigawatts of renewable energy capacity under various stages of construction. By the year 2030, installed electricity capacity from non-fossil fuels is expected to increase to 66 per cent of the total national electricity generation capacity.

In line with this projected change, India's renewable energy generation capacity addition was estimated at 16 gigawatts in the financial year 22-23, its highest ever annual addition.

There is a basis for national optimism. As of March 31, 2022, India's cumulative renewable energy generation capacity (including hydro) stood at 150 gigawatts and it is expected to accelerate from this point, with good reason. Due to India's favourable location in the solar belt (400 S to 400 N), India is one of the best solar energy recipients marked by abundant availability of sunlight.

In such a situation, the picture is expected to be stronger. Coal-based electricity is expected to account for just 33 per cent of the country's total installed capacity of 817 gigawatts in the year 2030 (53 per cent of the current installed capacity of 393 gigawatts) and just 10.5 per cent in the year 2047, according to the government's vision document.

This projection is in line with Prime Minister Narendra Modi's net-zero commitment to make India self-sufficient in its energy needs by the 100th year of Independence and increase the share of renewable energy from 22 per cent to 67 per cent by the year 2047. Of the 1,325 gigawatts of projected installed capacity by the year 2047, 1,125 gigawatts is expected to come from renewable energy, 140 gigawatts from coal, 10 gigawatts from gas, and 7 Giga Watt to 50 gigawatts of nuclear power generation capacity.

The following points give an optimistic summation of where India is and where it intends to go –

- ✓ India is the fifth largest country in the world in terms of solar rooftop installations and one of the fastest growing countries in terms of overall renewable energy capacity addition.
- ✓ The Government of India not only announced a strategic direction, it implemented numerous initiatives and reforms to promote and encourage domestic manufacturing of products.
- ✓ In the Union Budget for the financial year 2021-22, the government announced the allocation of ₹ 19,500 for Production Linked Incentive (PLI) to increase manufacturing of high-efficiency modules by giving priority to fully integrated manufacturing units in solar photovoltaic (PV) modules.
- ✓ In April 2021, a production-linked incentive programme was launched to push gigawatt-scale manufacturing of high-efficiency solar photovoltaic modules with an outlay of ₹ 45 billion.
- ✓ In June 2021, the Indian Renewable Energy Development Agency Limited (IREDA) invited bids from solar module manufacturers to set up solar manufacturing units under the central government's 4500 crore production linked incentive scheme.
- ✓ In July 2021, the Ministry of New and Renewable Energy announced its decision to launch Phase II of the Rooftop Solar Programme, which aims to install 4000 megawatts of RTS capacity in the residential sector by the year 2022, with provision for subsidies.

- ✓ Customs duty on solar inverters increased from 5 per cent to 20 per cent and on solar lanterns from 5 per cent to 15 per cent to encourage domestic production.

Adani Group forayed into solar manufacturing in the year 2017. The company's manufacturing units and Research & Development (R&D) facilities are located in the Electronics Manufacturing Cluster, are situated in a SEZ at Mundra, supported by manufacturing units for critical components (EVA, back-sheet, glass, junction boxes and solar cells and string interconnect ribbons). The company had a total capacity of 1.5 gigawatts by March 31, 2022.

The company is respected for its scale, speed and quality of operations. The company is India's first and largest vertically integrated solar company offering products and services across the photovoltaic spectrum. The company commissioned India's largest solar cell and module manufacturing facility with a total installed capacity of 1200 megawatts each (later de-bottlenecked to 1500 megawatts each). They have unmatched acumen to meet new challenges, adopt cutting edge technologies and deliver impeccable quality.

The company sources state-of-the-art technology equipment from best-in-class manufacturers. It has achieved cost leadership, high operational scale and transformation in standards at par with global standards. The manufacturing facility is likely to be scaled up to 3.5 gigawatts of modules and cells.

- ✓ The company recorded the highest annual sales volume among all Indian solar photovoltaic manufacturers.
- ✓ The company is India's leading module supplier in DCR (accounting for more than half of India's total DCR production).
- ✓ The company is India's largest solar PV module supplier in the CPSU segment.

- ✓ The company enjoys the largest solar rooftop market share of KUSUM schemes with over 50 per cent pan-India sharc.
- ✓ The company is the first and now the largest manufacturer of bifacial cells in India.
- ✓ The credit rating of the company has improved to A (positive outlook).
- ✓ The order book of the company stood at 700 megawatts at the end of the financial year.
- ✓ The company became a member of PV Cycle, a non-profit organization that aims to provide collective waste management and legal compliance services to companies and PV module waste holders worldwide.
- ✓ The company expanded its solar retail footprint to 21 states (covering over 2000 cities for distribution of solar panels in India).
- ✓ Solar product sales reached 1104 megawatts in the financial year 2021-22 as against 1158 megawatts in the financial year 2020-21, despite the Covid outbreak.
- ✓ The company sold around 251 megawatts under the Kusum scheme.
- ✓ sThe company is engaged in cost optimization, efficiency improvement in wafers, B grade cell reduction, reduced glue wastage, alternate source development for cell line and module line parts and life extension of high cost consumables.

❑

Adani-Hindenburg Controversy

In recent months, the Adani Group, one of India's largest conglomerates, has been embroiled in a controversy sparked by a bombshell report from short-selling firm Hindenburg Research. The report, titled "Adani Group: How the World's 3rd Richest Man is Pulling the Largest Con in Corporate History," leveled serious allegations against the group, accusing it of engaging in stock manipulation and accounting fraud on a massive scale. The fallout from the report has been significant, with billions of dollars wiped off the market value of Adani's stocks and widespread concern among investors. In this article, we will delve into the details of the Adani-Hindenburg controversy, exploring the allegations, the impact on the group, and the steps taken by Adani to seek redemption.

Hindenburg Research is a prominent short-selling firm based in the United States that specializes in forensic financial research. Led by Nathan Anderson, the firm has gained a reputation for targeting high-profile companies and exposing fraudulent practices. Hindenburg Research employs a team of analysts and former journalists with expertise in equity, credit, and derivatives analysis. The firm has previously exposed wrongdoings by companies such as Nikola Corporation and Aphria.

Hidenberg's Allegations Against the Adani Group

In its report, Hindenburg Research makes serious allegations against the Adani Group, accusing it of engaging in stock manipulation and accounting fraud schemes over several decades. The report claims that the group has orchestrated a brazen scheme amounting to ₹17.8 trillion (US$ 218 billion), involving offshore shell entities in tax havens to facilitate corruption, money laundering, and taxpayer theft. Hindenburg Research further alleges that the Adani family members have built and managed a complex network of offshore entities in countries like Cyprus, Mauritius, and the UAE.

The report contends that the Adani Group's stock valuations are significantly overvalued, even when considering their financials at face value. It also raises concerns about the group's compliance with shareholding limits set by the Securities and Exchange Board of India (SEBI).

The release of the Hindenburg Research report had immediate and significant consequences for the Adani Group. Within days, the group's stocks plummeted, resulting in billions of dollars in market value losses. The market volatility and uncertainty surrounding the allegations have led to concerns about the group's ability to repay its debts and the potential impact on Indian banks and institutions.

The report's findings have also affected major investors, including the Life Insurance Corporation of India (LIC), which reportedly lost over USD 2 billion in just two days. The broader implications of the report and the potential rise of non-performing assets in Indian banks have raised concerns about the stability of the financial sector.

In response to the Hindenburg Research report, the Adani Group vehemently denied the allegations, describing the report as malicious, mischievous, and unresearched. The group criticized the report's selective misinformation and baseless allegations, asserting that they had been tested and rejected by India's highest court. Adani also highlighted the report's admission that Hindenburg Research held short positions in Adani Group companies, suggesting a potential conflict of interest.

To restore investor confidence and address the allegations, the Adani Group has taken several steps. It has prepaid debt, bought back bonds, and conducted investor roadshows to showcase its financial stability and transparency. The group has sought to highlight its compliance with disclosure requirements under local laws and its commitment to addressing any concerns raised by regulators.

The Investigation and Regulatory Measures

India's markets regulator is currently conducting an investigation into the allegations made by Hindenburg Research. The investigation, which is expected to conclude by August 14, will determine if there were any regulatory failures or price manipulations within the Adani Group. The outcome of the investigation will play a crucial role in restoring investor trust and shaping the future of the group.

In response to the controversy, the regulator is also considering proposing additional disclosure requirements for foreign funds holding significant stakes in Indian stocks or companies. This move aims to address concerns about oversight and improve transparency in sprawling conglomerates like the Adani Group.

The release of the Hindenburg Research report had an immediate and substantial impact on the market value of Adani Group stocks. Over a span of just a few days, the group lost billions of dollars in market capitalization. The stocks of several Adani Group companies, including Adani Transmission, Adani Total Gas, and Adani Green Energy, experienced significant declines.

The decline in market value has also affected Gautam Adani's personal net worth. Bloomberg's Billionaires Index initially showed him as Asia's richest man and the fourth richest person globally. However, since the release of the report, his fortune has reportedly decreased by a fifth, amounting to a significant loss.

In a detailed 413-page response, the Adani Group countered the allegations made by Hindenburg Research. The group dismissed the report as a calculated attack on India, its institutions, and the growth story of the country. Adani accused Hindenburg of spreading misinformation and concealed facts to serve its own selfish motives.

The response also highlighted the group's compliance with disclosure requirements and the lack of independent or journalistic fact-finding in Hindenburg's questions. Adani claimed that the report lacked substance and was based on selective regurgitation of public disclosures and rhetorical innuendos.

The Supreme Court has deferred further hearings in the Adani-Hindenburg case to August. The case involves allegations made by US-based short-seller Hindenburg against the Adani Group, accusing it of accounting fraud, stock manipulation, and corporate governance lapses. The Adani Group denies these allegations.

The Chief Justice of India (CJI) had inquired about the status of the investigation during a hearing on July 11, to which the solicitor-general responded that the Securities and Exchange Board of India (Sebi) has time until August to conclude its investigations.

❑

Adani Group: Board of Directors, Companies and Achievements

As on March 31, 2022, the Board of the group company had eight members including four executive directors and four independent directors. There is one woman Independent Director on the Board.

Gautam Adani – Chairman, Adani Group

Gautam Adani is the founder and chairman of the Adani Group, which ranks among the top 3 industrial conglomerates in India. A first generation entrepreneur, Shri Adani is driven by the core philosophy of 'Growth with Goodness' with his nation-building vision. Each of the group's businesses focuses on helping build world-class infrastructure capabilities to help accelerate India's growth.

Adani Group comprises 7 publicly listed entities with a combined market capitalization of over 242.73 billion dollars (as on August 29, 2022) with businesses spread across energy, ports and logistics, mining and resources, gas, defence and aerospace, and airports. The group has established a leadership position in India in each of its business segments.

For Mr. Adani, nation building means transforming India's coastline by building ports and logistics hubs. For him, nation building also means strengthening the country's energy security and bridging the urban-rural divide by bringing electricity to millions of people living in India's hinterland. For Mr. Adani, nation building also includes promoting food security by building a modern agricultural supply chain and empowering farmers. Each of his industrial endeavours has created thousands of jobs.

Mr. Adani aims to make India one of the most important players in sustainable energy by investing in a renewable ecosystem spanning solar manufacturing, production and solar park businesses. He dreams of making India self-reliant in defence and security.

The group has a strong and robust track record of working with global business leaders keen to participate in India's growth story. The global expertise of these international companies in their respective businesses, combined with the project execution and market capabilities of the Adani Group, has forged an enduring partnership. Partners include Wilmar Group, Total SA and Elbit Systems.

Adani Foundation, the Corporate Social Responsibility arm of the group, is one of his key interest areas. The Foundation's pan-India initiatives in the critical areas of education, healthcare, sustainable livelihoods and community infrastructure development touch over 3.4 million lives annually in 2315 villages across 18 Indian states.

Dr. Priti Adani – Chairperson, Adani Foundation

An educationist and a qualified doctor with a Bachelor of Dental Surgery (BDS), Dr. Priti Adani works in the area of Corporate Social Responsibility (CSR). Focusing on the mantra of growth with goodness, Dr. Priti Adani is a business woman as well as a responsible citizen, helping to create sustainable solutions to complex problems.

She has led the Adani Foundation, founded by herself, for the last two decades—ensuring that the Adani Group helps to transform the lives of as many people as possible.

Under her guidance and leadership, Adani Foundation is carrying out its activities in four major areas, namely Education, Community Health, Sustainable Livelihood Development and Infrastructure Development. Presently, the foundation helps in the upliftment of 34 lakh people annually across 18 states of the country.

Rajesh S. Adani – Managing Director

He has been in charge of Adani Group's operations since inception and is responsible for business relations. His personal and proactive approach coupled with competitive spirit has catalysed the growth of the organization.

Pranav Adani – Director

He led the joint venture with the Wilmar Group in Singapore, turning it from a single refinery edible oil business into a pan-India food company.

He also heads the group's oil and gas, city gas distribution and agriculture infrastructure businesses. His understanding and analysis has helped businesses scale. Mr. Pranav Adani has been honoured with several awards, Global Man of the Year Award 2009 being one of them.

Malay Mahadevia - Whole Time Director - APSEZA and CEO - AAHL

Dr. Malay Mahadevia joined Adani in the year 1992 and worked on developing Mundra Port from concept to commissioning.

Dr. Malay Mahadevia was awarded the 'Outstanding Manager of the Year' by the Ahmedabad Management Association in the year 2002. In the year 2008, he was awarded a PhD degree by Gujarat University in the field of 'Coastal Ecology Around Mundra Region'.

He is a member of the Centre for Engineering and Technology (CEPT), Federation of Indian Chambers of Commerce and Industry (FICCI), The Associated Chambers of Commerce and Industry of India (ASSOCHAM), Gujarat University, Confederation of Indian Industry and Gujarat Chamber of Commerce and Industry, Maritime. He is a member of a number of professional bodies including the Advisory Board for Studies.

Before joining Adani Group, he worked at Government Dental College, Ahmedabad as Assistant Professor.

Anil Sardana - MD and CEO, Adani Transmission Limited

An Electrical Engineering graduate from University of Delhi, ICWAI alumnus and Postgraduate Diploma holder in Management, Anil Sardana's academic career is as diverse as his vast experience spanning Power Plants, EPC business, infrastructure sector in Coal Washeries, Power Transmission, Retail Power Distribution and Telecom.

He has also been the face of industry forums in diverse roles such as Chairman of the National Committee of Power and Business Advisory Board of CII, UN Women and Miracle Feet (Section 8 Company) and others. In a career spanning nearly four decades, he has held key positions with BSES and Tata

Group (16 years), NTPC (14 years), before joining the Adani Group in the year 2018.

Vinay Prakash – Director

He is a Mechanical Engineer with over 25 years of rich experience in Integrated Resource Management, Mining, Shipping, and Logistics and Port and Power sectors. Since inception, he has been involved in nurturing the integrated resource management and mining businesses of the company. The result is that AEL's Indian mining business has been featured among the Top 10 Great Places to Work in India in the year 2020, winning several awards across forums for commitment to environment, community engagement, sustainability, safety and CSR. Shri Prakash has held prominent positions in various professional bodies such as President.

He is the ASSOCHAM's National Council on Coal, Member of India-Indonesia CEO Forum, Chairman of Standing Committee on Coal and Industry in FMI. He has been recognized at several global forums including Global Business Excellence Award in Coal Sector at the World Petrocoal Congress 2017.

Hemant M Nerurkar – Independent and Non-Executive Director

He is associated with many professional organizations such as Tata Steel, Indian Institute of Metals, INSDAG and AIMA. With over 35 verticals of experience in the steel industry, Shri Nerurkar is an executive with multi-dimensional experience ranging from project execution, manufacturing, quality control, supply chain and marketing. During his illustrious career, Shri Nerurkar has received several awards including Tata Gold Medal in the year 2004, SMS Demag Excellence Award in the year 2002, and also have been awarded with prizes like Steel 80 Award—1990, SAIL Gold Medal - 1989, Visvesvaraya Award - 1988 and NMD Award in the year 1987.

V Subramanian - Independent and Non-Executive and Minister of Renewable Energy (MNRE)

Independent and Non-Executive and Minister of Renewable Energy (MNRE), where he took important initiatives for the reform and development of the renewable energy sector, including the introduction of feed-in tariff determination. As Additional Secretary and Financial Adviser, Ministry of Civil Aviation, Tourism and Culture, he was on the boards of Air India, Indian Airlines, Airports Authority of India, Helicopter Corporation of India and India Tourism Development Corporation. Later, as a financial advisor, in the Ministry of Rural Development, he implemented national rural development schemes including the National Rural Employment Guarantee Scheme. Currently, he is an independent consultant. He was the Business Development Advisor to the Council of Industrial and Scientific Research in New Delhi for one year after his retirement. He was the Chairman of the Research Council of the Indian Institute of Petroleum in an honorary capacity for three years. He led the Indian Wind Energy Association as General Secretary and later as President from the year 2008 to the year 2018. Currently, he is on the advisory board of the Indian Energy Exchange.

Mrs. Vijayalakshmi Joshi - Independent and Non-Executive Directors

Mrs. Vijayalakshmi Joshi Independent and Non-Executive Director has been appointed as Officer on Special Duty in the Ministry of Drinking Water and Sanitation. She led the Swachh Bharat Abhiyan, Swachh Bharat programme at the state level and is the Deputy Managing Director of Government companies like Gujarat Mineral Development Corporation Limited.

A 1980 batch IAS officer of the Gujarat Cadre, Mrs. Vijayalakshmi Joshi has served in various positions in the State and at the Centre. She has been Joint and Additional Secretary in the Ministry of Commerce between the years 2011 and 2014. She assumed the charge of Secretary, Ministry of Panchayati Raj on May 1, 2014. She has chaired prestigious councils and committees with the Indian Banks' Association and is the chairperson of the ASSOCHAM National Council for Banking and Finance.

Shri Narendra Marpadi - Independent and Non-Executive Director

A distinguished banking professional with over 40 years of professional experience, he is a certified member of the Indian Institute of Bankers. He began his career as an Officer Trainee with Corporation Bank. He was appointed as the CMD of Indian Overseas Bank in the year 2010 and retired as CMD in the year 2014. During his long career in the banking industry, he has achieved important benchmarks such as team building, brand enhancement, priority sector initiatives, branch expansion and risk management. Shri Narendra has been honoured with prestigious awards for his exceptional contribution to the banking industry. He has been a member of RBI's Technical Advisory Committee on Money, Foreign Exchange and Director Government Securities Markets.

Jayakumar Janakraj – CEO – Adani Global Singapore and Adani Conex

Jayakumar Janakraj joined the Adani Group in September 2013 and served as the Chief Executive Officer of the Adani Global in Singapore and the Chief Executive Officer of Adani's Data Centre business.

Jayakumar Janakraj has over 21 years of rich experience in resource uddioh, creation and development of world class mining projects and resource companies. Prior to joining the

Adani Group, Jayakumar Janakraj was with Sterlite Industries for 18 years, during which he held a number of executivc rolcs, most recently as CEO and Director of Konkola Copper Mines, Zambia. Jayakumar Janakraj holds a Mechanical Engineering degree from PSG College of Technology, Coimbatore.

In the year 2006, Jayakumar Janakraj was awarded the Gold Medal by the Indian Institute of Metallurgy for his significant contribution to the non-ferrous metallurgical industry and was also listed by the International Who's Who of Professionals (2009).

Sudipta Bhattacharya - CEO, Adani Group North America and CTO, Adani Group

Sudipta Bhattacharya is the CEO of Adani Group - North America. He is also the Chief Technology Officer (CTO) of the group. Prior to his current roles, he also held the positions of CEO of Adani Ports and SEZ (APSEZ) and Chief Strategy Officer for the group. Before joining the Adani Group, he was the CEO of Invensys' Security and Control and Software Business. Prior to Invensis Ltd., he was Senior Vice President of SAP's Supply Chain Management, Manufacturing and Engineering product portfolio. He also worked for the Tata Group in India for 10 years managing chemical plant operations, engineering projects and supply chain operations.

Vikram Tandon – Group Chief Human Resource Officer

Vikram is a seasoned HR professional with over three decades of experience across diverse businesses, geographies and cultures. His expertise lies in the thoughtful management of the intersection of strategy, talent and organization culture with wide-ranging results in organizational effectiveness, talent management, succession planning and leadership development.

Before joining the Adani Group, Vikram held several transformational leadership roles across global brands such as HSBC India, American International Group, Inchcap plc, Dubai and ANZ Grindlays Bank.

Vikram holds a Master's degree in Human Resources from XLRI Jamshedpur and certification in Leading Change, Management and Innovation from Harvard Business School. Vikram has also been the past President of National HRD Network, Mumbai Chapter and recipient of GNOSIS Excellence Award from XLRI.

Gaurav Gupta – CEO, Adani Capital

Gaurav Gupta joined the Adani Group in October 2016 to set up a financial services business. Gaurav has over 20 years of investment banking / corporate finance and advisory experience, having advised Indian and international clients on domestic and cross border M&A and capital market transactions.

Before joining the Adani Group, he was the Managing Director and India Head of Macquarie Capital, where he was instrumental in building the market-leading infrastructure advisory franchise. Gaurav is a qualified Chartered Accountant and has worked with multinational companies such as Nomura, Lehman, Rothschild and Arthur Andersen.

Anshu Malik – CEO of Adani Wilmar Limited

Mr. Malik has been a part of Adani Wilmar since its inception in 1999 and has risen from the position of a Deputy General Manager to his current role of Head of the organization. He was instrumental in the launch of Fortune as India's No.1 edible oil brand within just 20 months. His critical insight has ensured that Fortune has maintained its leadership position to this day.

Before joining Adani Wilmar, Shri Malik was associated with National Dairy Development Board (NDDB) as Head of

Operations in Dhara. Earlier, he worked with Gujarat Cooperative Milk Marketing Federation (Amul), Anand in sales, marketing, distribution and exports.

Shri Malik is a graduate in Dairy Technology from National Dairy Research Institute, Karnal and a Postgraduate Diploma in Rural Management from the Institute of Rural Management, Anand (IRMA).

Suresh Mangalani - CEO of Adani Gas Limited

Suresh is a seasoned professional with 29 years of diverse experience in many businesses. He has vast experience in oil and gas projects and has prime expertise in conceptualizing, negotiating, forming and successfully operating CT gas distribution business and joint ventures.

Suresh started his career with Kelvinator (now Whirlpool India) and later worked with GAIL, Mahanagar Gas (a joint venture between GAIL and Shell) and India Gas Solutions (a joint venture between RIL and BP). Prior to joining Adani Gas Limited, Suresh was working with Reliance Industries Limited as Senior Vice President and Commercial Head of Petroleum Retail Business. Suresh is a Cost Accountant by profession and holds the educational degrees of M.Com, LLB, ACMA, FCS.

Jayant Parimal - Advisor to the Chairman

With a diverse educational background and an illustrious career in the Indian Administrative Service, Mr. Jayant Parimal brings a wealth of experience to the Adani Group. An IAS officer of 1989 batch, he did BE in Electrical Engineering from MNIT Allahabad in 1988, CAF from ICFAI, Hyderabad in 2002, Masters in International Law and Economics from the World Trade Institute, Bern in 2004 and LLB from Gujarat University in 2007.

Mr. Parimal worked in various positions with the Government of Gujarat and the Government of India till 2006. He joined the Adani Group as Chief Executive Officer, handling the renewables business and served as an advisor to the Chairman. Prior to this he was the chairman at Reliance Industries Limited.

Pranav Vora - CEO, Shipping

A BSc from California State University, USA, Pranav Vora has over 18 years of experience in the field of shipping, especially in the commercial dry bulk sector.

Mr. Vora joined the Adani Group in the year 1993 and was responsible for cargo handling at ports, chartering Handymax for transportation of agricultural products, polymers, metallurgical coke and steam coal.

He currently leads the shipping business of the group and is based in Dubai, UAE.

Ashish Rajvanshi - President and Head, Office of the Speaker

Ashish Rajvanshi leads the Adani Group's philosophy of growth with stability as the Head of the Office of the Chairman. His deep passion for nation building and the phenomenal potential in India's defence and aerospace sector envisaged the group's foray into business.

Before joining Adani in the year 2014, Ashish led the energy and infrastructure agenda in international markets for the global management consulting firm Booz Allen Hamilton (later Booz & Company) in London. On the academic front, Ashish holds a Computer Science Engineering degree from the Delhi Institute of Technology (DIT) and an MBA from IIM Ahmedabad.

Adani Group Joint Ventures and Associates

1. Adani Road & OM Limited (a subsidiary of Adani Road Transport Limited, a wholly owned subsidiary of the Company).

2. Barakumari Karki Road Private Limited (a subsidiary of Adani Road Transport Limited, a wholly owned subsidiary of the Company).
3. Panagarh Palsit Road Private Limited (A subsidiary of Adani Road Transport Limited, which is a wholly owned subsidiary of the Company).
4. MUNDRA PETROCHEM LIMITED.
5. Mundra Solar Energy Limited (a subsidiary of Adani Tradecom Limited, a wholly owned subsidiary of the Company).
6. Mahanadi Mines and Minerals Private Limited.
7. MUNDRA WINDTECH LIMITED.
8. Adani Cement Industries Limited.
9. GVK Airport Developers Limited (a subsidiary of Adani Airport Holdings Limited, which is a wholly owned subsidiary of the Company).
10. GVK Airport Holdings Limited (a subsidiary of GVK Airport Developers Limited, which is a subsidiary of the Company).
11. Mumbai International Airport Limited (via GVK Airport Developers Limited and Adani Airport Holdings Limited, a subsidiary of the Company, a subsidiary company).
12. Navi Mumbai International Airport Limited (a subsidiary of Mumbai International Airport Limited, which is a step down subsidiary of the Company).
13. Bangalore Airport & Infrastructure Developers Limited (a subsidiary of GVK Airport Developers Limited, which is a subsidiary of the Company).
14. Bhagalpur Waste Water Limited.
15. Bowen Rail Operation Pte Ltd (a subsidiary of Adani Global Private Ltd, Singapore which is a subsidiary of the Company).

16. Bowen Rail Company Private Limited (a subsidiary of Bowen Rail Operation Private Limited, Singapore which is a step down subsidiary of the Company).
17. Adani Petrochemicals Limited.
18. Noida Data Centre Limited.
19. PLR Systems (India) Limited (A subsidiary of Ordefence Systems Limited, which is a subsidiary of the Company).
20. Adani Digital Labs Private Limited
21. Mumbai Travel Retail Pvt. (A subsidiary of Adani Airport Holdings Limited, which is a wholly owned subsidiary of the Company).
22. April Moon Retail Private Limited (a subsidiary of Adani Airport Holdings Limited, a wholly owned subsidiary of the Company).
23. Astraise Services IFSC Limited (A subsidiary of Adani Defence Systems & Technologies Limited, a wholly owned subsidiary of the Company).
24. Mundra Solar Technologies Limited (a subsidiary of Adani Infrastructure Private Limited, which is a wholly owned subsidiary of the Company).
25. Mundra Aluminium Limited.
26. Adani Data Network Limited.
27. Badaun Hardoi Road Pvt. Ltd.
28. Unnao Prayagraj Road Pvt. Ltd.
29. Hardoi Unnao Road Pvt. Ltd.
30. Adani New Industries Limited.
31. Bengal Tech Park Limited.
32. Adani Copper Tubes Limited.

33. Cleartrip Private Limited (20 per cent).

34. Adani Conex Private Limited (50 per cent)

Adani Enterprises FY 21-22 Performance

A snapshot of our financial year 2021-22 performance IRM volumes in the financial year 2021-22 stood at 64.4 MMT in the financial year 2021-22 as against 63.4 MMT in the financial year 2020-21. Mining services volume in the financial year 2021-22 increased by 58 per cent to 27.7 MMT. Solar module volume 1158 megawatts in the financial year 2020-21.

Acquisition

Mumbai and Navi Mumbai Airports. Jaipur, Guwahati and Thiruvananthapuram Airports completed initial public offerings and listed the equity shares of the joint venture Adani Wilmar on Indian stock exchanges. In the road business, won a major project worth ₹ 17,100 crore for construction and maintenance of 464 kilometres of green field Ganga Expressway projects in Uttar Pradesh.

Announced entry into a new green energy value chain under Adani New Industries to produce hydrogen at lowest cost. The revised Board Charter implemented and established new Board committees, including a Corporate Responsibility Committee, to provide assurance for all ESG commitments.

Consolidated EBITDA grew by 45 per cent to ₹ 4,726 crore, mainly due to Mumbai airport acquisition and better margins in IRM business.

IRM revenue grew 2X to ₹ 1,842 crore with a corresponding increase in EBITDA following improvement in realisations.

The airports business generated a healthy ₹ 1,091 crore EBITDA during the year following the acquisition of Mumbai airport.

Major Achievements of the Financial Year 21-22

✓ Growth in IRM segment and revenue growth due to higher JIS realisations.

✓ Growth in IRM due to better margins and airport business due to acquisition of MIAL.

✓ Decrease in PAT attributable to higher finance cost and depreciation in development of new businesses.

✓ Increase in net worth after acquisition of MIAL and listing of Adani Wilmar.

Financial Year 2021-22 Business-Performance

Airport Infrastructure

✓ Adani Airport handled 36.9 million passengers, over 320,000 air traffic movements and 6.65 lakh MT of cargo across seven operational airports.

Road and Highway Construction Business

✓ Concession agreement signed for ₹ 17,100 crore 464 kilometre long Ganga Expressway project in Uttar Pradesh under the BOT model.

✓ LOA received for 67 kilometre Kagal Satara project.

Maharashtra Under BOT Model

✓ Construction of 100 lane kilometres was completed during the year.

Canned and Branded Edible Oil

✓ Revenue of Adani Wilmar (50:50 Joint Venture and consolidated based on the equity method of consolidation revenue) grew by 46 per cent from ₹ 37,090 crore in the financial year 2020-21 to ₹ 54,214 crore in the financial year 2021-22.

✓ Fortune Brands continued to lead the domestic retail consumer pack market with 20 per cent market share.

58 Per Cent increase in Digging Volume

✓ 27.7 MMT, Revenue up 15 per cent at ₹ 2,360 crore, EBITDA at ₹1,075 crore.

✓ Production of 27.7 MMT includes 15 MMT from PEKB.

✓ 3.3 MMT from GPIII, 6.4 MMT from Talabira and 3.0 MMT from Kurmitar mine.

✓ Dispatch increased by 67.7 per cent to 25.2 MMT, which included 12.3 MMT from PEKB, 3.5 MMT from GPIII, 6.4 MMT from Talabira and 3.0 MMT from Kurmitar mine.

Integrated Resource Management

✓ Volume was 64.4 MMT (63.4 MMT in the financial year 2020-21).

✓ Revenue at ₹ 249,263 crore as against ₹ 24,280 crore due to improvement in receipts.

✓ Revenue and margin increased to ₹ 1,842 crore in line with the growth revenue from operations

In the financial year 2021-22, after recovering from the pandemic, there was an increase in gross sales, accompanied by higher material receipts.

Over the years, the company maintained operating performance growth as measured in terms of EBITDA. In the financial year 2021-22, there was strong growth from established and growing businesses.

As the company developed airports, roads and other new businesses, its profit declined in the financial year 2021-22 owing to higher finance cost and depreciation in infra-heavy businesses.

The company's net worth has increased every year during the last few years, indicating a firm financial foundation.

The company invested deeply in airports, roads and other new businesses and incurred higher finance costs, reducing its interest cover to 1.9 in the financial year 2021-22.

The Adani Group comprises seven publicly traded companies with a market capitalization of 206 billion US dollars as of April 29, 2022.

Situation

Adani Group has established itself as a leader in Transport Logistics and Energy Utility portfolio businesses in India. The group has focused on sizeable infrastructure development.

Reliability

The Adani Group comprises four IG-rated businesses and is India's only infrastructure investment grade bond issuer.

The robust 26 per cent growth in consolidated EBITDA of the group's listed companies in the financial year 2021-22 reflects the utility nature of the businesses.

APL EBITDA improved due to better tariff realization and higher prior period accruals.

AGAL's continued growth in EBITDA was supported by increased revenue and cost efficiency, driven through analytics-driven O&M.

ATL EBITDA increased due to higher revenue in transmission and distribution segment.

APSEZ EBITDA growth was driven by growth in volumes, operational efficiency and cost restructuring.

ATGL EBITDA increased due to increased sales volumes and improvements in operating margin and cost optimization.

AEL EBITDA grew due to better margins in IRM business and consolidation of Mumbai airport business.

APSEZ EBITDA excludes one time transaction cost of ₹ 60 crore in the financial year 2021-22 and donation of ₹ 80 crore in the financial year 2020-21. EBITDA excludes foreign exchange.

Competitive Advantage

The Adani Group recognizes that the ability to make a significant national contribution can only be derived from a comprehensive competitive advantage that is not dependent on any single factor but is the result of a comprehensive culture of excellence - the coming together of adjacent business presence, prosperous regional experience, timely project implementation, ability to commission projects faster than the regional curve, ability to do so at a cost below the industry average, foresight to not only serve the market but establish a decisive sustainable leadership to grow it to develop and position the company into a common name within its area of presence.

Relatively Immature Location

The Adani Group has chosen to enter businesses that can be considered 'maturely non-mature'. While some businesses may be classified as mature based on traditional interpretations of sustainable industry presence and their market potential, these same businesses may be considered non-mature based on their enormous market potential and superior Adani Group value proposition. The result is that the Adani Group addresses regional spaces not based on existing market demand, but on the basis of potential market growth following a superior Adani regional value proposition.

Big Size

The Adani Group has established a reputation for taking large stakes in select sectors and businesses without compromising on balance sheet safety. The group sets a larger capacity aspiration that sends a strong message of its long-term direction. Its large initial capacity establishes economies of scale within a relatively short time horizon that deters potential competition and generates substantial cost leadership (fixed and variable) across market cycles.

Technology

The Adani Group invests in today's best technology standards that can generate valuable additional basis points in profitability and help more than pay off the additional costs (if any) within a short period of time. This superior technology standard develops into a company's sustainable competitive advantage, respect, talent traction and profitability.

Execution Excellence

The Adani Group has built a distinct expertise in project execution, which is one of the most challenging segments in India. Samih has established benchmark credentials in executing projects faster than the regional average by drawing from Adani's multi-decade pool of managerial excellence across a range of competencies. This capacity has resulted in faster revenue flows, increased surplus and competitive project cost per unit of distributed generation.

Scalable Financial Structure

The Adani Group has built a strong financial foundation of ownership and borrowed funds (lowest ever cost for infrastructure construction companies in India). This enhanced credibility makes it possible for the Adani Group to raise resources from some of the largest global lenders at the lowest cost. This approach helps transform these key institutions from mere lenders to stable resource (funds or growth) providers for the long term.

Culture of Flexibility

Resilience is one characteristic that makes it possible to bounce back. It is the ability to face the unexpected, facing uncertainty with curiosity and optimism. The capacity within societies to recover from setbacks is difficult to predict because crisis drivers are more complex and interconnected. While there is always room for debate, looking at recent events, it cannot be denied that India deserves more credit for handling the Covid-19 crisis from a humanitarian and economic perspective than most emerged from developed economies. When it comes to Russia, India has been able to take a mature approach towards the ongoing conflict. And in this complex environment, India has emerged as the fastest growing major economy when other major nations are facing bearish trends. India is also one of the few countries that has accelerated its renewable energy footprint despite the energy crisis that has seen many countries stalling their efforts to achieve renewable energy targets. Credit must be given to the government for the way it has played its part and managed this all-round balancing act.

It is India's inherent resilience that provides our country with inherent optimism. Optimism comes from resilience. Resilience comes from faith and faith is optimism. In Adani's case, it is the optimism and belief in resilience that propels it forward. In the words of Adani Group, "The faith we have in our past defines our ability to believe in our future, which translates into the big bets we make in the present. We have never shied away from investing in India, we have never slowed down our investments, and we have never been afraid to enter uncharted territory in adjacent areas – our resilience is the strength of our country and our countrymen. From this comes unwavering faith and strong belief in aspirations. The success of the Adani Group is based on its alignment with India's growth story.

We have always firmly believed in the policies announced by the government, continue to invest in all economic cycles, focus on emerging sectors critical to the country's development, and enter new areas with confidence in our learning and operational capabilities. Have done and more importantly believe in yourself. We've grown admirably without vacillating on the traditional business model. We have built the infrastructure envisaging a bigger and bigger India, a confidence that has paid dividends.

In a journey of over 25 years, we have faced our share of woes, and stumbled at times, but have always stood on our feet and emerged stronger with more faith in ourselves. It is these experiences and belief in ourselves that have given us our resilience and optimism for a better future. This is the future that unfolded in the period 2021-22. This was the year we announced ourselves to the world".

Preparing for 'Green Change'

"The best evidence to demonstrate our trust and confidence in the future is our $70 billion investment in facilitating India's green transition. We are already one of the world's largest developers of solar energy.

Our strength in renewable energy will greatly empower us in our endeavour to make green hydrogen the fuel of the future. We are at the forefront of the race to transform India from a country that is a highly-dependent importer of oil and gas, to a country that can one day become a net exporter of clean energy – in an astonishingly short time 'never before' 'Change' over a period of time - a change that will help reshape India's energy footprint in an extraordinary way.

While we now have a leading global renewable energy portfolio, we have made significant progress in many other industries. In one stroke, we have become India's largest airport operator. We are engaged in the adjacent businesses of building aerotropolises and local community-based economic centres around the airports we operate today. We have forayed into sectors ranging from data centres, super apps and industrial cloud to defence and aerospace, metals and materials – all in line with the government's vision of a self-reliant India.

We continue to grow as India's infrastructure builders, winning some of the largest road contracts in the country, and increasing our already substantial market share in businesses such as ports, logistics, transmission and distribution, city gas and piped natural gas. Our successful IPO of Adani Wilmar makes us the largest FMCG company in the country. And now, we are also the second largest cement manufacturer in India.

This year (2022) our combined group market capitalization is set to exceed 200 billion dollars. We were able to raise billions of dollars from international markets – a direct validation of the belief in both India and the Adani growth story. Our growth and success has been recognized worldwide. Foreign governments are now approaching us to work in their geographies and help build their infrastructure. In the year 2022, we have also laid the foundation for a massive expansion beyond the borders of India".

Strong Results, Growing Numbers

Our growing market capitalization has been supported by strong and continued growth in our cash flow.

Group Highlights

✓ Our utility portfolio grew by 26 per cent.

✓ Our transportation and logistics portfolio grew by 19 per cent.

✓ Our FMCG portfolio grew by 34 per cent and

✓ Our incubator business represented by AEL grew by 45 per cent.

EBITDA growth of 26 per cent in the portfolio. Portfolio EBITDA stood at ₹ 42,623 crore. This growth was diversified and reflected across all our businesses whose results spoke for themselves.

The high growth of our incubator AEL provides the group with a solid foundation for the continued development of new businesses for another successful decade. AEL's unique business model has no parallel and we intend to further leverage it.

Segment Highlights

AGEL

✓ AGEL to add 1,940 megawatts of operational capacity in the financial year 2022 (Green field commissioning: 200 megawatts, Inorganic addition: 1,740 megawatt).

✓ AGEL's solar CUF to grow by 130 bps YoY to 23.8 per cent and wind CUF to grow by 400 bps YoY to 30.8 per cent in FY22.

ATL

✓ Adani Transmission Limited (ATL) added 1,519 circuits to its network, reaching 18,795 circuit km, and sold a record 7,972 million units during the year.

APSEZ

✓ APSEZ cargo volume grew by 26 per cent to 312 MMT in the financial year 2022. The journey from 200 MMT to 300 MMT in cargo volume was achieved in a record time of just three years.

✓ The APSEZ also handled a record container volume of 68.2 million TEUs, a growth of 14 per cent.

ATGL

✓ Adani Total Gas Limited (ATGL) added 117 CNG stations, 556 commercial, 154 industrial and 85840 domestic customers, achieving a combined volume of 697 MMSCM (CNG PNG).

Strategic Highlights

✓ Adani Green Energy completes acquisition of Soft Bank's 5.3 GW renewable energy portfolio.

✓ AEL started operations of its Bravas mine in Australia.

✓ AEL took over the operations of Guwahati, Jaipur.

What Have We Become

"What we have been able to build over two decades is India's largest integrated infrastructure business based on rapid expansion into adjacent businesses. As a result, we have transformed into an integrated 'Platform of Platforms', combining energy with logistics, taking us closer to unprecedented access to the Indian consumer. I don't know of any company today that has this business model and has unlimited B2B and B2C market access for the next several decades".

Milestone

"This is where I want to take a moment to reflect on the year 2022 as a year with special personal meaning. It represents the 100th birth anniversary of my inspirational father and role model Shri Shantilal Adani and my 60th birthday. To mark this milestone, the Adani family came together and decided to contribute ₹ 60,000 crore for charitable activities related to healthcare, education and skill development, especially with a focus on rural India. All these three sectors should be looked at holistically rather than in isolation, as they are collectively the drivers of an equitable and future-ready India. We have a decisive opportunity to permanently lift millions of people out of poverty in India.

We are responsible not only to ourselves but also to our country, to do whatever we can to catalyze this process. Our experience in planning and executing large projects and learnings from the work the Adani Foundation is doing will help us uniquely accelerate and implement these programmes in the communities that need them most."

"I am an incurable optimist. I have always believed that India is one of the greatest countries for an entrepreneur to learn, grow and thrive. Today, I see a genuine motivation among young Indians to reclaim their economic stature and regain their position as an important force in global affairs. Undoubtedly, the largest middle class that will ever exist has been fuelled by an increase in the working age and an increase in the quality of life consumed. I have no doubt that we will see it unfold in the next decade. India today is indeed the strongest pitch in the world to bat on". Gautam Adani, Chairman, Adani Group.

❑

Formula of Gautam Adani's Success

Gautam Adani is the world's busiest deal maker who earned maximum wealth in the year 2022. He started the business as a regular diamond merchant. Today it has ports, mines, electricity, solar energy, green energy, cement, housing, petrochemicals and everything. With his hard work and determination, Gautam Adani became the king of infrastructure. His assets in December 2021 were 9,62,322 crore. It is ₹ 18,64,579 crore in a year in December 2022. He earns 1600 crore every day, 67 crore every hour. He is the third richest man in the world.

Money Making Formula

This formula is not based on any mathematics, chemistry or physics. There is only one formula that works both in business and in our practical lives, and that is hard work, hard work and more hard work. Also family support, seniors support, good team and their support, and above all, God's blessings and mercy are also needed. Working with integrity and that is one reason and there is no shortcut. The success of any human being depends on honesty and diligence, and the rest is left to God, that is the only formula.

Gautam Adani does not get trapped in numbers. The biggest thing for him is what change he can bring to the country. If you talk about the ever-increasing wealth of Gautam Adani, then it can be said that the country is on the path of progress. And it is his belief that India's position today and in the coming 20-30 years will be invincible.

Gautam Adani passed his 10th Class in 15 years and came to Mumbai in search of work without completing studies or graduation due to a weak economic family condition. They had a journey of 4 years before returning to Ahmedabad. Mumbai taught him a lot, it taught him how to work hard. After this his business journey started. Belonging to a middle class family, a business family, he got into business and at the age of 15-19 he had the enthusiasm to do something beyond his family business. His family supported him and on that basis he kept moving forward. Money was limited, and they had to grow their business accordingly. There were several problems, there were many established players. But he has seen that at different points in his life, different people supported him to be successful and who he is today because of them.

However, Gautam Adani was good at studies and chose engineering as a technical subject. He was also proficient at maths. But the circumstances were such that he had to put his studies in cold storage and he got involved in business.

But he believes that studies are very important. Education makes a person wise. Adani could not choose that path and he considers it his misfortune. He chose the second path—perseverance and experience. That hard work and experience increased his intelligence. He says that sometimes he wonders that if he had so much hard work and experience as well as education, he would have become much bigger than today's Gautam Adani.

Despite having a fleet of jet aircraft and helicopters, Gautam Adani is a down to earth and practical man and even today he knows the mindset of a person travelling by scooter rickshaw, bus or jet, because he has been through it. Just because he travels by a jet, doesn't mean he isn't connected to the ground.

There was a time when people used to talk only about Tata-Birla, today they only talk about Adani-Ambani. But Gautam Adani believes that Tata and Birla are very respected industrialists of the country. He has done a lot in building this nation and is still doing so for the country. He believes that India has the potential to create many more such industrialists.

Business and Difficulties

Gautan Adani believes that no business is risk free. He says, "How much calculated risk does one take, how much is one's risk taking ability... I would not say that I have reached here without difficulty. But, one must have the determination to stay strong in favourable and unflavourable times and reach new heights with one's hard work. When you take risks, you must know your limits. We have taken risks in many places, and it is not that we have been successful in all, we have also faced failures in many places. You need to have that strength to survive through such times and for that you need to be strong. Difficulties will come. It is not that you will get success in every endeavour, you will also have to face difficulties. But with the right intention and right dedication, you will never face failure".

Gautam Adani's nature is to adapt to different situations. He believes that it is not in him to lose his peace over what is not in his control. He was abducted and released the next day. That night he slept well. So, he never feels that pressure.

Adani's Role in India's Renewable Energy Shift (AGEL)

As the world is increasingly realising the toll that carbon intensive fossil fuels are placing on the climate, countries have prioritised the transition to renewable energy sources. India's energy mix has also shifted towards renewable sources, supported by forward looking and supportive governmental regulations and policy initiatives. In February 2023, renewable energy sources accounted for 12% of the total energy output, which in turn consists of solar (7.5%), wind (2.5%) small hydro (0.4%), biomass and bagasse (0.8%). Of late, renewable energy has also benefited from transmission optimisations and better distribution infrastructure, leading to more efficient energy usage. The impact of energy security is wider than just climate change energy security has wide ranging ramifications—it has for long dictated critical areas such as our foreign policy. Energy independence or at least reduced dependence on fossil fuels will enable us to develop favourable policies and meet our global commitments.

Let us now have a brief look at India's stance on climate change. India has committed to achieve net zero emissions by 2070, almost 20 years after Europe. But then, these economies have had very different growth trajectories. Net zero emissions is achieved when all human generated emissions are counterbalanced by decarbonisation. This has essentially two parts: first, the reduction of emissions from fossil fuels and second decarbonisation by restoration of forests or reforestation.

Right in 2015, at the Paris Convention, India initiated the International Solar Alliance, which is a member-driven, collaborative platform for enhanced usage of solar energy technologies for mitigating the impact of climate change, driving energy security and transition for its member countries. Given India's rapid strides in renewable energy, the role of renewable energy in India's growth story is well understood and acknowledged. India proudly claims a number of achievements in renewable energy – it has the world's largest utility-scale solar park; a steadily growing wind power sector, and investments in other green technologies.

One of India's major renewable energy firms, Adani Green Energy Limited (AGEL), has a current project portfolio of 20,434 MW. AGEL has grown its footprint across 12 Indian states, creating a solid renewable energy infrastructure, boosting job growth and energy independence. With a portfolio of 54 active projects and 12 ongoing projects, AGEL is leading India's transition to renewable energy.

Adani realised that the fossil fuel dependent industries would soon make transition completely to renewable energy, as a result, companies which are developing and supplying renewable energy would be better poised for growth. The foray of the company into green technologies helped him realise this vision. Whether it was solar, wind or hydrogen, Adani invested capital and technology into creating the right infrastructure for the market. The market entry in this sector was also supported by its success in the infrastructure sector, with the Group's proven track record in transport, logistics, energy and utility space, and experience and knowledge in development and construction.

In line with the founder's vision for expansion into renewable energy, AGEL's vision is to be world's leading business that adds value to the lives of people and builds infrastructure through sustainable value generation across all sources of renewable energy, be it solar, wind or hydrogen.

The company aims to become the world's largest solar power company by 2025 and largest renewable power company by 2030. Its existing portfolio of renewable power generating assets stands at over 2.5 GW. The company expects to ramp this up to 3.5 GW, with projects implemented under construction capacity.

By 2025, the company hopes to increase this to 18 GW. Under the leadership of its founder, the company has committed to investing over 70% of the budgeted capex of the energy vertical into clean energy and energy-efficient systems.

The company's offerings comprise solar PV plants, solar parks, and wind farms throughout India. The company has an ambitious target of being a 25,000 MW renewable energy generator by 2025, and in order to achieve this objective, it is investing in infrastructure, technologies and innovation.

AGEL has invested in extensive R&D and innovation which has helped it create an unparalleled infrastructure of land, grid network, and technology. The company has invested in ESG compliance and any project execution considers impact on the neighbouring geographical areas, climate, and local facilities. The company has set up a solar PV manufacturing arm, thus reaping the benefits of upstream integration. It has also invested in technological leadership, helping it derive cost gains from its scale of operations. Currently, the company is building the world's first fully integrated of 10GW solar PV manufacturing unit at Mundra.

It is this vision that has powered the phenomenal growth of the Adani Group. Under the able leadership of its founder, AGEL shall continue to support the nation in meeting its climate action goals.

Adani realised the value of partnerships for global businesses such as AGEL. Partnerships are essential for better technology access, access to specific knowhow/knowledge, access to capital and building a global brand. Adani has pioneered the concept of value-added partnerships that have enhanced the Group's standing in India as well as abroad.

As part of his strategy, Adani has always sought strategic equity partners that are aligned with his long term goals. Under his leadership, the Group has forged strong partnerships with companies such as TotalEnergies, IFC, ADIA, and QIA.

In 2018, Total SA, acquired a 37.4% stake in Adani Gas and 50% stakc in Dhamra LNG project. During the course of this partnership, the companies expanded their partnership with Total acquiring a 50% stake in a 2.35 GW portfolio of operating solar assets owned by AGEL and a 20% stake in AGEL for around USD 2.5 billion.

This represents another deep strategic commitment between the two companies. Total is one of the biggest energy companies in the world, operating across exploration and production, operations, refining and petrochemicals and ship and market.

AGEL's partnership with Total provides it with not just market access routes, but also a global brand identity, and enhanced technological and skill expertise.

Adani had known that a renewable energy business was a wise investment from the long term perspective. The business was expected to have steady cash flows, if the Group was successful in getting long term PPAs. For driving better cost optimisations, there would be enhanced operational focus on preventive maintenance. One aspect of cost optimisation is derived from grid parity. As per the estimations of his team, grid parity was achievable in the long run. Grid parity happens when an alternative energy source can generate power at a cost less than or equal to the cost of electricity sourced from fossil fuels.

As more infrastructure gets built for renewable sources, more utility companies join the market, and this leads to a faster path to grid parity. Technological advancements also accelerate grid parity and generate net savings for consumers.

The company's current project portfolio is nearly 5,990 MW and operational capacity of 2,545 MW. The company's portfolio is split between solar projects (44%), wind (28%), and hybrid (28%).

The company has continued to pay off investments and has been profitable, with a consolidated EBITDA of INR 3,954 Crore in FY 2021–22, delivering 46% growth on year-on-year basis.

A US based clean energy communications, research, and consulting firm, Mercom has ranked AGEL as the global #1 solar power generation asset owner in a report announcing the 2021 top global large-scale solar PV developers.

The National Mission for Enhanced Energy Efficiency (NMEEE) aims to make the Indian market more climate resilient by creating supportive regulatory and policy mechanisms that drive innovation and sustainability. It has been at the forefront for driving a more balanced energy mix for the country.

India's energy portfolio is becoming increasingly inclined towards renewable energy. Globally, India is the third largest producer of renewable energy, with 40% of its installed electricity capacity coming from non-fossil fuel sources. Alongside India's commitment to achieve Net Zero Emissions are the following short term targets:

- ✓ Increasing the capacity of renewable energy to 500 GW by 2030, ™™ Meeting 50% of energy requirements from renewable sources of energy,
- ✓ Reducing cumulative emissions by one billion tonnes by 2030, and
- ✓ Reducing emissions intensity of India's gross domestic product (GDP) by 45% by 2030.

The above targets are supported by forward looking legislations which help India meet its climate pledges and undertake energy transformations to create a more balanced energy portfolio.

To realise its ambitious objectives, the company has acquired a large land bank, almost 200,000 acres, rich in solar and wind resources, located next to green corridors. The company is continuously planning for the future through initiatives such as creating a strong execution experience across 300+ sites across India, developing a strong vendor network, focusing on in-house R&D, and integrating technology across the operational lifecycle.

The company has developed a number of operational best practices, such as the constitution of a Cluster based operating model. This facilitates smooth governance across the 15 regional cluster teams, resources and helps allocate manpower efficiently.

The Energy Network Operations Centre (CENOC) helps drive predictive analytics leading to higher equipment performance and cost efficient O&M. ENOC offers the following advantages: it is platform agnostic, highly scalable, and vendor agnostic. All these technological advancements yield an unparalleled competitive advantage to AGEL.

Adani knew that an energy company would need to be ESG compliant. And he took massive steps in driving ESG alignment not just for compliance but for transforming the DNA of the company. AGEL has created a three pillar framework for assessing and promoting sustainability. These are:

- ✓ Commitment towards global climate action
- ✓ Corporate citizenship enabling social transformation
- ✓ Responsible business practices

The ESG principles are embedded deep within the Group's DNA, guiding and navigating the Group's support towards decarbonisation. All its sites are single-usage- plastic free, and over 100K+ hours of health and safety trainings are imparted to employees. The company has a dedicated internal ESG Risk Committee. As a result of its emphasis on ESG, it has received number of accolades. It was ranked second in the Indian electric utility sector in the global Corporate Sustainability Assessment by DJSI S&P, with a score of 66 out of 100, performing significantly better than the average World Electric Utility Score of 38 (out of

100). It has been rated 'A' by MSCI, and has received an FTSE ESG score of 'FTSE4Good'.

To reaffirm its commitment to climate change action, it became the title funder for the climate change gallery at the Science Museum in London.

In recognition for its efforts on sustainability, AGEL has been ranked first in Asia and among the top 10 companies globally in the renewable energy sector by ISS ESG, a leading global provider of Environmental, Social, and Governance (ESG) research and ratings. These rankings are based on a comprehensive assessment of a company's ESG performance, including its environmental impact, social responsibility, and corporate governance.

The company has also received the acclaimed "Water Positive" certification by DNV, an independent expert in assurance and risk management. The certification means that AGEL's water conservation is greater than consumption. For all operational sites having capacity of 200 MW or greater, the agency conducted extensive tests to assess the water balance index, the results indicating the index to be 1.12 (positive).

AGEL is helping the nation build future ready climate technologies and helping it become more climate resilient. One of the goals of the nation is to build a renewable energy portfolio to 450 GW by 2030. AGEL with its current portfolio is helping bring this vision to reality by taking on 10% of the target, that is, 45 GW, with an investment of US $50-$70 billion in the renewable space.

It has also signed a UN Energy Compact affirming to develop and operate renewable energy generation Capacity of 45 GW by 2030 and to keep the average tariff below Average Power Purchase Cost at the national level.

AGEL is helping the nation decarbonise and architect a climate transformation. The company's ambitious goals are helping not just enrich lives but also the environment. Its investments in processes, R&D, technology and innovation are drivers for future sustained growth.

Adani Finserv

The country's financial services sector consists of capital markets, insurance sector and Non-Banking Financial Companies (NBFCs). This sector has seen strong growth due to rising incomes, progressive government policies and the increasing pace of digital adoption.

Adani Finserv marks the entry of the Adani Group in the finance segment. AdaniFinserv operates two companies – Adani Capital and Adani Housing Finance.

This chapter will discuss the principles of business that we can learn from these two companies which have helped in the diversification of the Adani Group.

The Non-Banking Financial Companies (NBFCs) have been an integral part of credit access in a developing country like India. They help in democratising access to under-banked and unbanked sections of the Indian economy. Around 9,000 NBFCs are registered with the Reserve Bank of India (RBI) with assets of ₹ 42.05 lakh crore. Disbursing gold, personal and vehicle loans, to addressing the microfinance sector, NBFCs play an important role in India.

Launched in 2017, Adani Capital is the NBFC arm of the Adani Group. The focus of Adani Capital is to promote entrepreneurship, and provide credit access and capital availability to budding entrepreneurs and primary sector entrepreneurs through a direct-to-consumer distribution model. It offers loans for a wide range of products, including loans for farm equipment, commercial vehicles, business loans, and supply chain finance. According to the 2020-21 annual report, the company reported a net income of INR 163 million. The company has around 60,000 borrowers and has 150+ branches spread across eight states, operating in states, including Gujarat, Maharashtra, Rajasthan and Karnataka. The total business managed by the company is around 30 billion, with about 1% gross Non Performing Assets (NPAs).

Adani Capital received its license in January 2017 as a non-deposit taking systemically important NBFC, and after receiving its license commenced its operations in March 2017. The company disburses tractor loans (new, used/ refinanced), commercial vehicle loans (new, used/refinanced with a focus on small and light commercial vehicles), business loans (fully collateralised term loans to micro and small enterprises) and supply chain finance (working capital loans to SMEs). MSME term loans comprised 37% of disbursed loans, tractor loans, 29%; commercial vehicle, 19%; and supply chain, 15%.

As on March 2022 the total AUM (Assets Under Management) were INR 2050 crore, an increase of 58% year on year. Adani Capital is continuously expanding its portfolio, helping micro entrepreneurs' access credit.

Nowadays, large business houses are setting up NBFCs for quite some time to get access to the financial services market and commence their digital lending journey. However, current regulatory norms do not permit corporate houses to set up a bank.

Many conglomerates wanted to enter the NBFC segment to capitalise the retail lending boom. Also digitalisation has ensured that companies do not have to set up branches in remote corners of the country. Digital revolution has transformed way of doing business in banking, whether it is Know Your Customer or digital payments.

Adani realised that financial inclusion was much below the desired level in the country. However he understood that tapping this business opportunity would enable him to access a larger customer base. He was aware that financial services would also be complementary to his existing businesses. Adani knew that financial services would accelerate digitalisation of his existing businesses, and offer more expansion opportunities at significantly lower costs than some of his existing infrastructure businesses. Hence his foray in financial services can be seen not just as a way of leveraging his existing business but also as a prudent diversification strategy.

Adani Capital is focused on developing the rural sector, by helping small and medium enterprises to access capital and outreach best industry practices. The Group disburses loans in the band 3–30 lakhs. To demonstrate its contribution to nation building, it has established a collaboration with CSC e-Governance Services, has provided working capital to 1,500 Village Level Entrepreneurs (VLEs) in early 2023.

Common Service Centres (CSC) are a special purpose vehicle (SPV) under the Ministry of Electronics and IT (MeitY). In 2020, CSCs had launched Grameen e-Store offering and promoting products such as local handicrafts, groceries, consumer durables in the remote areas of the country.

Till date, there are approximately 10,000 VLEs empanelled with around 3.64 lakh Grameen e-Stores doing around INR 642.77 crores worth of business. The VLEs act as distributors on the digital rural marketplace helping facilitate last mile distribution of products ranging from FMCG to home appliances.

By supporting these micro entrepreneurs operating in rural and semi-urban areas, Adani Capital is helping in nation building.

The core competencies of the Adani Group are in the infrastructure and power industry. As the Group faces increasing challenges due to capital-intensive expansion, the increasingly tough economic environment is adding to their capital raising woes. Being in the NBFC segment, it offers them an easier growth and diversification path for the Group. As per reports, the Group planned to focus initially on working capital loans, acquisition loans, last-mile project financing, structured credit solutions, funding stressed assets before diversifying further.

The Adani Group has always evaluated multiple options for growth, both organically and inorganically. In 2020, the Group acquired Essel Finance's Micro, Small and Medium Enterprises (MSME) loan business. Through the acquisition, Adani Capital has secured a loan book of around INR 145 crore, operating out of 10 cities, comprising approximately 1,100 customers and 40 employees.

The acquisition was a synergistic one as it enabled Adani Capital access to two new markets: Noida and Chennai.

Both the companies operated in similar segments, which focused on lending to income-generating borrowers. The acquisition enabled the firm to increase its operational footprint, improve processes, leverage technology for productivity improvements.

An IPO (Initial Public Offering) is planned for Adani Capital in 2024, raising as much as INR 1500 crore ($188 million). The Group is targeting a valuation of $2 billion and is thinking of offloading a 10% stake.

The company manages credit risk through a balanced structured credit policy framework with oversight from a risk committee. The underwriting of the credit, capacity, collateral and capital is carried out by a team of experts. The company also uses technology to predict delinquency, improve collection efficiency and for evaluating credit worthiness of applicants. The team integrates multiple sources of data, including internal, transactional and behavioural data, and external, credit bureau and market information data. This helps the organisation to take proactive steps to manage any deterioration in portfolio quality.

The firm has seen numerous challenges arising out of an unpredictable economic environment, uncertain demand and an unanticipated contraction arising during COVID-19. However, in his typical indefatigable style, Adani has never let challenges faze him.

After the acquisition of Essel Finance, its NPAs shoot up from 1.49% to 9.12%. Adani Finserv injected almost INR 150 crore to revive the business.

In testament to his never-say-die spirit, the business revived and in the first six months of 2021-22, Adani Capital and Adani Housing reported a consolidated profit after tax of INR 39 crore, up from INR 2 crore the previous fiscal year. According to Crisil Ratings, Adani Capital's total borrowings stood at INR 1,902 crore in 2021-22, as against INR 983 crore in the previous fiscal.

In 2018, Adani Housing Finance was launched, marking the Adani Group's entry into the affordable housing finance segment. The company provides financial assistance to dream of owning a home.

Housing is an important driver of the economic growth engine. In developed economies, housing mortgage contributes to 88% of the total GDP. In other developing economies such as Brazil and China, its contribution is around 8% and 30%, respectively. In India, housing mortgage contributes only 10% of the total GDP. There is a huge gap between demand and supply in the low cost and affordable housing segment, leading up to 95% of housing shortage. Private investment in housing has been encouraged to meet demands and help provide sectoral and financial expertise.

In India, the mortgage market is driven by the following forces: an increasingly younger demographic, leading to a large working age population; increased migration to cities leading to urbanisation and rising nuclearisation; rising purchasing power and disposable income; and finally, government incentives such as credit linked subsidy schemes. All these drivers have led to a rise in the affordable housing finance market. The products offered by the company are home loans and mortgage loans.

The business can be broadly categorised as follows:

- ✓ Affordable housing financing
- ✓ Home loans: home purchase, home improvement, composite loans, balance transfer and top up loans.
- ✓ Loan against property: commercial purchase, loan against residential property and commercial property.
- ✓ Construction finance: construction finance loans to affordable builders.

In other Asian economies, mortgage penetration stands at 20–30% of GDP. As of FY22, India has a mortgage penetration rate stands at 13% GDP. This segment has come under spotlight as it is expected that home loans will double to $600 billion by 2027.

The housing finance market is expected to grow as there is anticipated demand for 25 million homes over FY17–FY22 in the medium and lower income group categories. Adani has always placed his bets in a growing market and this market was lucrative enough for a new strategic direction for the Group.

Home loans are considered to be low-risk as they are backed by collaterals which the banks prefer. Affordable housing loans have a lower ticket size and hence chances of NPAs are comparatively lesser, at 0.3-0.8%. HFCs can earn a spread of more than 5%, as their rate of borrowing is 7–8% and the lending rate is 12-13%. Affordable housing finance is a niche area, with high growth, higher return on assets, and increased profitability. Since the product is long- term in tenure, there is continuity of cash flow, it assumes the mechanics of an annuity business. Hence lower costs, higher yields and improved margins make this an attractive investment opportunity for many conglomerates.

Adani knew that with limited credit access in a majority of the country, with people having sufficient savings but not the income structure desired by banks for providing credit, HFCs would be poised for growth. It is this market potential of the untapped segment which Adani Finserv has capitalised on.

A report by CRISIL stated that the Assets Under Management (AUM) under housing finance companies are expected to grow by 10-12% in FY 2022-23 as compared to 8% in the previous financial year. However, it was also reported that banks would be better positioned to expand their market share at the expense of HFCs. The one segment where HFCs have grown competitively is the affordable housing segment because of lesser footprint of banks in that area.

Under Adani's guidance, the business has focused on the affordable housing finance market and has seen progressive growth.

The housing finance market is more vulnerable to changes in economic conditions than other industries. Due to COVID-19, many HFCs suffered operational losses. After two challenging years, the HFC market overtook pre-Covid-19 (2018-19) levels of disbursement of ₹ 2.42 trillion with ₹ 2.59 trillion of disbursements in FY 2022.

Adani incorporated Adani Housing Finance in September 2017. The Group then tried to enter the housing finance segment by first trying to acquire a housing finance company in 2018. It then applied for a license with the National Housing Bank, and explored the retail and housing space.

The HFC market has a number of operating challenges such as thin spreads, tightening regulatory conditions, forcing them to introspect about their business models. Just in the last financial year, the first half saw 2% Y-O-Y (year on year) growth but the second half saw 14% surge in annualised growth, highlighting how deeply market forces affect HFC operations.

The last two years placed huge stressors for the lending market. Adani Housing Finance also had to bear the brunt of contraction in demand. In addition to that, it had incurred high operating expenses for setting up the requisite infrastructure in the initial years of business. Adani Housing reported losses in fiscal 2019 and fiscal 2020.

However, under Adani's leadership and astute execution by his team, through gradual sale-up in the loan book, the earnings profile improved and profitability increased. In Fiscal 2021, Adani Housing Finance reported a profit of INR 6.9 crore.

The HFC segment is bolstered by favourable policies such as Pradhan Mantri Awas Yojana, RERA, and Urban Infrastructure Development Fund, and trends such as rising per-capita income, rise in desire for asset ownership, expanding labour mobility, all contributing to rising demand.

It is anticipated that the HFCs will grow at 12.3% y-o-y in FY24, slightly dipping from 12.6% in FY 23. This growth is predominantly driven by the affordable housing finance, growing at 16%.

Competitive pressures remain steady for HFCs, and many lenders are looking to diversify beyond housing to reduce pressures on thin margins.

In 2023, Adani Housing Finance had 3977 crores worth AUM, with 63% Y-o-Y growth, with gross disbursement of INR 2482 crore.

Adani Healthcare

The Indian healthcare industry is projected to reach US$638 billion by 2025. The sector comprises key segments such as hospitals, diagnostic providers, pharmaceuticals, medical equipment and supplies, medical insurance, and telemedicine. Hospitals constitute around 70% of the healthcare market, followed by pharmaceuticals (20%), and medical technology (10%).

The Adani Group had been a part of healthcare services for quite some time by contributing to Corporate Social Responsibility (CSR) activities. Its objective is to provide quality healthcare services for people at the grassroot level. It runs Mobile Health Care Units (MHCUs), healthcare institutions like hospitals and clinics, and health camps.

The Gujarat Adani Institute of Medical Sciences (GAIMS) was established as a Public Private Partnership between Government of Gujarat and the Adani Education and Research Foundation. GAIMS has the distinction of being the only medical college and multi-specialty modern teaching district hospital in the Kutchh District.

To further signify its interest in the healthcare segment, Adani Enterprises incorporated a wholly-owned subsidiary Adani Health Ventures on 18 May 2022. The venture is expected to run medical and diagnostic facilities, health aids, health tech-based facilities, research centres and allied activities.

The hospital industry in India offers huge investment opportunities for investors and presently there are 582 investment opportunities worth US$32.16 billion in the medical infrastructure sector. Up to 100% Foreign Direct Investment (FDI) is allowed for construction of hospitals under the automatic route for green field projects and for brownfield projects, up to 100% FDI is permitted under the government approval route.

Gautam Adani realised the tremendous scale of the healthcare industry and along with Apollo Hospitals expressed interest in picking up a majority stake in Mumbai based diagnostic chain of Metropolis Healthcare Ltd. The deal size was anticipated to be around ₹ 7,765 crore or USD 1 billion. The diagnostics market in India is quite lucrative owing to free cash flows, attractive return ratios, and expansion potential.

Estimated at USD 675 bl, and growing at 8-9% annually, the sector has demonstrated EBITDA margins between 25-40%, sector also has comparatively low entry barriers and high Return on Investment (RoI), and all of these factors make diagnostics an interesting investment opportunity.

This is evident from the fact that in August 2020, Reliance acquired a majority stake in Netmeds for INR 620 crore (Reliance Retail). In June 2021, Tata Digital acquired the online pharmacy 1MG in an all-cash deal for ₹ 720 crore. The sector also saw many entrenched pharma companies such as Lupin launch their own diagnostic lab - called Lupin Diagnostics in July 2022. Torrent Pharma, the Ahmedabad-headquartered pharma company, launched its venture in this space— Torrent Diagnostics Private Limited in February, 2022. The sector also saw considerable M&As (Merger & Acquisitions) and subsequent consolidation with the acquisition of diagnostic chain Thyrocare by PharmEasy in June 2021 for INR 4,546 Crore. Medplus, a pharmacy retailer also marked its entry in this segment in March 2022 by launching its diagnostic centre in Hyderabad.

The non-COVID revenues for the diagnostics sector grew 11-22%; and companies have planned to expand the network in tier 2-3 towns in the coming months.

Just like the diagnostic centres, the hospital segment is also expected to grow further in the coming years. As per a report cited in The Times of India, major private hospital chains have reported up to 23% revenue growth y-o-y. The Average Revenue Per Occupied Bed (ARPOB) was led by improvement in the case and payer mix. For example, for Apollo Hospitals, the revenue growth stood at 21.3% y-o-y while EBITDA margin was 11.3%.

Major hospitals have already charted out their expansion plans; Apollo Hospitals is planning to add 2000 beds in 3 years with a capex of INR 3000 CR. Fortis Healthcare is looking to add 1,400 beds within 5 years, while KIMS Hospitals is looking to add 1,500 beds over 3 years.

All these factors make the hospital segment also an investment worthy area.

The segment that occupies the highest rank in the healthcare industry is the pharmaceutical industry. The Indian pharmaceutical market is estimated to touch USD 130 billion in value by the end of 2030, and the global market is expected to increase up to USD 1 trillion in 2023. It is natural that the Adani Group would have considered inorganic growth in this segment as well. In 2021, the government had decided to offload a 100% stake in the public sector pharmaceutical firms, HLL Hindustan Lifecare Limited. The Group also evaluated the purchase and bid along with Piramal Healthcare.

The two biggest obstacles faced in health care in India are affordability and accessibility. The rural and urban healthcare experience varies greatly based on how these two variables play out in these two widely different settings9. The last few years have shown how the PPP model can be used to improve healthcare delivery across India, particularly in for hung rural areas.

The government spend on healthcare is 2.1% of GDP (OECD countries spend is around 9.7%); around 55% of the healthcare expenditure is Out of Pocket (OOP).

Crippling healthcare expenditures push around 55M people into poverty each year.

Hence it is timportant that private companies come forward to help the government in setting up institutions to transfer technology, processes, training of manpower to build the healthcare infrastructure of the nation.

Conglomerates like Adani, who have the systems and institutions to set up a seamless healthcare infrastructure will not only aid in nation building but also help in improving quality of life, improve access to services, and GDP.

An important metric in the healthcare system is the doctor-patient ratio. India has a dismal metric of 0.7 doctors and 1.5 nurses per 1,000 people compared to the World Health Organisation's (WHO's) average of 2.5 doctors and 2.5 nurses per 1,000 people. Compounding the challenges are the fact that India has only 1.3 hospital beds per 1,000 people, which is significantly lower than 3.5 beds per 1,000 people, the average defined by WHO.

Firming up its foray in the medical institutions segment, the company established the Gujarat Adani Institute of Medical Sciences' (GAIMS) as a PPP between Adani Group and Government of Gujarat in 2009. Located in Katchh, the institution produces trained medical professionals and provides quality clinical services to the patients from the surrounding region. The GAIMS hospital, that has around 750 beds is being upgraded to make it a model District Hospital.

To provide quality healthcare services to the people of Mundra, the company established the Adani Hospitals Mundra (AHMPL) in 2009, which is a 100-bed secondary care hospital in Mundra. Till 2014, Sterling Hospitals handled the operations and maintenance of the Hospital. From 2014, the Hospital was brought under the management control of the Adani Group. Since then, the team is involved in setting up a Nursing College and for the reconstruction of the district Hospital at Baran, Rajasthan.

The Adani Skill Development Centre has launched a skill development centre offering courses to learners – such as a course on general duty assistant for the healthcare and hospital industry, fire safety, occupational safety and health administration, disaster management, diet and nutrition. Students can access the courses through a VR headset and read the study material online. This is again a commendable effort by the company to upskill people in the healthcare segment.

As far as medical professionals are concerned, the doctor-patient ratio in the country is much lower than the WHO recommended average. Central government medical colleges are short of more than 3,000 doctors, while well known hospitals such as AIIMS, RML, Safdarjung, LHMC, JIPMER are severely short of faculty members.

There are around 700+ medical colleges for MBBS in the country. But these are still falling short of churning out trained medical professionals to meet the healthcare requirements of the entire nation. The Adani Group is planning to set up two medical colleges in Odisha to provide better access to healthcare in the districts of Bhadrak and Rayagada in Odisha. This will be a small initiative in helping to balance the abysmal doctor-patient ratio in the country and will go a long way in providing trained healthcare professionals ready to join the healthcare workforce.

The company has stated its objectives to establish centres of excellence to impart quality medical education, deliver best-in-class clinical services and conduct healthcare research. The company has reaffirmed its commitment to improve the national population health metrices and strengthen the health infrastructure of the nation. It remains steadfast in its goal to build a healthier India by providing high quality clinical services and improving the number and quality of medical professionals in the country, thereby addressing the challenges of low doctor-patient ratio.

India's public expenditure on healthcare stood at 2.1% of GDP in 2021-22 against 1.8% in 2020-21 and 1.3% in 2016-2019.

The government has launched a slew of programmes and initiatives to help improve healthcare access and affordability to the most marginalised sections of citizens.

In the Union Budget of 2023-24, the government allocated USD 10.76 B or INR 89,155 crore to the Ministry of Health and Family Welfare (MoHFW). The government, amongst the many healthcare reforms launched, is also planning to boost the country's healthcare infrastructure by introducing a credit incentive programme worth ₹ 500 billion (US$ 6.8 billion).

In 2020, the Tata Group had made solid investments in healthcare. It set up Tata Medical & Diagnostics, acquired 1MG, the e-pharmacy retailer. Reliance too acquired NetMeds. Analysts expect that the Group will acquire diagnostic laboratories and pharmacy retail chains to accelerate its healthcare play. The Group acquired a stake in Foresight Robotics, an Israeli start-up, for USD 20 M. Foresight offers the world's first Hybrid Intraocular Robotic Ophthalmic Platform, ORYOM, for advanced ophthalmic surgery to treat a wide range of conditions, including cataract, glaucoma, and other retinal diseases.

As part of its healthcare expansion, the establishment of a super-speciality healthcare centre in Ahmedabad in on the cards. The Adani Healthcare Services team also provides technical support and service to other healthcare initiatives of Adani Group. The Group is also planning to establish a Nursing College and Hostel and construction of a new 300-bed hospital in place of the existing District Hospital at Baran, Rajasthan. The Group has planned a USD 4B investment in healthcare. Under the leadership of its founder, the company realised that its presence in other infrastructure sectors, transport logistics and energy and utilities have added massive heft to the company's sphere of influence. Presence in the healthcare infrastructure space would be good as the company could leverage its infrastructure strengths from the other group companies. Analysts have speculated that the company is looking to diversify into high EBIDTA opportunities and might be exploring acquisitions of diagnostics chains, hospitals, and research centres. There is also conjecture that instead of being stand alone facilities, these might be parts of a large healthcare ecosystem/platform that will provide end-to-end services for patients. Experts have predicted that the Group might acquire diagnostic companies, hospitals, and also a platform to offer these services to patients across the country.

Adani Total Gas

India's energy policy have long been dominated by Fossil fuels, helping our nascent industries grow and flourish. However, as the world realised the devastating effects of fossil fuels on the environment, the global and local energy policies have focused on green/renewable fuels that are less harmful to the environment.

India is at an inflexion point. Our industries are dependent on fossil fuels, however, we are also uniquely placed to leverage renewable energy sources quicker than some of the developed countries. Interestingly, though India is the third largest energy consuming nation globally, but it is also ranked fourth globally in the world for renewable energy installed capacity (including Large Hydro). As per the REN21 Renewables 2022 Global Status Report, India is ranked fourth in wind and solar power capacity both. Our rising energy requirements go hand in hand with the national commitment to achieve net zero status by 2070.

With a growth rate of approximately 400% across last 8.5 years, India's installed non-fossil fuel capacity stands at 178.79 Giga Watts (including large Hydro). This is about 43% of the country's total capacity (as on May 2023). In 2022, India also saw the highest year on year growth in renewable energy additions, to the tune of 9.83%.

Natural gas is an important component in the energy mix. Natural gas is widely regarded as a bridge fuel, helping economies move from dirty fossil fuels such as coal and oil to renewable sources of energy such as solar and wind. Though not green, natural gas is a comparatively cleaner fuel, producing fewer conventional air pollutants, like sulfur dioxide and particulates, than does coal or oil.

At present, natural gas accounts for just about 6% in the total energy mix of the country, due to its low per capita consumption. To increase its relative share, the government has set an ambitious target of increasing the share of natural gas in the total energy mix to 15% by 2030.

The per capita consumption of natural gas is expected to increase as it is supported by favourable government policies and reforms. Concurrently, population in India is expected to grow to 1.44 billion by 2024 thereby increasing net energy demand. Increasing population, rising energy consumption, these are all expected to alter the energy mix prevalent in the country. In the meantime, there is a gradual preference and transformation for gas energy over oil energy as natural gas is one of the most convenient, safe and cost effective fuels.

Adani Total Gas Limited (ATGL) was founded in 2005, and is India's largest City Gas Distribution (CGD) company (annual report 2020-2021). The company has also ventured in generation and distribution of clean energy from biomass. The company covers almost 9100 km pipeline network, across 1820 industrial customers, 3856 commercial customers and 15 lakh residential customers. The company has reported around 22.5% CAGR in revenue growth.

ATGL covers 15 states, 71 districts, and around 8% of the population. It supplies Piped Natural Gas (PNG) to industrial, commercial, domestic (residential) sector and Compressed Natural Gas (CNG) to the transport sector.

The company has already set up city gas distribution networks in Ahmedabad and Vadodara in Gujarat, Faridabad in Haryana and Khurja in Uttar Pradesh. In addition, the development of Allahabad, Chandigarh, Ernakulam, Panipat, Daman, Dharwad, and Udham singh Nagar gas distribution is awarded to a consortium of Adani Total Gas Ltd and Indian Oil Corporation Ltd.

The company is also focused on developing technologies that help in achieving carbon neutrality by providing energy efficiency services and investing in carbon sinks (natural sinks, CCUS).

The company has affirmed its commitment to cut the greenhouse gas emissions of their operations by 15% between 2015 and 2025.

Let us look at the principles of business that we can learn from Adani Total Gas led by its founder, Gautam Adani.

There is a huge gap in the country's natural gas output and requirements. As a result, 50% of the demand is met through imports. The total consumption of natural gas in India in 2020–21 was 48 Million Metric Tonnes (MMT), domestic production was around 25 MMT, and the rest was imported.

The largest consumer of natural gas is the fertiliser sector, followed by City Gas Distribution and Power.

Adani placed huge bets on this sector knowing the importance of alternate energy sources in the days to come. The government has framed highly investor-friendly policies to encourage generation and distribution of non-fossil fuels.

Adani realised the huge opportunity that natural gas distribution could have on the state of the economy and therefore, market entry into this segment made perfect business sense.

India's natural gas infrastructure consists of six LNG storage and regasification terminals with combined capacity of 42.5 MMT. There is additional infrastructure development in progress which will help in capacity expansion to 61.5

MMT. At present, around 20,000 km of gas pipelines are operational. The government has invested nearly 120,000 crore for infrastructure development.

The company realigned its strategic areas to focus more on natural gas and low-carbon technology.

The strategies emphasise on:

1. **Natural Gas:** Strengthening their presence across the entire natural gas chain.
2. **Low-Carbon Electricity:** Focusing on renewable sources for electricity generation and gas, reducing the emissions from operations, and promoting the use of biofuels.
3. **Contributing to Carbon Neutrality:** The company has also affirmed its commitment to energy efficiency and carbon sinks.

To support India's ambitious growth targets, India's energy consumption will reach 2,300 Million Tonnes of Oil Equivalent (MTOE) by 2047, of which natural gas will contribute almost 173 MTOE under the determined effect scenario.

India's dependence on other countries for gas imports makes it vulnerable as far as energy security is concerned. Having a robust natural gas import diversification strategy was highly needed as it dictates our energy relationships with other gas producing countries, amid changing geopolitical dynamics.

ATGL has helped in not just improving India's PNG footprint but also made natural gas a fuel of choice for the industry. Through ATGL, the company has advanced and advocated the use of natural gas, and made its consumption easier, convenient and comfortable.

One of the reasons for the success of Adani Gas is because of partnerships. Partnerships are important for the growth of any organisation in the public infrastructure as it helps bridge talent/ expertise gaps, provides technical know-how, capital and also helps organisations in managing the regulatory requirements.

Adani Total Gas has some very strong partnerships in its portfolio, right from Total Gas to Indian Oil Corporation.

Total is one of France's largest oil and gas companies and the world's second largest LNG company. Total first partnered with Adani in 2018 for a liquefied natural gas (LNG) venture. Eventually, Total cndcd up acquiring a 19.75% stake in Adani Green Energy Ltd and a stake in solar assets for USD 2.5 billion in 2020–219. It also acquired a 37.4% in Adani Total Gas Ltd, the firm that retails CNG to automobiles and piped natural gas to household kitchens and industries. Till date, this has also been the largest FDI in India's CGD sector by a global energy major.

Adani's partnership with Total reinforces the existing partners' strategic partnership to invest in one of the emerging energy markets to create one of the largest integrated gas utility providers, a sign of India's growth in the energy markets. Total's further expansion in the partnership, that is, acquisition of joint control, represents a natural expansion of the existing LNG and fuel retail partnership. The partnership has also enabled the companies to explore significant synergies in the areas of gas distribution, fuel retail and LNG businesses. The partnership has helped Adani Gas to serve 7.5% of India's population across 38 geographical areas across India. The company has also been able to set up a successful fuel retail business, by setting up nearly 1500 outlets.

Adani launched a 50-50% joint venture with Indian Oil Corporation (Indian Oil–Adani Gas Private Limited (IOAGPL) in 2013, which operates CGD network in 19 geographic areas across Punjab, Haryana, Uttarakhand, Karnataka amongst other states.

Natural Gas Regulatory Board (PNGRB) for laying, building, operating or expanding City Gas Distribution (CGD) projects across the districts of Ernakulam, Kozhikode, Wayanad, Malappuram, Palakkad, Thrissur (Kerala), Chandigarh (UT), SAS Nagar District (Mohali), Prayagraj, Bulandshahr, Aligarh, Hathras, Bhadohi, Kaushambi, Jaunpur and Ghazipur (Uttar Pradesh), Daman (UT of Daman & Diu), Udhamsingh Nagar (Uttarakhand), Dharwad- Hubli (Karnataka), Panipat (Haryana),

South Goa (Goa), Gaya and Nalanda (Bihar), Kannur-Kasaragodu and Mahé (Kerala &Puducherry), Burdwan (West Bengal).

Some of the biggest emission sources are industries such as manufacturing, logistics, mining– traditionally, behemoths and slightly impervious to change. For India to achieve a transition to renewable power and to achieve radical decarbonisation, the entire energy infrastructure needs to be made green first and has to be led from the carbon spewing industries up front.

How important is renewable energy in India's strategy can be assessed through India's four-plank energy security strategy - It prioritises diversifying supplies, increasing exploration and production, alternate energy sources and energy transition through a gas-based economy, Green Hydrogen etc., (Press release, Jan 23).

It is this reason why the government has prioritised CNG/ LPG adoption. CNG is a better fuel option than petroleum, as natural gas possesses an octane rating of 127. CNG vehicles experience less knocking, no vapour locking and superior starting. CNG fuel tanks are safer and generate eliminates the need for safety protocols for home use, and is more economical and convenient.

The government's mandate to increase natural gas use from 6.5% of the primary fuel mix to 15% by 2030 will enable India to meet its commitments to COP26 for achieving carbon neutrality by 2070. Adani Total Gas has reinforced India's commitment in developing sustainable energy by widening its footprint in city gas distribution network.

In October 2015, at the 26th edition of the COP, India submitted its proposed Nationally Determined Contribution (NDC) to UNFCCC. The 2015 NDC comprised eight goals; with quantitative targets for three goals time-lined till 2030. These are:

- ✓ Cumulative electric power installed capacity from non-fossil sources to reach 40%.
- ✓ Reduction in the emissions intensity of GDP by 33 to 35% compared to 2005 levels.
- ✓ Creation of additional carbon sink of 2.5 to 3 billion tonnes of CO_2 equivalent through additional forest and tree cover.

As per the updated NDC, India has committed to reduce emissions intensity of its GDP by 45% by 2030, from 2005 level and achieve about 50% cumulative electric power installed capacity from non-fossil fuel-based energy resources by 2030.

In addition to massive investments in creating a green ecosystem, ATGL has reaffirmed its commitment to greenification by the launch of the initiative "Greenmosphere", which involves mass plantation projects, recruiting green millennials and energy audits.

Greenmosphere: Mass plantation will be used as a platform for spreading awareness on energy conservation for our community circle. The initiative uses the "Miyawaki" methodology, helping afforestation even on adverse soil and climatic conditions. It provides 30 times denser forest, 30 times more carbon dioxide consumption and minimum 30 native species can be planted in the same area in cluster plantations.

Green millennials: It aims at awareness generation of Millennials across all schools and colleges. Through a structured programme, youngsters will be informed about green technology, energy efficiency and conservation with deep empathy for sustainable living.

Energy audits: Energy Audits will be conducted across Industrial, Commercial and Residential sectors energy efficiency of all the stakeholders, business owners and consumers by providing them with energy-efficient solutions.

What the Group is planning to do is also based on how India's energy trajectory will change in the next decade.

India is expected to overtake European Union as the world's third largest energy consumer by 2030. India's primary energy consumption is expected to double to 1123M Tonnes of Oil Equivalent by 2040. India is poised to account for a quarter of global energy demand growth.

The government has spend USD 60 bn in creating a national gas infrastructure (annual report 2020-2021) till 2024 consisting of pipelines, LNG terminals, and city gas distribution network. Till 2022, India had 4434 CNG stations in India, which is projected to increase to 15000 stations and this number is projected to increase to 30M households.

Adani has planned to invest INR 20,000 cr in city gas distribution network by 2030, addressing around 9% of the population. This investment will widen distribution across 9 M households, across 95 districts, 33 geographical areas across 12 states.

The 26th edition of the Conference of the Parties (COP26) was held in Glasgow from 1-12 November 2021. Jointly hosted by the UK and Italy, it is one of the world's most significant events on climate change. The summit was attended by the countries that signed the United Nations Framework Convention on Climate Change (UNFCCC) – a treaty that came into force in 1994.

At the conference, Indian Prime Minister Narendra Modi announced an aggressive set of targets for low-carbon power by 2030 and a net zero target by 2070 across all greenhouse gases.

India had made the following commitments at COP 26:

- ✓ To reach 500 GW non-fossil energy capacity by 2030.
- ✓ Acquire 50% of its energy requirements from renewable energy by 2030.

- ✓ Reduce of total projected carbon emissions by one billion tonnes from now to 2030.
- ✓ Reduce of the carbon intensity of the economy by 45 by 2030, over 2005 levels.
- ✓ Achieve the target of net zero emissions by 2070.

We can expect more investments and initiatives which will help align India to its global commitments.

The energy sector is governed by present demands, future planning and national interests. This sometimes makes policy making difficult. This makes firms operating in the energy sector highly vulnerable and dependent on favourable regulations for their operations and growth.

For example, the Hydrocarbon Vision 2025, released in 1999, projected the share of gas would reach 20% of the primary energy mix by 2025, while India's current vision puts this target at 15% by 2030. India nearly lost a decade due to policy inaction.

Despite being fast tracked by the government, the CGD growth has taken time to scale. The first eight bidding rounds, conducted across 10 years covered 92 geographic areas, the next three rounds conducted across 2 years, covered 201 GAs. The first eight bidding rounds covered just 20% of the country's population, in contrast, the last three bidding rounds covered approximately 70% of the population.

Due to macroeconomic uncertainty, India's LPG imports are picking up after seeing years of weak demand. India had boldly committed to increase the share of gas in the gas-energy mix to 15% by 2030 and become one of the world's biggest LNG importers, helping attract a wave of infrastructure investment.

But because of external variables such as COVID, Russia's invasion of Ukraine, LNG import market contracted, pushing up prices far higher than coal. India's LNG imports increased for three consecutive months starting in March, with imports in May reaching 2.7bn cubic metres. Demand is expected to expand further, the 66% growth in imports in May compared to February providing a much needed boost to India's LNG sector.

India is also struggling with low utilisation rate of its LNG import terminals. India is the fourth largest LNG buyer and has 6 LNG import terminals with a capacity of 42.5 million tons annually. Due to lack of downstream takeaway capacity, terminals are suffering from low usage. Apart from the Petronet's Dahej terminal in Gujarat, the other LNG import terminals had a utilisation rate lower than 40%. After LNG prices shot through the roof, demand contracted and import plans were shelved, leading to delay in commissioning of two floating import terminals.

The Group was supposed to commission a new terminal on the eastern coast in the second quarter of this year. However, capacity utilisation may be a challenge as the downstream value chain has not secured overseas supplies.

All these factors make operating in this sector highly risky and challenging. However, under the leadership of Adani, the Group has managed to circumvent all these problems and has focused on other promising areas such as electric mobility, which are more consumer-led with a slightly more stable demand cycle.

In March 2022, Adani Total Gas announced its investment in the area of electric mobility by launching its first Electric Vehicle Charging (EVC) station in Ahmedabad through a special purpose vehicle, Adani Total Energies Mobility.

The company announced its growth targets by outlining that it was planning to set up 1,500 EVCs across the country depending on the demand generation and momentum of the EV ecosystem in the country. After having commissioned 104 EV charging points across 26 locations, the company announced its plans of scaling up to 3000 stations in the next 12-18 months.

ATGL has received the letter of award for installing, testing, commissioning, operating, and maintaining EV charging stations in Ahmedabad, Bengaluru, Chennai, Delhi, Kolkata, Mumbai, Pune, and Surat on a Build, Own, and Operate (BOO) model.

This was again an astute business bet from Adani as he was well aware that given India's commitment to emission reduction and transition to green energy, an investment in setting up the EV infrastructure of the country would yield excellent results.

Adani Cement

India is fortunate to be blessed with rich limestone deposits, which provide it with the raw materials for being the second largest cement producer in the world. Around 7% of the global installed capacity is generated in India, around 500 Metric Tonnes Per Annum (MTPA). The production capacity is almost 298 MTPA. The sector generates about 1.2% GDP, and employs more than half a million people.

The boom in the cement industry is driven by housing demand in rural and urban areas, government's focus on infrastructure spending and development. The sector has seen a CAGR of almost 6% in the period FY16–22, driven by commercial and residential construction. The entire production capacity, almost 98%, is with the private sector, with only a miniscule 2% being controlled by the public sector. The sector follows the Pareto principle where the top 20 companies control around 70% of the production volume, giving them immense autonomy in price determination and production control.

Cement is a huge driver of economy and a large array of factor influence the cost of cement, right from energy costs to logistics cost, making the supply chain highly vulnerable. The oligopolistic nature of the cement industry makes it more susceptible to cartelisation and price collusion. However, the government has been proactive on this front, launching investigations and holding companies accountable for malpractices.

The Adani Group forayed into cement in 2021, and within a year, through inorganic expansion, it became the second largest cement manufacturer in the country. Its rise and expansion has been meteoric, and is largely driven by the vision and the zeal of its founder, Gautam Adani.

Let us now look at the principles of business that can be learnt from Adani for the incorporation and expansion of Adani Cement.

Adani has always had an astute sense of growth, and the same could be seen in the market entry strategy for cement. Despite being the second largest producer of cement in the world, the per capita consumption in India is just 250 kg as compared to the per capita consumption in China, which is around 1,600 kg. Adani realised that there was almost a 7 times greater opportunity for growth, given the government's focus on infrastructure projects.

Infrastructure sector and the cement sector presented the right set of adjacencies to help build its portfolio further. The group's presence in core infrastructure sectors right from ports to logistics and power gave it a competitive edge over its peers.

In terms of capex outlay, a 1 MTPA green field cement plant requires an investment of INR 700-800 crore. Acquisition could prove to be an expensive proposition but would give Adani an immediate entry to a market with a known brand. Hence it commenced operations with a focus on inorganic growth and began exploring the market for suitable acquisition opportunities.

However, Adani did not focus just on acquiring and creating yet another cement manufacturing company. The focus of the business was to build on its strength in renewable energy and use that to create a clear differentiation from the other cement manufacturers in the country, with a focus on green cement6. This is also in line with the Group's focus on sustainability and circular economy. It has an ambitious target to become the largest cement manufacturer by 2030.

Let us look at how the cement industry evolved over the past few decades. A handful of companies, UltraTech, Ambuja/ACC, Shree, JSW, Dalmia, JK Lakshmi, have dominated the cement industry in India. The market itself is oligopolistic in nature, with these few manufacturers holding almost half of the total installed manufacturing capacity. For many years, the industry has seen friction, conflict, and regulations that have identified malpractices such as cartelisation, none of which deterred Adani in expanding in this area. He knew that the focus of the government was on infrastructure, and launching a new business aligned to the core infrastructure strategy would reap dividends. He also knew that competing with established players like UltraTech, Dalmia organically would be a challenge. Hence, the Group launched itself into this category inorganically, through acquisitions. All of this was made possible through the visionary leadership of Gautam Adani.

Cement presented a business proposition adjacent to Adani's infrastructure business. Growth in this sector would help to fortify Adani's infrastructure enterprise. Building on his market entry strategy of inorganic growth, Adani evaluated acquiring Holcim's stake in two key cement manufacturing companies, Ambuja Cement and ACC. Sweden based Holcim is the world's largest cement manufacturer and was looking to exit some of its emission heavy investments. Adani expressed interest, structured the deal and on completion, this acquisition catapulted the Group to become India's second largest manufacturer in a single shot.

It wasn't a cakewalk for Adani - bidding was competitive, and his bid was lower than that of his peers, UltraTech and JSW Cement. However, through a combination of financial astuteness and market savvy, he was able to swing the deal in his favour. At that time, it was the largest M&A transaction in India's infrastructure and materials space valued at USD 10.50 billion. Acquisition of Holcim's stake lent Adani control over 13-14% of the market, superseded only by 25% controlled by

UltraTech. Post the transaction, Adani held 63.15% in Ambuja Cements and 56.69% in ACC (of which 50.05% is held through Ambuja Cements). The acquisition gave Adani access to the entire infrastructure of the two companies, 23 cement plants, 14 grinding stations, 80 ready-India.

The acquisition yielded Adani the stature of the second largest cement player, at 70 MTPA. Adani is preceded by UltraTech and followed by Shree Cements and Dalmia Cement which sit at third and fourth places respectively. Adani's ambitious growth plans include doubling capacity to 140 MTPA.

Both Ambuja Cements and ACC have benefited from the synergies with the Adani conglomerate, with improved access to raw materials, energy and logistics. Ambuja and ACC have also benefited from the Group's focus on ESG and circular economy. Despite being a fossil fuel heavy industry, Adani has differentiated the companies as they are deeply aligned to UN Sustainability Development Goals (SDGs).

Unlike other infrastructure companies, the Adani Group has prioritised and focused R&D and innovation under the leadership of Gautam Adani. ACC and Ambuja Cements have launched a Cement and Concrete Research & Development facility at Kalamboli, Navi Mumbai. The facility is dedicated to transforming the cement industry, create new sustainable products, and drive cost optimisation. This focus on new product development, energy optimisation and environment, is a novel move in an industry typically not recognised for innovation.

The Group has charted out a joint operational strategy for the ACC and Ambuja Cements by a capital expenditure plan worth USD 5.58 Billion. Investments will be allocated equally between the two subsidiaries, maintaining the two distinct brands. After the completion of the current expansion plan, the Group will cease expansion for sometime to maximise efficiency gains from the investment, across supply chain and logistics, before embarking on any new investments.

It is expected that there will be further consolidation in the cement industry. Smaller players such as Nuvoco Vistas (capacity of 25 MTPA), India Cements (15 MTPA) and Sanghi Cement (6 MTPA) will face margin pressures and will become more susceptible for acquisitions.

As part of its expansion strategy, Ambuja Cements was recently announced as the preferred bidder for the Uskalvagu limestone block in Odisha's Malkangiri district through an e-auction. The block covers 547 hectares and has almost 140 MT of limestone resources, further equipping the Group with the right raw materials. The Group is now under due process to secure statutory licences and permits for commencing mining operations.

The Group is focused on not just sustainability but also safety. At the Occupational Health, Safety and Sustainability Association of India (OHSSAI) Awards 2023, Adani Cement was the recipient of four awards. It won two manufacturing site awards-the OHSSAAI Safety Silver Award and the OHSSAI Road Safety Gold Award - and two individual awards.

For a critical sector like cement which is fossil fuel intensive and is susceptible to multiple factors, managing labour unions is crucial. Upon completing the acquisition of Ambuja and ACC Cements, the Adani Group started contract renegotiations for freight in Himanchal Pradesh.

The company leadership felt that the unions were trying to stall and control all operational decisions and were keeping freight costs artificially high.

Against the last rate offered by Ambuja, INR 10.58 per km and ACC (INR 11.41 per km), the Adani Group wanted to offer INR 6 per tonne per km (PTPK). As discussions aborted, the group shut down its Ambuja plant at Darlaghat and ACC plant in Bilaspur after the unions rejected their proposal.

This lasted in a deadlock for nearly 68 days between the Group and the truck operators. Finally, after intervention by the state government, the two sides joined the negotiations again and finalised INR 10.3 per km for single axle and INR 9.3 for multi axle transport.

Another challenge that the industry faced was cartelisations- The industry has faced several accusations of cartelisation– price collusion, anti-competitive conduct against the consumer interest. In its investigation, Competition Commission of India (CCI) found out that nearly 20 companies, and their top leaderships, were involved in regulating production, restricting supplies and increasing prices in tandem. These 20 companies controlled more than half of the total installed cement making capacity in India. Even the industry body, Cement Manufacturers Association (CMA), was found to have facilitated the anti- competitive conduct among companies. Eventually the CCI instituted and imposed fines worth INR 6,700 crore on 11 companies, including Ambuja Cements and ACC. The fine for Ambuja was around 1,164 crore and for ACC was 1,148 crore.

In June 2023, the Adani Group, representing Ambuja Cements and ACC, exited the Cement Manufacturers Association, signalling the Groups intent to distance itself from malpractices involved with cartelisation.

Another challenge that the Group faced was how to continue profitable operations after the acquisition. Acquiring Holcim's stake in Ambuja and ACC Cements was an expensive proposition for Adani. For Holcim's stake in Ambuja and ACC, the group has paid USD 10.5 b, which translates into EV/T of USD 164/ tonne, clearly making this the most expensive acquisition in this space till date. To help place the metric in perspective, in 2018, Ultratech Cement paid USD 150/tonne for Binani Cement.

To deliver stakeholder value, Adani Cements will have to continue with a premium brand positioning so that they can deliver double-digit ROE and ROCE.

Earnings Before Interest, Taxes, Depreciation, and Amortisation (EBITDA) is indicative of the profitability of a company and tracks the net income. As per a report by Jeffries, in the cement industry, to deliver ROE and ROCE of 10.6% greenfield and brownfield opportunities need to make an EBITDA/T of INR 1,500 and ₹ 900 respectively. To deliver ROE and ROCE of greater than 10%, the Adani Group entity will need to make an EBITDA/T of INR 2,000 to get similar margins - [ROE of 10.8% and a ROCE of 10.7%].

The reason why Adani has to deliver a higher than industry average EBITDA is because the capital cost per tonne, or the acquisition price is far greater than what it would cost to put up similar capacities through greenfield or brownfield expansion. Typical green field projects cost INR 7,700/T and brownfield projects cost INR 4,620/T, whereas the acquisition cost for this project is INR 12,782/T.

Since EBITDA is higher, it could also mean premium valuation leading to pressures on delivering higher targeted unit profitability, which can arise from brand premium and efficiencies and synergies derived from the Group's other businesses.

Despite the fact that profitability is a critical financial metric at this stage, experts do not anticipate an acquisition fuelled competitive price war for maintaining market share. Fortunately for Adani, both Ambuja and ACC enjoy high brand recognition and recall, which helps it have a very high trade sales component of ~80%, but as non-trade sales catch up, brand retention will be key.

Despite facing many challenges, the Group has persevered to deliver on its ambitious growth targets and continues to generate employment, revenue and brand value in this infrastructure critical sector.

Two Near Death Experiences

On 26/11 terrorists attacked Taj Hotel and Gautam Adani was in the hotel. He still remembers everything and when the terrorists fired their first round, he saw the terrorists in front of him. He has had two near death experiences and feels that it is the grace of God that he survived.

Gautam Adani was having dinner with the CEO of Dubai Port at Masala Craft restaurant in the Taj on 26/11 when the incident took place around 10 pm. Five minutes before this, he had paid the bill and was ready to go. However, his friend wanted to discuss further, so he stayed for coffee and that's when the incident happened. He sometimes feels that if he had paid the bill and left at that time, he would have been stuck in the lobby area. Since they stayed back, he was trapped inside the restaurant. Today he says that the dedication shown by the Taj Group employees, whether they were waiters or any of them, is very rare to see in organizations today.

He was stuck there the whole night. Taj's staff took him through the back passage of the kitchen to the chamber. He was there the whole night. At around 7 am in the morning the commandos arrived and came to know that many people were trapped there. So, with full security, the commandos escorted them outside the hotel premises. He left the next day around 7:30-8 am in the morning.

Rahul ji Senior Leader of the Congress Party

In his speeches, Rahul Gandhi often keeps taking the name of Gautam Adani. Rahul says that the Modi government handed over all India's ports, airports, gas, transmission, electricity, mining, green energy, gas, everything to Gautam Adani.

Gautam Adani says about him that Rahul ji is a senior leader of the Congress Party. He feels that being an industrialist, it is not proper for him to comment on the data. He is a respected leader, and he also wants the country to progress. He (Rahul) says some things because of his political leanings, but he (Gautam) does not take it as more than a political gimmick.

They believe that Rahul is a respected leader. A political party runs, they have an ideological fight and there will be allegations and counter-allegations.

But when those allegations are made, then also consider whether anything happens without speaking. Is there any business they entered without bidding or qualifying? He also knows that doing so in India will create controversy. The Adani Group has a principle that nothing should be touched without bidding. Be it their ports, airports, roads, power houses, not a single business is done without bidding. It is like questioning the first person in the exam. Rahul also did not allege that there was some disturbance in the bidding process.

Rahul says that whatever money he is investing in different infrastructure projects, it is a loan that he has taken from different banks. Gautam Adani has a debt of 2,00,000 crore, which is all public money, on the basis of which he is making his fortune.

Gautam Adani says that when you build an infrastructure project, you have a bank there and you have equity on it. You will have to invest 30-40 per cent of your own money and 60-70 per cent can be borrowed from the bank. The question is, what is the rating of the loan you have taken?

He says that the Adani Group is the only group in India which has high rating in the market and this rating is not given by any political party or bank, it is given by an independent agency after their complete financial analysis. And on the basis of that a loan is given to the eligible people. They have that rating for India, Indian banks and each and every corporate.

Today, each Adani Group company is assigned a rating equivalent to India's overall rating, which is the sovereign rating. Such is the discipline and rating of Adani Group that in Gautam

Adani's tenure of 25 years, he has never delayed payments or defaulted on interest, and even more so whenever he needed funds for any development activity. Everyone is prepared to lend them money.

On the other hand, Rahul Gandhi says that Modiji is making sure that he is getting all this. Rahul says that most of the loans have been given to him by government banks and 40 per cent of the loans have been given between the year 2020 and the year 2022.

Gautam Adani says that earlier he used to accept 80 per cent money from Indian banks. That stands at 35 per cent today. After that, he entered the international market with global ratings. On the global front, no one lends based on what someone says, they lend purely by looking at their ratings and governance. Based on his company ratings and disclosures, one of his companies has been awarded the third ESG level worldwide. Gautam Adani says that this is an absolutely baseless allegation. He understands that he needs to say a few things politically, but there is no estrangement between lenders and borrowers.

In the last 10 years, his loan interest rate has increased by 11 per cent and his income has increased by 24 per cent. Their ratings have improved because of their profitability and their borrowings increase their ratings further.

Many people say that if ever the Adani bubble bursts, all the banks will collapse. On this, Gautam Adani says that 'some people have such a dream'. But Adani's assets are 3-4 times more than their debt, so no one's money is unsafe. And as long as India is making progress this balloon will keep flying.

Rahul Gandhi has another allegation that Modi ji supports him so much that drugs worth 20,000 crore were seized in September 2021 in the first port Mundra Port Trust he ran. Drugs worth 500 crore were caught in May 2022 and then drugs worth 375 crore were caught in July 2022. He asks who is saving Adani? Rahul

Gandhi and the Congress Party allege that Adani or his men were never questioned even after repeated drug seizures.

According to Gautam Adani, "You have to see that these drugs have been caught. You need to look at it from the point of view that any drug passing through the port is intercepted. It does not mean that there is no investigation of the previous case. But today I want to congratulate every agency, be it customs, police, or DRI, they worked with complete dedication and caught this smuggling of drugs. When we run a port, we don't have any additional powers like a government. When you run a port, you are only in charge of loading and unloading cargo. You have no policing powers, no inspection powers, and no power to arrest. This is the job of various agencies of the government who mislead people. What is being caught is being informed to the government – who is the sender, who is doing it, how is it coming and the government has settled all these.

Whenever there is an investigation, it is a 360-degree investigation and there is an inquiry. It has never happened that anyone has been able to bypass the government investigation. So I disagree that the Adani group is getting some special privileges".

Adani is a regular industrialist. He does his work and Rahul Gandhi does his politics.

Even if the slogan of the Congress Party is, "*Aam Aadmi Behaal, Adani Malamaal*". They have even invested 68,000 crore in Congress ruled Rajasthan. Gautam Adani says that the Adani group is committed to the development of the potential not only in Rajasthan, but also in all the states. Rahul Gandhi has appreciated his investment in his press conference. Rahul Gandhi has no such policy which is against development. So their goal is to go to every state, wherever possible, and invest as much as possible.

Ashok Gehlot's government provided them land for a power project, there were MDO projects for mining, and all this was done through bidding. Whatever help they have given is under the policy. His policies were very clear and when you are a serious player and you are asking something within the policy, Adani believes that not only Ashok Gehlot's Congress government, he is also working with the Left government in Kerala, working with Didi (Mamata), also working with Naveen Patnaik, with Jaganji, with KCR, so they work in every state and all have different governments, some regional party. Congress, is also a left party, so today he says with absolute confidence that he never had any problem with any government. So Bayan and all are in a different place and when you are a serious player in infrastructure and whatever you are making promises to all the states and developing accordingly, then they did not have a problem with any government.

Today he is working in 22 states, and all these states are not BJP ruled. He had no complaint because he had no problem with any state government.

₹60,000 crore in Andhra Pradesh, 57,000 crore in Odisha, 35,000 crore in West Bengal, but still people say Modi is Adani's chowkidar. People say that Modi has made Adani what it is today. There are very few people who give such statements who have problems with Modi or because of ideological push-ups. But as Gautam Adani's experience says, all he can say is that most people like Modi ji and don't see any problem with Adani's development model.

'Narendra Modi gave him land for the Mundra port at Re 1 per square feet'. On this, Gautam Adani says that the land we got for Re 1 was not the land at all. When the high tide came, the land went under the sea water and they did reclamation about 10 feet, 3-4 metres above and the cost of reclamation is much more than the cost of the land. Even today when people give the example of Mundra Port, it is a unique example. They have not taken even an acre of land from any farmer. So today after making such a huge investment in the port for infrastructure, the price of the land has gone up. So people blame today's land price, but considering when they got the land, when it was not developed and today's price, it is not fair.

In Mundra till date they have not taken a single piece of land from the farmer. Whatever land they have taken, it is government, unsurveyed land, sea water used to come on that land and they have developed by reclamation and that development has happened due to the investment and cost of ₹ 50,000 to 1 lakh crores. The amount of land has increased appreciably and the farmers get its full benefits. The Adani Group in Mundra is able to grow more and more because of all the farmers and community with whom they are working shoulder to shoulder.

When that land was being developed, Gautam Adani used to wake up every morning at 4 am and go there. Gautam Adani says that if you do not have dedication and hard work, then infrastructure projects will never stand. Not only that, all his employees worked together with him, that's why Mundra Port is standing. He developed it in such a way that in 10 years it became India's biggest port and the government did not invest even a single rupee in it. He made all the road connections. Built a private railway line of 100 kilometres. An airport was built there. The government only gave land, gave the right to development, nothing else. Whenever he needed any permission, whatever government was there in Gujarat, he helped him completely.

This is not just the spirit of the Adani Group. There are also industrialists in Gujarat, this is the sentiment of all. The governments of Gujarat have been friendly to the industrialists. That's why whatever policies are made, they are made to attract industrialists. Otherwise Gujarat does not have the resources. Before the water of Narmada canal came, there used to be happiness every 2-3-4 years. Despite this it was ahead in industrialization. Gujarat was ahead even before Adani was born, so it is not that Adani has any special favour.

Those who were agitating farmers in Delhi were saying that Narendra Modi has brought these three agricultural laws to benefit Adani. But it would be fair to say that Adani has very limited exposure to agriculture. They have built some godowns for the Food Corporation of India and the wheat in those godowns was not purchased by the Adani group nor was it ever owned. The food corporation buys from farmers at the minimum support price, stores it and supplies it to people below the poverty line. Therefore, they only provided a basic framework. The farmer produces produce, he does not know what is the demand in the market, so when his produce comes out, the market is closed, there is no place to store it.

India's 40-50 per cent population is directly or indirectly dependent on agriculture and India has the potential to supply food to the whole world and the major problem is limited infrastructure, people are not getting things by rail. No cold storage, lack of warehousing. In such a situation, the customers are not getting acceptable things and the farmers are not getting a regular income. If such laws had come, he would have invested more in infrastructure which would have benefited the farmers.

They are building ports, airports, roads, power houses and these are not for providing ports and electricity to the Adani group, they are for the people of the country. People have seen the condition of electricity 15 years ago. Now getting uninterrupted. Today there are so many advantages in airports, the roads are good. It has to be said that infrastructure is helpful in the development of the country and the aspirations of all the youth are increasing, so many jobs are being created, so there is no way other than infrastructure for further development of the country.

According to Gautam Adani, you cannot expect personal help from Modi ji. You can talk about policies. You can talk about how you can take our country forward and what is happening on the ground. So you make policies for everyone and the Adani Group also gets the benefit of the policies which are for everyone.

The break that Gautam Adani got in his life was given by the Rajiv Gandhi government, due to which Global Trading Houses were started. Then he got the second break from the Narasimha Rao government, due to which the Public Private Partnership developed and showed the country a new direction of industrialization and the third Keshubhai government. His experience with the Modi government of Gujarat was also very good.

According to Gautam Adani, 'The country is progressing tremendously. The country is celebrating 75 years of independence, after independence it took India 58 years to achieve 1 trillion dollar economy, 12 more years to achieve 2 trillion Dollar economy, and 3 trillion dollar economy It took five years to do and the way the aspirations of the country's youth are increasing and India's place in the world today, the country's economy will exceed 30 trillion dollars by the year 2050. Job opportunities will increase. No one can stop India with governance in the times to come.

According to Gautam Adani, 'This country has innumerable opportunities. If you try to analyse it and work hard and never think that you will be successful by resorting to shortcuts. Everyone becomes successful, it takes time, some become quick, some take time. If you continuously follow the target, then the door of success will open for you. You should like, not as I saw him, I want to be like him. Don't fall into it whatever interest you have for anything, you go ahead with it.

According to Gautam Adani, 'I am a man of the land, so in my every process the common man is in my eyes. Let me give you an cxamplc. 10 days ago on my 60th birthday my family members were sitting and discussing what gift to give me on my 60th birthday. So I said that if you wants to gift me something, then give 60,000 crore to the foundation from the wealth of our family. It's not just me, it's my whole family and they very happily said it's a great idea and gave it. You start with whatever you feel from within. So when we gave this 60,000 crore to the foundation, then we thought what to do now, how to use it. So we took up three sectors—health, education and skill development. We are talking to the experts of these three sectors. You will see that in the coming 2-2 months we will make a big announcement and use it in such a way that it will benefit the poorest of the poor. I have it in my mind to use it for good '.

Family Life

Gautam Adani's wife Preeti mostly looks after the work of the Adani Foundation. Gautam Adani says that 'Preeti ji is my pillar and she takes full care of the family, two children and my granddaughters and she is also a doctor. She left her profession and is supporting me. She fully supported the family, took care of the family, brought up and raised the children and when the children grew up, she took care of all the activities of the Foundation. So, today I am very satisfied that for the activities of the foundation, Preeti is working at most 7-8 hours daily on this. Secondly, there is great professionalism in our foundation and many development works are in progress under the guidance of Preeti.

Despite a busy schedule, Gautam finds regular time for the family.

He is out of Ahmedabad three days a week, when he is there for four days he goes to the office late around 11 or 12 as he comes late at night. That's why the morning time—two hours—is spent with the family. Second, he has made it a rule that even if he is in the office at lunchtime, his family has the lunch available there. So he basically spends time with them.

He sees Dhirubhai Ambani as a role model. This is because the economy of Reliance Industries was not open at that time in his office, then it opened later and he has been very impressed with the way he showed the direction of thinking big to the country, later Mukesh Ambani took it a lot further. But from the first generation point of view and when you don't have money but the vision is very big, they always attract you and especially first generation entrepreneurs like Adani, so he naturally sees that he has done a commendable job.

Mukesh Ambani is a close friend of Gautam and he respects him. The new direction he gave to Reliance Industries in Jio, Technology, Retail and of course his traditional business of Petrochemicals and Refinery, the thirteen he has worked with, have contributed immensely to the development of the country.

Prime Minister of UK, Deputy Prime Minister of Singapore visit Adani Group Headquarters. It is not important, they come to our country and how they see India and because different Prime Ministers and dignitaries come, they see India in a completely different way. It is very satisfying that now they are basically looking at India and Indian industrialists very seriously.

Due to the specific working style of Prime Minister Narendra Modi, now he treats Indians with completely different respect, so this is his contribution, which is most commendable.

❑

Timeline

1988: Gautam Adani lays the foundation for the Adani Group with a small trading business focused on commodities.

1991: A substantial contract from the Gujarat state government boosts the Adani Group's credibility and provides financial resources for ambitious business moves.

1993: The Adani Group ventures into the global marketplace by importing and exporting commodities worldwide, expanding its operations beyond national boundaries.

1995: The Adani Group enters the port development sector and starts the Mundra Port project, eventually becoming India's largest private port.

1996: Mundra Port becomes operational, highlighting the group's commitment to efficient project delivery and infrastructure development.

1998: Adani Power Limited is established, marking the group's entry into the power generation sector.

2001: Adani Wilmar Limited is established, diversifying the group's operations into the agribusiness sector and the edible oil business.

2002: Adani Enterprises becomes a publicly-traded company, increasing its financial standing and visibility among investors.

2006: The Mundra Special Economic Zone (SEZ) is successfully constructed, driving industrialization and economic growth in the region.

2008: Adani Ports and SEZ Limited (APSEZ) is established, consolidating the group's port operations and driving growth in the sector.

2009: Adani Power becomes India's largest private thermal power producer, showcasing the group's strategic planning and execution skills.

2011: Adani Green Energy Limited is established, marking the group's entry into the renewable energy market.

2013: Adani Group starts working on the world's largest single-area solar power project in Gujarat, demonstrating its commitment to sustainable energy.

2015: The group acquires Dhamra Port in Odisha, expanding its port operations and geographical reach.

2017: Adani Transmission becomes India's largest private power transmission company, enhancing the country's power infrastructure.

2018: The group's solar manufacturing arm becomes India's largest manufacturer of solar panels and solar cells, reinforcing its dedication to renewable energy.

2019: The Adani Group makes its first significant international investment by investing in Australia's Carmichael Coal Mine and Rail Project.

2020: The Adani Group becomes the third Indian company to surpass $100 billion in market capitalization, showcasing its growth and economic strength.

2021: The group lays out the world's largest solar power plant in Tamil Nadu, further emphasizing its commitment to renewable energy and sustainability.

2022: The Adani Group continues to expand and diversify its operations, contributing significantly to India's economic growth and establishing itself as a versatile conglomerate.

2023 (Additional update):

The Adani Group continues to innovate and invest in emerging industries, such as artificial intelligence and clean technology, positioning itself as a leader in cutting-edge sectors.

The group partners with various international organizations to work on global sustainability projects and supports initiatives to address climate change and environmental challenges.

Adani Group's philanthropic efforts expand, with various social welfare projects initiated to uplift underprivileged communities and promote education and healthcare.

In recognition of its sustainable practices and commitment to social responsibility, the Adani Group receives several prestigious awards and accolades in the fields of business and sustainability.

❑

References

For writing this book, in addition to various information sources and personal contacts, cooperation has been taken from the following information sources, for which the author expresses heartfelt gratitude.

- ✓ 'Billionaire Survivor of Ransom', bloomberg.com. Retrieved on 13th December 2020.
- ✓ 'Two accused of kidnapping Gautam Adani 20 years ago acquitted', *Indian Express*, 1st December 2018.
- ✓ 'Adani Green hits new highs by winning world's largest solar bid worth $7 billion', *Business Standard*, 10th June 2020.
- ✓ 'Adani acquires Holcim India assets for $10.5 billion', *Times of India*.
- ✓ 'Profile of billionaire Gautam Adani at a glance', *India Today*, 20th August 2011.
- ✓ 'Cryogenic Tank Imported from Saudi Arabia by Adani Group to Improve Oxygen Availability', Asianet News Network Pvt Ltd, 11th May 2021.
- ✓ 'Gautam Adani donates ₹ 100 crore to PM fund to fight corona virus', indiatvnews.com, 1st April 2020.
- ✓ 'Gautam Adani, President, Adani Group', outlookbusiness.com, 10th July 2015.

- ✓ 'Gautam Adani, Nita Ambani and KM Birla Top Philanthropic Leaders in India', *The Economic Times*, 15th January 2022.
- ✓ 'Throwback: When India's fifth richest man was kidnapped for ransom', Times Now News, 14th June 2020.
- ✓ 'India's 10 Richest Billionaires 2021', *Forbes*, 1st July 2021.
- ✓ 'Indian billionaire Gautam Adani becomes Asia's richest person', *Forbes*, 11th February 2022.
- ✓ 'Top 10 Gujarati Billionaires', India TV, 1st August 2015.
- ✓ https://www.adani.com/About-us/Chairman-Message
- ✓ https://economictimes.indiatimes.com/adani-power-ltd/chairmanspeech/companyid-23479.cms
- ✓ https://www.business-standard.com/company/adani-transmissi-66273/annual-report/chairman-speech
- ✓ https://english.revoi.in/gautam-adanis-speech-at-the-2022-bengal-global-business-summit/
- ✓ https://www.adaniwatch.org/freedom_of_speech_about_adani_stifled_by_officials_in_adani_s_home_state_of_gujarat

❑❑❑